D1243713

Using Docker

Adrian Mouat

Beijing · Boston · Farnham · Sebastopol · Tokyo

Using Docker

by Adrian Mouat

Copyright © 2016 Adrian Mouat. All rights reserved.

Printed in the United States of America.

Published by O'Reilly Media, Inc., 1005 Gravenstein Highway North, Sebastopol, CA 95472.

O'Reilly books may be purchased for educational, business, or sales promotional use. Online editions are also available for most titles (*http://safaribooksonline.com*). For more information, contact our corporate/institutional sales department: 800-998-9938 or *corporate@oreilly.com*.

Editor: Brian Anderson	**Indexer:** WordCo Indexing Services
Production Editor: Melanie Yarbrough	**Interior Designer:** David Futato
Copyeditor: Christina Edwards	**Cover Designer:** Randy Comer
Proofreader: Amanda Kersey	**Illustrator:** Rebecca Demarest

December 2015:   First Edition

Revision History for the First Edition

2015-12-07:   First Release
2016-04-08:   Second Release
2016-08-12:   Third Release

See *http://oreilly.com/catalog/errata.csp?isbn=9781491915769* for release details.

The O'Reilly logo is a registered trademark of O'Reilly Media, Inc. *Using Docker*, the cover image of a bowhead whale, and related trade dress are trademarks of O'Reilly Media, Inc.

While the publisher and the author have used good faith efforts to ensure that the information and instructions contained in this work are accurate, the publisher and the author disclaim all responsibility for errors or omissions, including without limitation responsibility for damages resulting from the use of or reliance on this work. Use of the information and instructions contained in this work is at your own risk. If any code samples or other technology this work contains or describes is subject to open source licenses or the intellectual property rights of others, it is your responsibility to ensure that your use thereof complies with such licenses and/or rights.

978-1-491-91576-9

[LSI]

To those who try, whether they fail or succeed.

Table of Contents

Part III.   Tools and Techniques

Preface

Containers are a lightweight and portable store for an application and its dependencies.
Written down by itself, this sounds dry and boring. But the process improvements made possible by containers are anything but; used correctly, containers can be game-changing. So persuasive is the lure of the architectures and workflows made possible by containers that in the span of a year, it feels like every major IT company has gone from never having heard of Docker or containers to actively investigating and using them.

The rise of Docker has been astonishing. I don't remember any technology that has had such a fast and profound effect on the IT industry. This book is my attempt to help you understand *why* containers are so important, *what* you stand to gain from adopting containerization, and most importantly, *how* to go about it.

Who Should Read This Book

This book tries to take a holistic approach to Docker, explaining the reasons for using Docker and showing how to use it and how to integrate it into a software development workflow. The book covers the entire software lifecycle, from development through to production and maintenance.

I have tried to avoid assuming too much of the reader beyond a basic knowledge of Linux and software development in general. The intended readership is primarily software developers, operations engineers, and system administrators (particularly those keen to develop a DevOps approach), but technically informed managers and enthusiasts should also be able to get something out of this book.

Why I Wrote This Book

I was in the fortunate position to learn about and use Docker while it was still in the early stages of its meteoric rise. When the opportunity to write this book appeared, I leapt at it with both hands. If my scribblings can help some of you to understand and make the most of the containerization movement, I will have achieved more than I have in years of developing software.

I truly hope that you enjoy reading this book and that it helps you on the path to using Docker in your organization.

Navigating This Book

This book is roughly organized as follows:

- Part I starts by explaining what containers are and why you should be interested in them, before going into a couple tutorial chapters showing the basics of Docker. It concludes with a lengthy chapter explaining the fundamental concepts and technology in Docker, including an overview of the various Docker commands.

- Part II explains how to use Docker in a software development lifecycle. It starts by showing how to set up a development environment, before building a simple web application that is used as an ongoing example throughout the subsequent chapters. This part covers development, testing, and integration, as well as how to deploy containers and how to effectively monitor and log a production system.

- Part III goes into advanced details and the tools and techniques needed to run multihost clusters of Docker containers safely and reliably. If you are already using Docker and need to understand how to scale up or solve networking and security issues, this is for you.

Conventions Used in This Book

The following typographical conventions are used in this book:

Italic
Indicates new terms, URLs, email addresses, filenames, and file extensions.

`Constant width`
Used for program listings, as well as within paragraphs to refer to program elements such as variable or function names, databases, data types, environment variables, statements, and keywords.

`Constant width bold`
Shows commands or other text that should be typed literally by the user.

`Constant width italic`
Shows text that should be replaced with user-supplied values or by values determined by context.

This element signifies a tip or suggestion.

This element signifies a general note.

This element indicates a warning or caution.

Using Code Examples

Supplemental material (code examples, exercises, etc.) is available for download at *https://github.com/using-docker/*.

This book is here to help you get your job done. In general, if example code is offered with this book, you may use it in your programs and documentation. You do not need to contact us for permission unless you're reproducing a significant portion of the code. For example, writing a program that uses several chunks of code from this book does not require permission. Selling or distributing a CD-ROM of examples from O'Reilly books does require permission. Answering a question by citing this book and quoting example code does not require permission. Incorporating a significant amount of example code from this book into your product's documentation does require permission.

We appreciate, but do not require, attribution. An attribution usually includes the title, author, publisher, and ISBN. For example: "*Using Docker* by Adrian Mouat (O'Reilly). Copyright 2016 Adrian Mouat, 978-1-491-91576-9."

If you feel your use of code examples falls outside fair use or the permission given above, feel free to contact us at *permissions@oreilly.com*.

Safari® Books Online

 *Safari Books Online* is an on-demand digital library that delivers expert content in both book and video form from the world's leading authors in technology and business.

Technology professionals, software developers, web designers, and business and creative professionals use Safari Books Online as their primary resource for research, problem solving, learning, and certification training.

Safari Books Online offers a range of plans and pricing for enterprise, government, education, and individuals.

Members have access to thousands of books, training videos, and prepublication manuscripts in one fully searchable database from publishers like O'Reilly Media, Prentice Hall Professional, Addison-Wesley Professional, Microsoft Press, Sams, Que, Peachpit Press, Focal Press, Cisco Press, John Wiley & Sons, Syngress, Morgan Kaufmann, IBM Redbooks, Packt, Adobe Press, FT Press, Apress, Manning, New Riders, McGraw-Hill, Jones & Bartlett, Course Technology, and hundreds more. For more information about Safari Books Online, please visit us online.

How to Contact Us

Please address comments and questions concerning this book to the publisher:

O'Reilly Media, Inc.
1005 Gravenstein Highway North
Sebastopol, CA 95472
800-998-9938 (in the United States or Canada)
707-829-0515 (international or local)
707-829-0104 (fax)

We have a web page for this book, where we list errata, examples, and any additional information. You can access this page at *http://bit.ly/using-docker*.

To comment or ask technical questions about this book, send email to *bookquestions@oreilly.com*.

For more information about our books, courses, conferences, and news, see our website at *http://www.oreilly.com*.

Find us on Facebook: *http://facebook.com/oreilly*

Follow us on Twitter: *http://twitter.com/oreillymedia*

Watch us on YouTube: *http://www.youtube.com/oreillymedia*

Acknowledgments

I am immensely grateful for all the help, advice, and criticism I received during the writing of this book. If I missed your name in the following list, please accept my apologies; your contribution was appreciated whether I acted on it or not.

For their generous feedback, I would like to thank Ally Hume, Tom Sugden, Lukasz Guminski, Tilaye Alemu, Sebastien Goasguen, Maxim Belooussov, Michael Boelen, Ksenia Burlachenko, Carlos Sanchez, Daniel Bryant, Christoffer Holmstedt, Mike Rathbun, Fabrizio Soppelsa, Yung-Jin Hu, Jouni Miikki, Dale Bewley, Alex Ott and Thomas Demmig.

For technical conversations and input on specific technologies in the book, I would like to thank Andrew Kennedy, Peter White, Alex Pollitt, Fintan Ryan, Shaun Crampton, Spike Curtis, Alexis Richardson, Ilya Dmitrichenko, Casey Bisson, Thijs Schnitger, Sheng Liang, Timo Derstappen, Puja Abbassi, Alexander Larsson, and Kelsey Hightower. For allowing me to reuse monsterid.js, I would like to thank Kevin Gaudin.

For all their help, I would like to thank the O'Reilly staff, in particular my editors, Brian Anderson and Meghan Blanchette, for starting the whole process.

Diogo Mónica and Mark Coleman—thanks to both of you for answering my last-minute plea for help.

A particular shout-out has to go to two companies: Container Solutions and CloudSoft. Jamie Dobson and Container Solutions kept me busy blogging and speaking at events, and put me in contact with several people who had an impact on this book. The folks at CloudSoft graciously allowed me to use their office during the writing of this book and hosted the Edinburgh Docker meetup, both of which were very important to me.

For putting up with my obsession and moaning over the book, I would like to thank all my friends and family; you know who you are (and are unlikely to read this anyway).

Finally, I would like to thank the BBC 6 Music DJs who provided the soundtrack to this book, including Lauren Laverne, Radcliffe and Maconie, Shaun Keaveny, and Iggy Pop.

PART I
Background and Basics

The first part of this book begins by taking a look at what containers are and why they are becoming so popular. This is followed by an introduction to Docker and the key concepts you need to understand to make the most of containers.

CHAPTER 1

The What and Why of Containers

Containers are fundamentally changing the way we develop, distribute, and run software. Developers can build software locally, knowing that it will run identically regardless of host environment—be it a rack in the IT department, a user's laptop, or a cluster in the cloud. Operations engineers can concentrate on networking, resources, and uptime—and spend less time configuring environments and battling system dependencies. The use and uptake of containers is increasing at a phenomenal rate across the industry, from the smallest startups to large-scale enterprises. Developers and operations engineers should expect to regularly use containers in some fashion within the next few years.

Containers are an encapsulation of an application with its dependencies. At first glance, they appear to be just a lightweight form of virtual machines (VMs)—like a VM, a container holds an isolated instance of an operating system (OS), which we can use to run applications.

However, containers have several advantages that enable use cases that are difficult or impossible with traditional VMs:

- Containers share resources with the host OS, which makes them an order of magnitude more efficient. Containers can be started and stopped in a fraction of a second. Applications running in containers incur little to no overhead compared to applications running natively on the host OS.

- The portability of containers has the potential to eliminate a whole class of bugs caused by subtle changes in the running environment—it could even put an end to the age-old developer refrain of "but it works on my machine!"

- The lightweight nature of containers means developers can run dozens of containers at the same time, making it possible to emulate a production-ready distributed system. Operations engineers can run many more containers on a single host machine than using VMs alone.

- Containers also have advantages for end users and developers outside of deploying to the cloud. Users can download and run complex applications without needing to spend hours on configuration and installation issues or worrying about the changes required to their system. In turn, the developers of such applications can avoid worrying about differences in user environments and the availability of dependencies.

More importantly, the fundamental goals of VMs and containers are different—the purpose of a VM is to fully emulate a foreign environment, while the purpose of a container is to make applications portable and self-contained.

Containers Versus VMs

Though containers and VMs seem similar at first, there are some important differences, which are easiest to explain using diagrams.

Figure 1-1 shows three applications running in separate VMs on a host. The hypervisor[1] is required to create and run VMs, controlling access to the underlying OS and hardware as well as interpreting system calls when necessary. Each VM requires a full copy of the OS, the application being run, and any supporting libraries.

In contrast, Figure 1-2 shows how the same three applications could be run in a containerized system. Unlike VMs, the host's kernel[2] is shared with the running containers. This means that containers are always constrained to running the same kernel as the host. Applications Y and Z use the same libraries and can share this data rather than having redundant copies. The container engine is responsible for starting and stopping containers in a similar way to the hypervisor on a VM. However, processes running inside containers are equivalent to native processes on the host and do not incur the overheads associated with hypervisor execution.

Both VMs and containers can be used to isolate applications from other applications running on the same host. VMs have an added degree of isolation from the hypervisor and are a trusted and battle-hardened technology. Containers are comparatively new, and many organizations are hesitant to completely trust the isolation features of containers before they have a proven track record. For this reason, it is common to

---

1 The diagram depicts a *type 2* hypervisor, such as VirtualBox or VMware Workstation, which runs on top of a host OS. *Type 1* hypervisors, such as Xen, are also available where the hypervisor runs directly on top of the bare metal.

2 The kernel is the core component in an OS and is responsible for providing applications with essential system functions related to memory, CPU, and device access. A full OS consists of the kernel plus various system programs, such as init systems, compilers, and window managers.

---

find hybrid systems with containers running inside VMs in order to take advantage of both technologies.

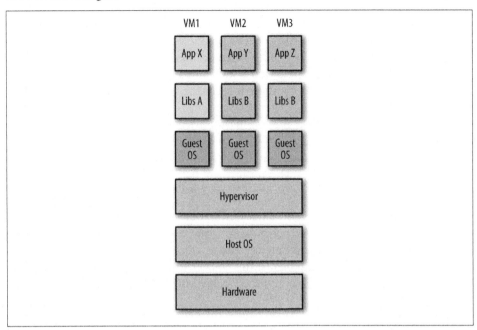

Figure 1-1. Three VMs running on a single host

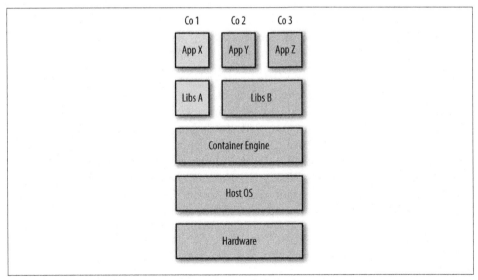

Figure 1-2. Three containers running on a single host

Docker and Containers

Containers are an old concept. For decades, Unix systems have had the `chroot` command, which provides a simple form of filesystem isolation. Since 1998, FreeBSD has had the jail utility, which extended chroot sandboxing to processes. Solaris Zones offered a comparatively complete containerization technology around 2001 but was limited to the Solaris OS. Also in 2001, SWsoft (now Parallels, Inc.) released the commercial Virtuozzo container technology for Linux and later open sourced the core technology as OpenVZ in 2005.[3] Then Google started the development of CGroups for the Linux kernel and began moving its infrastructure to containers. The Linux Containers (LXC) project started in 2008 and brought together CGroups, kernel namespaces, and chroot technology (among others) to provide a complete containerization solution. Finally, in 2013, Docker brought the final pieces to the containerization puzzle, and the technology began to enter the mainstream.

Docker took the existing Linux container technology and wrapped and extended it in various ways—primarily through portable images and a user-friendly interface—to create a complete solution for the creation and distribution of containers. The Docker platform has two distinct components: the Docker Engine (which is responsible for creating and running containers); and the Docker Hub (a cloud service for distributing containers).

The Docker Engine provides a fast and convenient interface for running containers. Before this, running a container using a technology such as LXC required significant specialist knowledge and manual work. The Docker Hub provides an enormous number of public container images for download, allowing users to quickly get started and avoid duplicating work already done by others. Further tooling developed by Docker includes Swarm, a clustering manager; Kitematic, a GUI for working with containers; and Machine, a command-line utility for provisioning Docker hosts.

By open sourcing the Docker Engine, Docker was able to grow a large community around Docker and take advantage of public help with bug fixes and enhancements. The rapid rise of Docker meant that it effectively became a *de facto* standard, which led to industry pressure to move to develop independent formal standards for the container runtime and format. In 2015, this culminated in the establishment of the Open Container Initiative, a "governance structure" sponsored by Docker, Microsoft, CoreOS, and many other important organizations, whose mission is to develop such a standard. Docker's container format and runtime forms the basis of the effort.

The uptake of containers has largely been driven by developers, who for the first time were given the tools to use containers effectively. The fast startup time of Docker con-

---

3 OpenVZ never achieved mass adoption, possibly because of the requirement to run a patched kernel.

tainers is essential to developers who crave quick and iterative development cycles where they can promptly see the results of code changes. The portability and isolation guarantees of containers ease collaboration with other developers and operations; developers can be sure their code will work across environments, and operations can focus on hosting and orchestrating containers rather than worrying about the code running inside them.

The changes brought about by Docker are significantly changing the way we develop software. Without Docker, containers would have remained in the shadows of IT for a long time to come.

The Shipping Metaphor

The Docker philosophy is often explained in terms of a shipping metaphor, which presumably explains the Docker name. The story normally goes something like this: when goods are transported, they have to pass through a variety of different *means*, possibly including trucks, forklifts, cranes, trains, and ships. These means have to be able to handle a wide variety of goods of different sizes and with different requirements (e.g., sacks of coffee, drums of hazardous chemicals, boxes of electronic goods, fleets of luxury cars, and refrigerated racks of lamb). Historically, this was a cumbersome and costly process, requiring the manual labor of dock workers to load and unload items by hand at each transit point (Figure 1-3).

The transport industry was revolutionized by the introduction of the intermodal container. These containers come in standard sizes and are designed to be moved between modes of transport with a minimum of manual labor. All transport machinery is designed to handle these containers, from the forklifts and cranes to the trucks, trains, and ships. Refrigerated and insulated containers are available for transporting temperature-sensitive goods, such as food and pharmaceuticals. The benefits of standardization also extend to other supporting systems, such as the labeling and sealing of containers. This means the transport industry can let the producers of goods worry about the contents of the containers so that it can focus on the movement and storage of the containers themselves.

The goal of Docker is to bring the benefits of container standardization to IT. In recent years, software systems have exploded in terms of diversity. Gone are the days of a LAMP[4] stack running on a single machine. A typical modern system may include JavaScript frameworks, NoSQL databases, message queues, REST APIs, and backends all written in a variety of programming languages. This stack has to run partly or completely on top of a variety of hardware—from the developer's laptop and the in-house testing cluster to the production cloud provider. Each of these environments is different, running different operating systems with different versions of libraries on

---

4 This originally stood for Linux, Apache, MySQL, and PHP—common components in a web application.

different hardware. In short, we have a similar issue to the one seen by the transport industry—we have to continually invest substantial manual effort to move code between environments. Much as the intermodal containers simplified the transportation of goods, Docker containers simplify the transportation of software applications. Developers can concentrate on building the application and shipping it through testing and production without worrying about differences in environment and dependencies. Operations can focus on the core issues of running containers, such as allocating resources, starting and stopping containers, and migrating them between servers.

Figure 1-3. Dockers working in Bristol, England, in 1940 (by Ministry of Information Photo Division Photographer)

Docker: A History

In 2008, Solomon Hykes founded dotCloud to build a language-agnostic platform-as-a-service (PaaS) offering. The language-agnostic aspect was the unique selling point for dotCloud—existing PaaSs were tied to particular sets of languages (e.g., Heroku supported Ruby, and Google App Engine supported Java and Python). In 2010, dot-

Cloud took part in Y Combinator's accelerator program, where it was exposed to new partners and began to attract serious investment. Some companies might have been reluctant to make such as decision (who wants to give away their magic beans), but the major turning point came in March 2013 when dotCloud recognized that Docker would benefit enormously from becoming a community-driven project.

Early versions of Docker were little more than a wrapper around LXC paired with a union filesystem, but the uptake and speed of development was shockingly fast. Within six months, it had more than 6,700 stars on GitHub and 175 nonemployee contributors. This led dotCloud to change its name to Docker, Inc., and to refocus its business model. Docker 1.0 was announced in June 2014, just 15 months after the 0.1 release. Docker 1.0 represented a major jump in stability and reliability—it was now declared "production ready," although it had already seen production use in several companies, including Spotify and Baidu. At the same time, Docker started moving toward being a complete platform rather than just a container engine, with the launch of the Docker Hub, a public repository for containers.

Other companies were quick to see the potential of Docker. Red Hat became a major partner in September 2013 and started using Docker to power its OpenShift cloud offering. Google, Amazon, and DigitalOcean were quick to offer Docker support on their clouds, and several startups began specializing in Docker hosting, such as Stack Dock. In October 2014, Microsoft announced that future versions of Windows Server would support Docker, representing a huge shift in positioning for a company traditionally associated with bloated enterprise software.

DockerConEU in December 2014 saw the announcement of Docker Swarm, a clustering manager for Docker and Docker Machine, a command-line interface (CLI) tool for provisioning Docker hosts. This was a clear signal of Docker's intention to provide a complete and integrated solution for running containers and not allowing themselves to be restricted to only providing the Docker engine.

That same December, CoreOS announced the development of rkt, its own container runtime, and the development of the appc container specification. In June 2015, during DockerCon in San Francisco, Solomon Hykes from Docker and Alex Polvi from CoreOS announced the formation of the Open Container Initiative (then called the Open Container Project) to develop a common standard for container formats and runtimes.

Then, in June 2015, the FreeBSD project announced that Docker was now supported on FreeBSD, using ZFS and the Linux compatibility layer. In August 2015, Docker and Microsoft released a "tech preview" of the Docker Engine for Windows server.

With the release of Docker 1.8, Docker introduced the content trust feature, which verifies the integrity and publisher of Docker images. Content trust is a critical component for building trusted workflows based on images retrieved from Docker registries.

Plugins and Plumbing

As a company, Docker, Inc., has always been quick to recognize that it owes a lot of its success to the ecosystem. While Docker, Inc., was concentrating on producing a stable, production-ready version of the container engine, other companies such as CoreOS, WeaveWorks, and ClusterHQ were working on related areas, such as orchestrating and networking containers. However, it quickly became clear that Docker, Inc., was planning to provide a complete platform out of the box, including networking, storage, and orchestration capabilities. In order to encourage continued ecosystem growth and ensure users had access to solutions for a wide range of use cases, Docker, Inc., announced it would create a modular, extensible framework for Docker where stock components could be swapped out for third-party equivalents or extended with third-party functionality. Docker, Inc., called this philosophy "Batteries Included, But Replaceable," meaning that a complete solution would be provided, but parts could be swapped out.[5]

At the time of writing, the plugin infrastructure is in its infancy, but is available. There are several plugins already available for networking containers and data management.

Docker also follows what it calls the "Infrastructure Plumbing Manifesto," which underlines its commitment to reusing and improving existing infrastructure components where possible and contributing reusable components back to the community when new tools are required. This led to the spinning out of the low-level code for running containers into the runC project, which is overseen by the OCI and can be reused as the basis for other container platforms.

64-Bit Linux

At the time of writing, the only stable, production-ready platform for Docker is 64-bit Linux. This means your computer will need to run a 64-bit Linux distribution, and all your containers will also be 64-bit Linux. If you are a Windows or Mac OS user, you can run Docker inside a VM.

Support for other native containers on other platforms, including BSD, Solaris, and Windows Server, is in various stages of development. Because Docker does not

---

5 Personally, I've never liked the phrase; all batteries provide much the same functionality and can only be swapped with batteries of the same size and voltage. I assume the phrase has its origins in Python's "Batteries Included" philosophy, which it uses to describe the extensive standard library that ships with Python.

natively do any virtualization, containers must always match the host kernel—a Windows Server container can only run on a Windows Server host, and a 64-bit Linux container will only run on a 64-bit Linux host.

Microservices and Monoliths

One of the biggest use cases and strongest drivers behind the uptake of containers are *microservices*.

Microservices are a way of developing and composing software systems such that they are built out of small, independent components that interact with one another over the network. This is in contrast to the traditional *monolithic* way of developing software, where there is a single large program, typically written in C++ or Java.

When it comes to scaling a monolith, commonly the only choice is to *scale up*, where extra demand is handled by using a larger machine with more RAM and CPU power. Conversely, microservices are designed to *scale out*, where extra demand is handled by provisioning multiple machines the load can be spread over. In a microservice architecture, it's possible to only scale the resources required for a particular service, focusing on the bottlenecks in the system. In a monolith, it's scale everything or nothing, resulting in wasted resources.

In terms of complexity, microservices are a double-edged sword. Each individual microservice should be easy to understand and modify. However, in a system composed of dozens or hundreds of such services, the overall complexity increases due to the interaction between individual components.

The lightweight nature and speed of containers mean they are particularly well suited for running a microservice architecture. Compared to VMs, containers are vastly smaller and quicker to deploy, allowing microservice architectures to use the minimum of resources and react quickly to changes in demand.

For more information on microservices, see *Building Microservices* by Sam Newman (O'Reilly) and Martin Fowler's Microservice Resource Guide (*http://martinfowler.com/microservices/*).

CHAPTER 2

Installation

This chapter will briefly cover the steps required to install Docker. There are a few gotchas, depending on which operating system you're using; but with any luck, it should be a straightforward and painless affair. If you already have a recent version of Docker installed (say 1.8 or newer), you can safely skip to the next chapter.

Installing Docker on Linux

By far the best way to install Docker on Linux is through the installation script provided by Docker. While most of the major Linux distributions have their own packages, these tend to lag behind Docker releases, which is a serious issue, given the pace of Docker development.

Docker Requirements

Docker doesn't have many requirements, but you do need to be running a reasonably modern kernel (version 3.10 or above, at the time of writing). You can check this by running uname -r. If you are using RHEL or CentOS, you will need version 7 or later.

Also remember that you need to be running on a 64-bit architecture. You can check this by running uname -m; the result should be x86_64.

You should be able to the use the script provided at *https://get.docker.com* to automatically install Docker. The official instructions will tell you to simply run curl -sSL https://get.docker.com | sh or wget -qO- https://get.docker.com | sh, and you're welcome to do that, but I recommend you inspect the script before running it to verify you are happy with the changes it will make to your system:

```
$ curl https://get.docker.com > /tmp/install.sh
$ cat /tmp/install.sh
...
$ chmod +x /tmp/install.sh
$ /tmp/install.sh
...
```

The script will do a few checks, then install Docker using the appropriate package for your system. It will also install some extra dependencies for security and filesystem features if they are missing.

If you simply don't want to use the installer, or you would like to use a different version of Docker than the one provided by the installer, you can also download a binary from the Docker website. The downside to this approach is that no checks for dependencies will be done, and you will have to manually install updates. For more information and links to binaries, see the Docker Binary page (*https://docs.docker.com/installation/binaries/*).

Tested with Docker 1.8

At the time of writing, Docker is at version 1.8. All commands have been tested against this version.

Run SELinux in Permissive Mode

If you are running a Red Hat–based distribution, including RHEL, CentOS, and Fedora, you will probably have the SELinux security module installed.

When getting started with Docker, I recommend running SELinux in *permissive* mode, which will log, rather than enforce, errors. If you run SELinux in *enforcing* mode, you are likely to see various cryptic "Permission Denied" errors when running examples from this book.

To check your SELinux mode, run `sestatus` and check the output. For example:

```
$ sestatus
SELinux status:                 enabled
SELinuxfs mount:                /sys/fs/selinux
SELinux root directory:         /etc/selinux
Loaded policy name:             targeted
Current mode:                   enforcing ❶
Mode from config file:          error (Success)
Policy MLS status:              enabled
Policy deny_unknown status:     allowed
Max kernel policy version:      28
```

❶   If you see "enforcing" here, SELinux is enabled and enforcing rules.

To change SELinux into permissive mode, just run `sudo setenforce 0`.

For more information on SELinux and why you should consider enabling it once you are confident with Docker, see "SELinux".

Running without sudo

As Docker is a privileged binary, by default, we need to prefix commands with `sudo` in order for them to run. This quickly gets boring. We can get around this by adding our user to the `docker` group. On Ubuntu, you should be able to do the following:

```
$ sudo usermod -aG docker
```

This will create the docker group (if it doesn't exist already), and add the current user. You'll then need to log out and log in again. Other Linux distributions should be similar.

You'll also need to restart the `docker` service, which is distribution dependent. On Ubuntu, this looks like:

```
$ sudo service docker restart
```

For the sake of brevity, this book omits `sudo` from all Docker commands.

 Adding a user to the `docker` group is equivalent to giving that user root privileges. As such, it has security implications you should be aware of, especially if you are using a shared machine. For further information, see the Docker security page (*https://docs.docker.com/articles/security/*).

Installing Docker on Mac OS or Windows

If you are using Windows or Mac OS, you will need some form of virtualization in order to run Docker.[1] You can download a full VM solution and follow the Linux instructions to install Docker, or alternatively, you can install the Docker Toolbox (*https://www.docker.com/toolbox*), which includes the minimal boot2docker VM as well as other Docker tools we will use in this book, such as Compose and Swarm. If you use Homebrew to install applications on your Mac, there is a brew recipe available for boot2docker; but in general, I recommend using the official Toolbox installation to avoid issues.

---

[1] Windows and Docker have announced a joint initiative to support Docker on Windows Server. This will allow Windows Server users to launch Windows-based images without virtualization.

Once the Toolbox is installed, you can access Docker by opening the Docker quick-start terminal.[2] Alternatively, you can configure an existing terminal by entering the following commands:

```
$ docker-machine start default
Starting VM...
Started machines may have new IP addresses. You may need to rerun the
`docker-machine env` command.
$ eval $(docker-machine env default)
```

This will set up your environment with the settings needed to access the Docker Engine running in the VM.

Be aware of the following when using the Docker Toolbox:

- The examples in this book assume Docker is running on the host machine. If you're using the Docker Toolbox, this won't be the case. In particular, you will need to change references to localhost to the IP address of the VM. For example:

  ```
  $ curl localhost:5000
  ```

  will become something like:

  ```
  $ curl 192.168.59.103:5000
  ```

  You can easily discover the IP of the VM by running docker-machine ip default, which allows for some automation:

  ```
  $ curl $(docker-machine ip default):5000
  ```

- Mapped volumes between your local OS and the Docker container must be cross-mounted inside the VM. The Docker Toolbox automates this to some extent, but be aware that this is happening if you have issues when using Docker volumes.

- You may need to change settings inside the VM if you have special requirements. The file */var/lib/boot2docker/profile* inside the boot2docker VM has various settings, including the Docker Engine configuration. You can also run your own scripts after VM initialization by editing the */var/lib/boot2docker/bootlocal.sh* file. Refer to the boot2docker GitHub repository (*https://github.com/boot2docker/boot2docker*) for full details.

- Some of the code in the book will only work with Unix line endings. If you are on Windows, make sure all files have the correct line endings. The dos2unix utility may be of help here.

---

2 The Docker Toolbox also includes Kitematic, a GUI for running Docker containers. We won't cover Kitematic in this book, but it is certainly worth investigating, especially when getting started with Docker.

If you have any problems following the examples in this book, try logging in to the VM directly with `docker-machine ssh default` and running the commands from there.

Docker Experimental Channel

As well as the normal, stable build, Docker maintain an *experimental* build that contains the latest features for testing purposes. As these features are still being discussed and developed, they are likely to change significantly before making it into a stable build. The experimental build should only be used for investigating new features before they are officially released and should never be used in production.

The experimental build can be installed on Linux using the script:

```
$ curl -sSL https://experimental.docker.com/ | sh
```

or by downloading a binary version from the Docker website (*http://bit.ly/1Q8g39C*). Note that the build is updated nightly, and hashes are available for verifying the download.

A Quick Check

Just to make sure everything is installed correctly and working, try running the `docker version` command. You should see something like this:

```
$ docker version
Client:
 Version:      1.8.1
 API version:  1.20
 Go version:   go1.4.2
 Git commit:   d12ea79
 Built:        Thu Aug 13 02:35:49 UTC 2015
 OS/Arch:      linux/amd64

Server:
 Version:      1.8.1
 API version:  1.20
 Go version:   go1.4.2
 Git commit:   d12ea79
 Built:        Thu Aug 13 02:35:49 UTC 2015
 OS/Arch:      linux/amd64
```

If so, you're all set and ready for the next chapter. If you instead get something like the following, it means the Docker daemon isn't running (or the client can't access it):

```
$ docker version
Client:
 Version:      1.8.1
 API version:  1.20
```

```
Go version:     go1.4.2
Git commit:     d12ea79
Built:          Thu Aug 13 02:35:49 UTC 2015
OS/Arch:        linux/amd64
Get http:///var/run/docker.sock/v1.20/version: dial unix /var/run/docker.sock:
no such file or directory.
* Are you trying to connect to a TLS-enabled daemon without TLS?
* Is your docker daemon up and running?
```

To investigate the problem, try starting the Docker daemon manually by running
sudo docker daemon—this should give you some information on what is going
wrong and help in searching for an answer. (Note that this will only work on a Linux
host. If you're using the Docker Toolbox or similar, you'll need to check the documentation for more help.)

CHAPTER 3

First Steps

This chapter will guide you through your first steps with using Docker. We start by launching and using some simple containers to give you a feel for how Docker works. Then we move onto *Dockerfiles*—the basic building block of Docker containers—and *Docker Registries*, which support the distribution of containers. The chapter concludes with a look at how to use a container to host a key-value store with persistent storage.

Running Your First Image

To test that Docker is installed correctly, try running:

```
$ docker run debian echo "Hello World"
```

This may take a little while, depending on your Internet connection, but eventually you will get something similar to the following:

```
Unable to find image 'debian' locally
debian:latest: The image you are pulling has been verified
511136ea3c5a: Pull complete
638fd9704285: Pull complete
61f7f4f722fb: Pull complete
Status: Downloaded newer image for debian:latest
Hello World
```

So what's happened here? We've called the docker run command, which is responsible for launching containers. The argument debian is the name of the image[1] we want to use—in this case, a stripped-down version of the Debian Linux distribution. The first line of the output tells us we don't have a local copy of the Debian image. Docker

---

[1] Images will be defined in more detail later; for the moment, just consider them "templates" for containers.

then checks online at the Docker Hub and downloads the newest version of the Debian image. Once the image has been downloaded, Docker turns the image into a running container and executes the command we specified—echo "Hello World"—inside it. The result of running this command is shown in the last line of the output.

If you run the same command again, it will immediately launch the container without downloading. The command should take around one second to run, which is astounding if you consider the amount of work that has happened: Docker has provisioned and launched our container, executed our echo command, and then shut down the container again. If you were to try to do something similar with a traditional VM, you would be waiting several seconds, possibly minutes.

We can ask Docker to give us a shell inside a container with the following command:

```
$ docker run -i -t debian /bin/bash
root@622ac5689680:/# echo "Hello from Container-land!"
Hello from Container-land!
root@622ac5689680:/# exit
exit
```

This will give you a new command prompt inside the container, very similar to sshing into a remote machine. In this case, the flags -i and -t tell Docker we want an interactive session with a TTY attached. The command /bin/bash gives us a bash shell. When you exit the shell, the container will stop—*containers only run as long as their main process.*

The Basic Commands

Let's try to understand Docker a bit more by launching a container and seeing what effect various commands and actions have. First, let's launch a new container; but this time, we'll give it a new hostname with the -h flag:

```
$ docker run -h CONTAINER -i -t debian /bin/bash
root@CONTAINER:/#
```

What happens if we break a container?

```
root@CONTAINER:/# mv /bin /basket
root@CONTAINER:/# ls
bash: ls: command not found
```

We've moved the */bin* directory and made the container pretty useless, at least temporarily.[2] Before we get rid of this container, let's see what the ps, inspect, and diff

---

2 I normally use rm rather than mv when demonstrating this in presentations, but the fear of someone running the command on their host forced me to use mv here.

commands tell us about it. Open a new terminal (leave the container session running), and try running docker ps from the host. You will see something like this:

```
CONTAINER ID  IMAGE   COMMAND       ...   NAMES
00723499fdbf  debian  "/bin/bash"   ...   stupefied_turing
```

This tells us a few details about all the currently running containers. Most of the output should be self-explanatory, but note that Docker has given the container a readable name that can be used to identify it from the host—in this case, "stupefied_turing".[3] We can get more information on a given container by running docker inspect with the name or ID of the container:

```
$ docker inspect stupefied_turing
[
{
    "Id": "00723499fdbfe55c14565dc53d61452519deac72e18a8a6fd7b371ccb75f1d91",
    "Created": "2015-09-14T09:47:20.2064793Z",
    "Path": "/bin/bash",
    "Args": [],
    "State": {
        "Running": true,
...
```

There is a lot of valuable output here, but it's not exactly easy to parse. We can use grep or the --format argument (which takes a Go template[4]) to filter for the information we're interested in. For example:

```
$ docker inspect stupefied_turing | grep IPAddress
    "IPAddress": "172.17.0.4",
    "SecondaryIPAddresses": null,
$ docker inspect --format {{.NetworkSettings.IPAddress}} stupefied_turing
172.17.0.4
```

Both give us the IP address of the running container. But for now, let's move onto another command, docker diff:

```
$ docker diff stupefied_turing
C /.wh..wh.plnk
A /.wh..wh.plnk/101.715484
D /bin
A /basket
A /basket/bash
A /basket/cat
```

---

3 Docker-generated names are a random adjective followed by the name of a famous scientist, engineer, or hacker. You can instead set the name by using the --name argument (e.g., docker run --name boris debian echo "Boo").

4 As in the templating engine for the Go programming language. This is a fully featured templating engine that provides a lot of flexibility and power for filtering and selecting data. You can find more information on how to use inspect at the Docker website (*https://docs.docker.com/reference/commandline/inspect/*).

```
A /basket/chacl
A /basket/chgrp
A /basket/chmod
...
```

What we're seeing here is the list of files that have changed in the running container—in this case, the deletion of /bin and addition of everything in /basket, as well as the creation of some files related to the storage driver. Docker uses a union filesystem (UFS) for containers, which allows multiple filesystems to be mounted in a hierarchy and to appear as a single filesystem. The filesystem from the image has been mounted as a read-only layer, and any changes to the running container are made to a read/write layer mounted on top of this. Because of this, Docker only has to look at the topmost read-write layer to find the changes made to the running system.

The last thing I want to show you before we're finished with this container is docker logs. If you run this command with the name of your container, you will get a list of everything that's happened inside the container:

```
$ docker logs stupefied_turing
root@CONTAINER:/# mv /bin /basket
root@CONTAINER:/# ls
bash: ls: command not found
```

We're finished with our broken container now, so let's get rid of it. First, exit from the shell:

```
root@CONTAINER:/# exit
exit
$
```

This will also stop the container, because the shell was the only running process. If you run docker ps, you should see there are no running containers.

However, this doesn't tell the whole story. If you type docker ps -a, you will get a list of all containers including *stopped* containers (officially called *exited* containers). An exited container can be restarted by issuing docker start (although we've broken the paths in this container, so in this case, you won't be able to start it). To get rid of the container, use the docker rm command:

```
$ docker rm stupefied_turing
stupefied_turing
```

Cleaning Up Stopped Containers

If you want to get rid of all your stopped containers, you can use the output of docker ps -aq -f status=exited, which gets the IDs of all stopped containers. For example:

```
$ docker rm -v $(docker ps -aq -f status=exited)
```

This is a common operation, so you might want to put it into a shell script or alias. Note that the -v argument will delete any Docker-managed volumes that aren't referenced by other containers.

You can avoid piling up stopped containers by giving the --rm flag to docker run, which will delete the container and associated filesystem when the container exits.

OK, let's see how we can build a new, useful container we actually want to keep.[5] We're going to create a Dockerized cowsay application. If you don't know what cowsay is, I suggest you brace yourself. Start by launching a container and installing some packages:

```
$ docker run -it --name cowsay --hostname cowsay debian bash
root@cowsay:/# apt-get update
...
Reading package lists... Done
root@cowsay:/# apt-get install -y cowsay fortune
...
root@cowsay:/#
```

Give it a whirl!

```
root@cowsay:/# /usr/games/fortune | /usr/games/cowsay
 _____
/ Writing is easy; all you do is sit \
| staring at the blank sheet of paper |
| until drops of blood form on your   |
| forehead.                           |
|                                     |
\ -- Gene Fowler                      /
 -----------------------------------
        \   ^__^
         \  (oo)_____
            (__)\       )\/\
                ||----w |
                ||     ||
```

---

5 Well, I say useful, but that's not *strictly* accurate.

Excellent. Let's keep this container.[6] To turn it into an image, we can just use the docker commit command. It doesn't matter if the container is running or stopped. To do this, we need to give the command the name of the container ("cowsay") a name for the image ("cowsayimage") and the name of the repository to store it in ("test"):

```
root@cowsay:/# exit
exit
$ docker commit cowsay test/cowsayimage
d1795abbc71e14db39d24628ab335c58b0b45458060d1973af7acf113a0ce61d
```

The returned value is the unique ID of our image. Now we have an image with cowsay installed that we can run:

```
$ docker run test/cowsayimage /usr/games/cowsay "Moo"
 _____
< Moo >
 ------
        \   ^__^
         \  (oo)_____
            (__)\       )\/\
                ||----w |
                ||     ||
```

This is great! However, there are a few problems. If we need to change something, we have to manually repeat our steps from that point. For example, if we want to use a different base image, we would have to start again from scratch. More importantly, it isn't easily *repeatable*; it's difficult and potentially error-prone to share or repeat the set of steps required to create the image. The solution to this is to use a *Dockerfile* to create an automated build for the image.

Building Images from Dockerfiles

A Dockerfile is simply a text file that contains a set of steps that can be used to create a Docker image. Start by creating a new folder and file for this example:

```
$ mkdir cowsay
$ cd cowsay
$ touch Dockerfile
```

And insert the following contents into *Dockerfile*:

```
FROM debian:wheezy

RUN apt-get update && apt-get install -y cowsay fortune
```

The FROM instruction specifies the base image to use (debian, as before; but this time, we have specified that we want to use the version tagged wheezy). All Dockerfiles

---

6 Just play along. It's easier that way.

must have a `FROM` instruction as the first noncomment instruction. `RUN` instructions specify a shell command to execute inside the image. In this case, we are just installing cowsay and fortune in the same way as we did before.

We can now build the image by running the `docker build` command inside the same directory:

```
$ ls
Dockerfile
$ docker build -t test/cowsay-dockerfile .
Sending build context to Docker daemon  2.048 kB
Step 0 : FROM debian:wheezy
 ---> f6fab3b798be
Step 1 : RUN apt-get update && apt-get install -y cowsay fortune
 ---> Running in 29c7bd4b0adc
...
Setting up cowsay (3.03+dfsg1-4) ...
 ---> dd66dc5a99bd
Removing intermediate container 29c7bd4b0adc
Successfully built dd66dc5a99bd
```

Then we can run the image in the same way as before:

```
$ docker run test/cowsay-dockerfile /usr/games/cowsay "Moo"
```

Images, Containers, and the Union File System

In order to understand the relationship between images and containers, we need to explain a key piece of technology that enables Docker—the *UFS* (sometimes simply called a *union mount*). Union filesystems allow multiple filesystems to be overlaid, appearing to the user as a single filesystem. Folders may contain files from multiple filesystems, but if two files have the exact same path, the last mounted file will hide any previous files. Docker supports several different UFS implementations, including AUFS, Overlay, devicemapper, BTRFS, and ZFS. Which implementation is used is system dependent and can be checked by running `docker info` where it is listed under "Storage Driver." It is possible to change the filesystem, but this is only recommended if you know what you are doing and are aware of the advantages and disadvantages.

Docker images are made up of multiple *layers*. Each of these layers is a read-only filesystem. A layer is created for each instruction in a Dockerfile and sits on top of the previous layers. When an image is turned into a *container* (from a `docker run` or `docker create` command), the Docker engine takes the image and adds a read/write filesystem on top (as well as initializing various settings such as the IP address, name, ID, and resource limits).

Because unnecessary layers bloat images (and the AUFS filesystem has a hard limit of 127 layers), you will notice that many Dockerfiles try to minimize the number of layers by specifying several Unix commands in a single `RUN` instruction.

A container can be in one of several states: *created, restarting, running, paused*, or *exited*. A "created" container is one that has been initialized with the docker create command but hasn't been started yet. The exited status is commonly referred to as "stopped" and indicates there are no running processes inside the container (this is also true of a "created" container, but an exited container will have already been started at least once). A container exits when its main processes exits. An exited container can be restarted with the docker start command. A stopped container is *not* the same as an image. A stopped container will retain changes to its settings, metadata, and filesystem, including runtime configuration such as IP address that are not stored in images. The restarting state is rarely seen in practice and occurs when the Docker engine attempts to restart a failed container.

But we can actually make things a little bit easier for the user by taking advantage of the ENTRYPOINT Dockerfile instruction. The ENTRYPOINT instruction lets us specify an executable that is used to handle any arguments passed to docker run.

Add the following line to the bottom of the Dockerfile:

```
ENTRYPOINT ["/usr/games/cowsay"]
```

We can now rebuild and run the image without needing to specify the cowsay command:

```
$ docker build -t test/cowsay-dockerfile .
...
$ docker run test/cowsay-dockerfile "Moo"
...
```

Much easier! But we've also lost the ability to use the fortune command inside the container as input to cowsay. We can fix this by providing our own script for the ENTRYPOINT, which is a common pattern when creating Dockerfiles. Create a file named *entrypoint.sh* with the following contents and save it in the same directory as the Dockerfile:[7]

```
#!/bin/bash
if [ $# -eq 0 ]; then
    /usr/games/fortune | /usr/games/cowsay
  else
    /usr/games/cowsay "$@"
fi
```

Set the file to be executable with chmod +x entrypoint.sh.

---

7 Be careful not to confuse users when writing ENTRYPOINT scripts—remember the script will swallow any commands given to docker run, which they may not be expecting.

All this script does is pipe input from fortune into cowsay if it is called with no arguments; otherwise, it calls cowsay with the given arguments. We next need to modify the Dockerfile to add the script into the image and call it with the `ENTRYPOINT` instruction. Edit the Dockerfile so that it looks like this:

```
FROM debian

RUN apt-get update && apt-get install -y cowsay fortune
COPY entrypoint.sh / ❶

ENTRYPOINT ["/entrypoint.sh"]
```

❶ The `COPY` instruction simply copies a file from the host into the image's filesystem, the first argument being the file on the host and the second the destination path, very similar to `cp`.

Try building a new image and running containers with and without arguments:

```
$ docker build -t test/cowsay-dockerfile .
...snip...
$ docker run test/cowsay-dockerfile
 _____
/ The last thing one knows in  \
| constructing a work is what to put |
| first.                        |
|                               |
\ -- Blaise Pascal             /
 ------------------------------------
        \   ^__^
         \  (oo)_____
            (__)\       )\/\
                ||----w |
                ||     ||
$ docker run test/cowsay-dockerfile Hello Moo
 _____
< Hello Moo >
 ------------
        \   ^__^
         \  (oo)_____
            (__)\       )\/\
                ||----w |
                ||     ||
```

Working with Registries

Now that we've created something amazing, how can we share it with others? When we first ran the Debian image at the start of the chapter, it was downloaded from the official Docker registry—the Docker Hub. Similarly, we can upload our own images to the Docker Hub for others to download and use.

The Docker Hub can be accessed from both the command line and the website. You can search for existing images with the Docker search command or use *https://hub.docker.com*.

Registries, Repositories, Images, and Tags

There is a hierarchical system for storing images. The following terminology is used:

Registry
> A service responsible for hosting and distributing images. The default registry is the Docker Hub.

Repository
> A collection of related images (usually providing different versions of the same application or service).

Tag
> An alphanumeric identifier attached to images within a repository (e.g., `14.04` or `stable`).

So the command `docker pull amouat/revealjs:latest` will download the image tagged `latest` within the `amouat/revealjs` repository from the Docker Hub registry.

In order to upload our cowsay image, you will need to sign up for an account with the Docker Hub (either online or using the `docker login` command). After you have done this, all we need to do is tag the image into an appropriately named repository and use the `docker push` command to upload it to the Docker Hub. But first, let's add a `MAINTAINER` instruction to the Dockerfile, which simply sets the author contact information for the image:

```
FROM debian

MAINTAINER John Smith <john@smith.com>
RUN apt-get update && apt-get install -y cowsay fortune
COPY entrypoint.sh /

ENTRYPOINT ["/entrypoint.sh"]
```

Now let's rebuild the image and upload it to the Docker Hub. This time, you will need to use a repository name that starts with your username on the Docker Hub (in my case, `amouat`), followed by / and whatever name you want to give the image. For example:

```
$ docker build -t amouat/cowsay .
...
$ docker push amouat/cowsay
The push refers to a repository [docker.io/amouat/cowsay] (len: 1)
```

```
e8728c722290: Image successfully pushed
5427ac510fe6: Image successfully pushed
4a63ead8b301: Image successfully pushed
73805e6e9ac7: Image successfully pushed
c90d655b99b2: Image successfully pushed
30d39e59ffe2: Image successfully pushed
511136ea3c5a: Image successfully pushed
latest: digest: sha256:bfd17b7c5977520211cecb202ad73c3ca14acde6878d9ffc81d95...
```

As I didn't specify a tag after the repository name, it was automatically assigned the `latest` tag. To specify a tag, just add it after the repository name with a colon (e.g., `docker build -t amouat/cowsay:stable.`).

Once the upload has completed, the world can download your image via the `docker pull` command (e.g., `docker pull amouat/cowsay`).

Private Repositories

Of course, you might not want the world to have access to your image. In this case, you have a couple of choices. You can pay for a hosted private repository (on the Docker Hub or a similar service such as Quay.io), or you can run your own registry. For more information on private repositories and registries, see Chapter 7.

Image Namespaces

Pushed Docker images can belong to one of three namespaces, which can be identified from the image name:

- Names prefixed with a string and /, such as `amouat/revealjs`, belong to the "user" namespace. These are images on the Docker Hub that have been uploaded by a given user. For example, `amouat/revealjs` is the revealjs image uploaded by the user `amouat`. It is free to upload public images to the Docker Hub, which already contains thousands of images from the whimsical `supertest2014/nyan` to the very useful `gliderlabs/logspout`.

- Names such as `debian` and `ubuntu`, with no prefixes or /s, belong to the "root" namespace, which is controlled by Docker, Inc., and reserved for the official images for common software and distributions available from the Docker Hub. Although curated by Docker, the images are generally maintained by third parties, normally the providers of the software in question (e.g., the `nginx` image is maintained by the nginx company). There are official images for most common software packages, which should be your first port of call when looking for an image to use.

- Names prefixed with a hostname or IP are images hosted on third-party registries (not the Docker Hub). These include self-hosted registries for organizations,

---

as well as competitors to the Hub, such as Quay.io. For example, `localhost:5000/wordpress` refers to an WordPress image hosted on a local registry.

This namespacing ensures users cannot be confused about where images have come from; if you're using the `debian` image, you know it is the official image from the Docker Hub and not some other registry's version of the `debian` image.

Using the Redis Official Image

OK, I admit it: you probably won't get a lot of mileage out of the cowsay image. Let's see how we can use an image from one of the official Docker repositories—in this case, we'll have a look at the official image for Redis, a popular key-value store.

Official Repositories

If you search the Docker Hub for a popular application or service, such as the Java programming language or the PostgreSQL database, you will find hundreds of results.[8] The official Docker repositories are intended to provide curated images of known quality and provenance and should be your first choice where possible. They should be returned at the top of searches and marked as official.

When you pull from an official repository, the name will have no user portion, or it will be set to `library` (e.g., the MongoDB repository is available from `mongo` and `library/mongo`). You will also get a message saying, "The image you are pulling has been verified," indicating the Docker daemon has validated the checksums for the image and therefore has verified its provenance.

Start by getting the image:

```
$ docker pull redis
Using default tag: latest
latest: Pulling from library/redis

d990a769a35e: Pull complete
8656a511ce9c: Pull complete
f7022ac152fb: Pull complete
8e84d9ce7554: Pull complete
c9e5dd2a9302: Pull complete
27b967cdd519: Pull complete
3024bf5093a1: Pull complete
e6a9eb403efb: Pull complete
c3532a4c89bc: Pull complete
```

---

8 At the time of writing, there are 1,350 PostgreSQL images.

```
35fc08946add: Pull complete
d586de7d17cd: Pull complete
1f677d77a8fa: Pull complete
ed09b32b8ab1: Pull complete
54647d88bc19: Pull complete
2f2578ff984f: Pull complete
ba249489d0b6: Already exists
19de96c112fc: Already exists
library/redis:latest: The image you are pulling has been verified.
Important: image verification is a tech preview feature and should not be re...
Digest: sha256:3c3e4a25690f9f82a2a1ec6d4f577dc2c81563c1ccd52efdf4903ccdd26cada3
Status: Downloaded newer image for redis:latest
```

Start up the Redis container, but this time use the -d argument:

```
$ docker run --name myredis -d redis
585b3d36e7cec8d06f768f6eb199a29feb8b2e562288445263377216 9695b94a
```

The -d tells Docker to run the container in the background. Docker starts the container as normal, but rather than printing the output from the container, it returns the container's ID and exits. The container is still running in the background, and you can use the docker logs command to see any output from the container.

OK, so how do we use it? Obviously we need to connect to the database in some way. We don't have an application, so we'll just use the redis-cli tool. We could just install the redis-cli on the host, but it's easier and more informative to launch a new container to run redis-cli in and link the two:

```
$ docker run --rm -it --link myredis:redis redis /bin/bash
root@ca38735c5747:/data# redis-cli -h redis -p 6379
redis:6379> ping
PONG
redis:6379> set "abc" 123
OK
redis:6379> get "abc"
"123"
redis:6379> exit
root@ca38735c5747:/data# exit
exit
```

Pretty neat—we've just linked two containers and added some data to Redis in a few seconds. So how did this work?

Docker Networking Changes

Throughout this book, we use the `--link` command to network containers. Forthcoming changes to the way networking works in Docker mean that in the future, it will be more idiomatic to "publish services" rather than link containers. However, links will continue to be supported for the foreseeable future, and the examples in this book should work without changes.

For more information on the upcoming changes to networking, see "New Docker Networking".

The linking magic happened with the `--link myredis:redis` argument to `docker run`. This told Docker that we wanted to connect the new container to the existing "myredis" container, and that we want to refer to it by the name "redis" inside our new container. To achieve this, Docker set up an entry for "redis" in */etc/hosts* inside the container, pointing to the IP address of the "myredis". This allowed us to use the hostname "redis" in the `redis-cli` rather than needing to somehow pass in, or discover, the IP address of the Redis container.

After that, we run the Redis `ping` command to verify that we are connected to a Redis server before adding and retrieving some data with `set` and `put`.

This is all good, but there is still an issue: how do we persist and back up our data? For this, we don't want to use the standard container filesystem—instead, we need something that can be easily shared between the container and the host or other containers. Docker provides this through the concept of *volumes*. Volumes are files or directories that are directly mounted on the host and not part of the normal union file system. This means they can be shared with other containers and all changes will be made directly to the host filesystem. There are two ways of declaring a directory as a volume, either using the VOLUME instruction inside a Dockerfile or specifying the `-v` flag to `docker run`. Both the following Dockerfile instruction and `docker run` command have the effect of creating a volume as */data* inside a container:

```
VOLUME /data
```

and:

```
$ docker run -v /data test/webserver
```

By default, the directory or file will be mounted on the host inside your Docker installation directory (normally */var/lib/docker/*). It is possible to specify the host directory to use as the mount via the `docker run` command (e.g., `docker run -d -v /host/dir:/container/dir test/webserver`). It isn't possible to specify a host directory inside a Dockerfile for reasons of portability and security (the file or directory may not exist in other systems, and containers shouldn't be able to mount sensitive files like *etc/passwd* without explicit permission).

So, how do we use this to do backups with the Redis container? The following shows one way, assuming the myredis container is still running:

```
$ docker run --rm -it --link myredis:redis redis /bin/bash
root@09a1c4abf81f:/data# redis-cli -h redis -p 6379
redis:6379> set "persistence" "test"
OK
redis:6379> save
OK
redis:6379> exit
root@09a1c4abf81f:/data# exit
exit
$ docker run --rm --volumes-from myredis -v $PWD/backup:/backup \
        debian cp /data/dump.rdb /backup/
$ ls backup
dump.rdb
```

Note that we have used the -v argument to mount a known directory on the host and --volumes-from to connect the new container to the Redis database folder.

Once you've finished with the myredis container, you can stop and delete it:

```
$ docker stop myredis
myredis
$ docker rm -v myredis
myredis
```

And you can remove all leftover containers with:

```
$ docker rm $(docker ps -aq)
45e404caa093
e4b31d0550cd
7a24491027fc
...
```

Conclusion

We've now finished our brief tutorial on getting started with Docker. It's been a whirlwind tour, but by now, you should feel confident about creating and running your own containers. In the next chapter, we'll go into details about the architecture of Docker and some of the fundamental concepts.

CHAPTER 4

Docker Fundamentals

In this chapter, we'll expand on the fundamental Docker concepts. We'll start by looking at the overall architecture of Docker, including the technologies it builds on. This is followed by more in-depth sections on building Docker images, networking containers, and handling data in volumes. The chapter concludes with an overview of the remaining Docker commands.

As this chapter contains a lot of reference material, you may prefer to skim the main points and move onto Chapter 5, referring back to this chapter as needed.

The Docker Architecture

In order to understand how best to use Docker and some of the more unusual behavior in Docker, it's good to have a rough understanding of how the Docker platform is put together under the covers.

In Figure 4-1, we can see the major components of a Docker installation:

- At the center is the *Docker daemon*, which is responsible for creating, running, and monitoring containers, as well as building and storing images, both of which are represented on the right of the diagram. The Docker daemon is launched by running docker daemon, which is normally taken care of by the host OS.

- The Docker client is on the lefthand side and is used to talk to the Docker daemon via HTTP. By default, this happens over a Unix domain socket, but it can also use a TCP socket to enable remote clients or a file descriptor for systemd-managed sockets. Because all communication must be done over HTTP, it's easy to connect to remote Docker daemons and develop programming language bindings, but it also has implications for how features are implemented, such as requiring a *build context* for Dockerfiles, as explained in "The Build Context"). The API used for communication with daemon is well defined and documented, allowing developers to write programs that interface directly with the daemon, without using the Docker client. The Docker client and daemon are distributed as a single binary.

- Docker registries store and distribute images. The default registry is the Docker Hub, which hosts thousands of public images as well as curated "official" images. Many organizations run their own registries that can be used to store commercial or sensitive images, which also avoids the overhead of needing to download images from the Internet. See "Running Your Own Registry" for information on running your own registry. The Docker daemon will download images from registries in response to docker pull requests. It will also automatically download images specified in docker run requests and in the FROM instruction of Dockerfiles if they are not available locally.

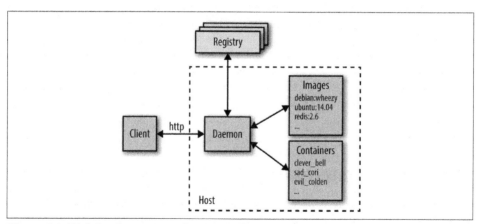

Figure 4-1. High-level overview of major Docker components

Underlying Technologies

The Docker daemon uses an "execution driver" to create containers. By default, this is Docker's own runc driver, but there is also legacy support for LXC. Note that runc is very closely tied to the following kernel features:

cgroups
> Responsible for managing resources used by a container (e.g., CPU and memory usage). They are also responsible for *freezing* and *unfreezing* containers, as used in the docker pause functionality.

namespaces

Responsible for isolating containers; making sure that a container's filesystem, hostname, users, networking, and processes are separated from the rest of the system.

Libcontainer also supports SELinux and AppArmor, which can be enabled for tighter security. See Chapter 13 for more information.

Another major technology underlying Docker is the Union File System (UFS), used to store the layers for containers. The UFS is provided by one of several storage drivers, either AUFS, devicemapper, BTRFS, or Overlay. See the previous discussion of UFS in "Images, Containers, and the Union File System".

Surrounding Technologies

The Docker engine and the Docker Hub do not in and of themselves constitute a complete solution for working with containers. Most users will find they require supporting services and software, such as cluster management, service discovery tools, and advanced networking capabilities. As described in "Plugins and Plumbing", Docker, Inc., plans to build a complete out-of-the-box solution that includes these features but allows users to easily swap out the default components for third-party ones. The "swappable batteries" strategy primarily refers to the API level—allowing components to hook into the Docker Engine—but can also be seen as allowing supporting Docker technology packaged as independent binaries to be easily replaced with third-party equivalents.

The current list of supporting technologies supplied by Docker includes:

Swarm

Docker's clustering solution. Swarm can group together several Docker hosts, allowing the user to treat them as a unified resource. See Chapter 12 for more information.

Compose

Docker Compose is a tool for building and running applications composed of multiple Docker containers. It is primarily used in development and testing rather than production. See "Automating with Compose" for more details.

Machine

Docker Machine installs and configures Docker hosts on local or remote resources. Machine also configures the Docker client, making it easy to swap between environments. See Chapter 9 for an example.

Kitematic

Kitematic is a Mac OS and Windows GUI for running and managing Docker containers.

Docker Trusted Registry

Docker's on-premise solution for storing and managing Docker images. Effectively a local version of the Docker Hub that can integrate with an existing security infrastructure and help organizations comply with regulations regarding the storage and security of data. Features include metrics, role-based access control (RBAC), and logs, all managed through an administrative console. This is currently the only non–open source product from Docker, Inc.

There is already a large list of services and applications from third parties that build on or work with Docker. Several solutions have already emerged in the following areas:

Networking

Creating networks of containers that span hosts is a nontrivial problem that can be solved in a variety of ways. Several solutions have appeared in this area, including Weave (*http://weave.works/net/*) and Project Calico (*http://www.project calico.org/*). In addition, Docker will soon have an integrated networking solution called Overlay. Users will be able to swap out the Overlay driver for other solutions using Docker's networking plugin framework.

Service discovery

When a Docker container comes up, it needs some way of finding the other services it needs to talk to, which are typically also running in containers. As containers are dynamically assigned IP addresses, this isn't a trivial problem in a large system. Solutions in this area include Consul (*https://consul.io/*), Registrator (*https://github.com/gliderlabs/registrator*), SkyDNS (*https://github.com/skynetservi ces/skydns/*), and etcd (*https://github.com/coreos/etcd*).

Orchestration and cluster management

In large container deployments, tooling is essential in order to monitor and manage the system. Each new container needs to be placed on a host, monitored, and updated. The system needs to respond to failures or changes in load by moving, starting, or stopping containers appropriately. There are already several competing solutions in the area, including Google's Kubernetes (*http://kubernetes.io/*); Marathon (*https://github.com/mesosphere/marathon*), a framework for Mesos (*https://mesos.apache.org/*); CoreOS's Fleet (*https://github.com/coreos/fleet*); and Docker's own Swarm tooling.

All of these topics are covered in more depth in Part III. It is worth pointing out that there are also alternatives to the Docker Trusted Registry, including the CoreOS Enterprise Registry (*https://coreos.com/products/enterprise-registry/*) and JFrog's Artifactory (*http://www.jfrog.com/open-source/#os-arti*).

In addition to the previously mentioned network driver plugins, Docker also supports *volume plugins* for integration with other storage systems. Notable volume plugins include Flocker (*https://github.com/ClusterHQ/flocker*), a multihost data management and migration tool, and GlusterFS (*https://github.com/calavera/docker-volume-glusterfs*) for distributed storage. More information on the plugin framework can be found at the Docker website (*https://docs.docker.com/extend/plugins/*).

An interesting side effect of the rise of containers is the new breed of operating systems designed to host them. While Docker runs happily on most current Linux distributions such as Ubuntu and Red Hat, there are several projects underway to create minimal and easy-to-maintain distributions that are focused entirely on running containers (or containers and VMs), especially within a context of powering a datacenter or cluster. Examples include Project Atomic (*http://www.projectatomic.io/*), CoreOS (*https://coreos.com/*), and RancherOS (*http://rancher.com/rancher-os/*).

Docker Hosting

We'll cover Docker hosting in more detail in Chapter 9, but it's worth pointing out some of the many choices here. Many of the traditional cloud providers, including Amazon, Google, and Digital Ocean, have brought out some level of Docker offering. Google's Container Engine may be the most interesting of these, as it is built directly on top of Kubernetes. Of course, even when a cloud provider doesn't have a specific Docker offering, it's normally still possible to provision VMs that can run Docker containers.

Joyent has also entered the space with its own container offering, called Triton, built on top of SmartOS. By implementing the Docker API with its own container and Linux emulation technology, Joyent was able to create a public cloud that interfaces with the standard Docker client. Importantly, Joyent believes its container implementation is secure enough to run directly on bare metal rather than having to be placed in VMs, meaning it can result in large efficiency savings, especially in terms of I/O.

There are also several projects that build a PaaS platform on top of Docker, including Deis (*http://deis.io/*), Flynn (*https://flynn.io/*), and Paz (*http://paz.sh*).

How Images Get Built

We saw in "Building Images from Dockerfiles" that the primary way to make new images is through Dockerfiles and the `docker build` command. This section will look at what happens here in a little more depth and end with a guide to the various instructions that can be used in a Dockerfile. It's handy to have some understanding of how the build command works internally, as its behavior can sometimes be surprising.

The Build Context

The docker build command requires a Dockerfile and a *build context* (which may be empty). The build context is the set of local files and directories that can be referenced from ADD or COPY instructions in the Dockerfile and is normally specified as a path to a directory. For example, we used the build command docker build -t test/cowsay-dockerfile . in "Building Images from Dockerfiles", which sets the context to '.', the current working directory. All the files and directories under the path form the build context and will be sent to the Docker daemon as part of the build process.

In cases where a context is not specified (if only a URL to a Dockerfile is given or the contents of a Dockerfile are piped from STDIN), the build context is considered to be empty.

Don't Use / as the Build Context

As the build context is gathered into a tarball and sent to the Docker daemon, you *really* don't want to use a directory with lots of files in it already. For example, using */home/user*, *Downloads*, or / will result in a long delay while the Docker client bundles everything up and transfers it to the daemon.

If a URL beginning with *http* or *https* is given, it is assumed to be a direct link to a Dockerfile. This is unlikely to be very useful, as no context is associated with the Dockerfile (and links to archives are not accepted).

A git repository can also be given as the build context. In this situation, the Docker client will clone the repository and any submodules to a temporary directory that is then sent to the Docker daemon as the build context. Docker will interpret the context as a git repository if the path begins with *github.com/*, *git@*, or *git://*. In general, I would suggest avoiding this method and instead checking out repositories by hand, which is more flexible and leaves less chance for confusion.

The Docker client can also take input on STDIN by giving a "-" as an argument in place of the build context. The input can either be a Dockerfile with no context (e.g., docker build - < Dockerfile) or an archive file that constitutes the context and includes a Dockerfile (e.g., docker build - < context.tar.gz). Archive files can be in *tar.gz*, *xz*, or *bzip2* format.

The location of the Dockerfile within the context can be specified with the -f argument (e.g., docker build -f dockerfiles/Dockerfile.debug .). If unspecified, Docker will look for a file called *Dockerfile* at the root of the context.

Use a .dockerignore File

In order to remove unneeded files from the build context, you can use a *.dockerignore* file. The file should contain the names of files to exclude, separated by newlines. The wildcard characters * and ? are allowed. Here's an example *.dockerignore* file:

```
.git ❶
*/.git ❷
*/*/.git ❸
*.sw? ❹
```

❶   Will ignore a *.git* file or directory in the root of the build context, but allow it any subdirectory (i.e., *.git* is ignored, but *dir1/.git* isn't).

❷   Will ignore a *.git* file or directory exactly one directory below the root (i.e., *dir1/.git* is ignored but *.git* and *dir1/dir2/.git* aren't).

❸   Will ignore a *.git* file or directory exactly two directories below the root (i.e., *dir1/dir2/.git* is ignored but *.git* and *dir1/.git* aren't).

❹   Will ignore *test.swp*, *test.swo*, and *bla.swp* but not *dir1/test.swp*.

Full regular expressions such as [A-Z]* are not supported.

At the time of writing, there isn't a way to match files over all subdirectories (e.g., you can't ignore both */test.tmp* and */dir1/test.tmp* in one expression).

Image Layers

New Docker users are often thrown by the way images are built up. Each instruction in a Dockerfile results in a new image *layer*, which can also be used to start a container. The new layer is created by starting a container using the image of the previous layer, executing the Dockerfile instruction and saving a new image. When a Dockerfile instruction successfully completes, the intermediate container will be deleted, unless the --rm=false argument was given.[1] Because each instruction results in a static image—essentially just a filesystem and some metadata—all running processes in the instruction will be stopped. This means that while you can start long-lived processes, such as databases or SSH daemons in a RUN instruction, they will not be running when the next instruction is processed or a container is started. If you

---

[1] Don't worry if I've lost you here. It should make more sense after looking at the output of docker build in our debug example.

want a service or process to start with the container, it must be launched from an ENTRYPOINT or CMD instruction.

You can see the full set of layers that make up an image by running the docker history command. For example:

```
$ docker history mongo:latest
IMAGE          CREATED       CREATED BY                                    ...
278372cb22b2   4 days ago    /bin/sh -c #(nop) CMD ["mongod"]
341d04fd3d27   4 days ago    /bin/sh -c #(nop) EXPOSE 27017/tcp
ebd34b5e9c37   4 days ago    /bin/sh -c #(nop) ENTRYPOINT &{["/entrypoint.
f3b2b8cf226c   4 days ago    /bin/sh -c #(nop) COPY file:ef2883b33ed7ba0cc
ba53e9f50f18   4 days ago    /bin/sh -c #(nop) VOLUME [/data/db]
c537910de5cc   4 days ago    /bin/sh -c mkdir -p /data/db && chown -R mong
f48ad436057a   4 days ago    /bin/sh -c set -x
df59596772ab   4 days ago    /bin/sh -c echo "deb http://repo.mongodb.org/
96de83c82d4b   4 days ago    /bin/sh -c #(nop) ENV MONGO_VERSION=3.0.6
0dab801053d9   4 days ago    /bin/sh -c #(nop) ENV MONGO_MAJOR=3.0
5e7b428dddf7   4 days ago    /bin/sh -c apt-key adv --keyserver ha.pool.sk
e81ad85ddfce   4 days ago    /bin/sh -c curl -o /usr/local/bin/gosu -SL "h
7328803ca452   4 days ago    /bin/sh -c gpg --keyserver ha.pool.sks-keyser
ec5be38a3c65   4 days ago    /bin/sh -c apt-get update
430e6598f55b   4 days ago    /bin/sh -c groupadd -r mongodb && useradd -r
19de96c112fc   6 days ago    /bin/sh -c #(nop) CMD ["/bin/bash"]
ba249489d0b6   6 days ago    /bin/sh -c #(nop) ADD file:b908886c97e2b96665
```

When a build fails, it can be very useful to launch the layer before the failure. Here's an example *Dockerfile*:

```
FROM busybox:latest

RUN echo "This should work"
RUN /bin/bash -c echo "This won't"
```

If we try to build it:

```
$ docker build -t echotest .
Sending build context to Docker daemon 2.048 kB
Step 0 : FROM busybox:latest
 ---> 4986bf8c1536
Step 1 : RUN echo "This should work"
 ---> Running in f63045cc086b ❶
This should work
 ---> 85b49a851fcc ❷
Removing intermediate container f63045cc086b ❸
Step 2 : RUN /bin/bash -c echo "This won't"
 ---> Running in e4b31d0550cd
/bin/sh: /bin/bash: not found
The command '/bin/sh -c /bin/bash -c echo "This won't"' returned a non-zero
code: 127
```

❶ ID of the temporary *container* Docker launched to run our instruction in.

❷   ID of the *image* created from the container.

❸   The temporary container is now deleted.

While, in this case, the problem is fairly clear from the error, we can run the image created from the last successful layer in order to debug the instruction. Note that we are using the last *image* ID here (85b49a851fcc), not the ID of the last *container* (e4b31d0550cd):

```
$ docker run -it 85b49a851fcc
/ # /bin/bash -c "echo hmm"
/bin/sh: /bin/bash: not found
/ # /bin/sh -c "echo ahh!"
ahh!
/ #
```

And the problem becomes even more obvious: the busybox image doesn't include the bash shell.

Caching

Docker also caches each layer in order to speed up the building of images. This caching is very important for efficient workflows, but is somewhat naive. The cache is used for an instruction if the previous instruction was found in the cache *and* there is a layer in the cache that has exactly the same instruction and parent layer (even spurious spaces will invalidate the cache).

Also, in the case of COPY and ADD instructions, the cache will be invalidated if the checksum or metadata for any of the files has changed.

This means that RUN instructions that are not guaranteed to have the same result across multiple invocations *will still be cached*. Be particularly aware of this if you download files, run apt-get update, or clone source repositories.

If you need to invalidate the cache, you can run docker build with the --no-cache argument. You can also add or change an instruction before the point where you want to invalidate the cache; and for this reason, you may sometimes see Dockerfiles with lines like this:

```
ENV UPDATED_ON "14:12 17 February 2015"
RUN git clone....
```

I would advise against using this technique, as it tends to confuse later users of the image, especially when the image was built on a different date than the line suggests.

Base Images

When creating your own images, you will need to decide which base image to start from. There are a lot of choices, and it's worth taking the time to understand the various advantages and disadvantages of each.

The best case scenario is that you don't need to create an image at all—you can just use an existing one and mount your configuration files and/or data into it. This is likely to be the case for common application software, such as databases and web servers, where there are official images available. In general, you are much better off using an official image than rolling your own—you get the benefit of other people's work and experience in figuring out how best to run the software inside a container. If there is a particular reason an official image doesn't work for you, consider opening an issue on the parent project, as it is likely others are facing similar problems or know of workarounds.

If you need an image to host your own application, first have a look to see if there is an official base image for the language or framework you are using (e.g., Go or Ruby on Rails). Often you can use separate images for building and distributing your software (e.g., you could use the `java:jdk` image to build a Java application but then distribute the resulting JAR file using the smaller `java:jre` image, which gets rid of the unnecessary build tooling). Similarly, some official images (such as `node`) have special "slim" builds that remove a lot of development tools and headers.

Sometimes you really just need a small but complete Linux distro. If I'm going for true minimalism, I'll use the `alpine` image, which is only just over 5 MB in size but still has an extensive package manager for easily installing applications and tools. If I want a more complete image, I'll normally use one of the `debian` images, which are much smaller than the also common `ubuntu` images but have access to the same packages. If your organization is tied to a particular distribution of Linux, you should also be able to find a Docker image for it. This may make more sense than moving to a new distribution that your organization doesn't support or have experience with.

A lot of the time, it's not necessary to go overboard with making sure images are as small as possible. Remember that base layers are shared between images, so if you already have the `ubuntu:14.04` image and pull an image from the Hub that is based on it, you will only pull the changes rather than the full image. However, minimal images are definitely a big bonus when aiming for fast deploys and easy distribution.

It is possible to go ultra minimal and ship images with only binaries. To do this, write a Dockerfile that inherits from the special `scratch` image (a completely blank filesystem) and simply copies your binary in and sets an appropriate `CMD` instruction. Your binary will need to include all its required libraries (no dynamic linking) and have no possibility of calling external commands. In addition, remember the binary will need to be compiled for the architecture of the container, which may be different than the architecture of the machine running the Docker client.[2]

While the minimalist approach can be very tempting, note that it can leave you in a difficult situation when it comes to debugging and maintenance—busybox won't have a lot tools to work with; and if you've used scratch, you won't even have a shell.

Phusion Reaction

Another interesting choice of base image is phusion/baseimage-docker. The Phusion developers created this base image in reaction to the official Ubuntu image, which they claim is missing several essential services. Several core Docker developers disagreed with Phusion's standpoint, which led to various exchanges across blogs, IRC, and Twitter. The main points of contention are:

The need for an init service

The view of Docker is that each container should only run a single application and ideally a *single process*. If you only have a single process, there is no need for an init service. The main argument put forth by Phusion is that the lack of an init service can lead to containers full of zombie processes—processes that have not been killed correctly by their parent processes or reaped by a supervising process. While this argument is correct, the only way zombie processes can occur is from bugs in the application code; the vast majority of users should not run into this problem; and if they do, the best solution is to fix the code.

A running cron daemon

The base ubuntu and debian images do not start the cron daemon by default, but the phusion image does. Phusion argues that many applications are dependent on cron, so it is essential to have it running. The Docker view—which I'm inclined to agree with—is that cron should only be running if your application is dependent on it.

An SSH daemon

The default images do not install or run an SSH daemon by default. The normal way of getting a shell is to use the docker exec command (see "Managing Containers"), which avoids the penalty of running an unnecessary process per con-

---

2 It's actually possible to take this concept of minimal computing even further by abandoning Docker and the full Linux kernel in favor of a *unikernel* approach. In a unikernel architecture, applications are combined with a kernel containing only the features used by the application, which is then run directly on a hypervisor. This gets rid of several unnecessary layers of code and unused drivers, resulting in a much smaller and faster application (unikernels commonly boot in under a second—that is, they can be started in direct response to user requests). If you'd like to learn more about this, take a look at "Unikernels: Rise of the Virtual Library Operating System" (*https://queue.acm.org/detail.cfm?id=2566628*) by Anil Madhavapeddy and David J. Scott and MirageOS (*http://www.openmirage.org/*).

tainer. Phusion seems to accept this and has disabled their SSH daemon by default, but their image is still considerably bloated by the inclusion of the daemon and its libraries.

Personally, I would only recommend using the Phusion base image if you have a specific need to run multiple processes, cron, and `ssh` inside your container. Otherwise, I would stick with images from the official Docker repositories, such as `ubuntu:14.04` and `debian:wheezy`.

> **Rebuilding Images**
>
> Note that when `docker build` is run, Docker will look at the `FROM` instruction and attempt to pull the image if it doesn't exist locally. If it does exist, Docker will use that image without checking to see if there is a newer version available. This means that just doing a `docker build` isn't enough to ensure your images are completely up to date; you also have to either explicitly `docker pull` all ancestor images or delete them in order to force the build command to download the latest versions.
>
> This becomes very important when common base images, such as `debian`, are updated with security patches.

Dockerfile Instructions

This section briefly covers the various instructions available for use in Dockerfiles. It doesn't go deep into details, partly because things are still changing and likely to quickly get out of date and partly because there is comprehensive and always up-to-date documentation available on the Docker website (*http://docs.docker.com/reference/builder/*). Comments in Dockerfiles are indicated by starting the line with a #.

> **Exec Versus Shell Form**
>
> Several instructions (`RUN`, `CMD`, and `ENTRYPOINT`) take both a *shell* format and an *exec* format. The exec form takes a JSON array (e.g., `["executable", "param1", "param2"]`) that assumes the first item is the name of an executable that is then executed with the remaining items as parameters. The shell format is a freeform string that will be interpreted by passing to `/bin/sh -c`. Use the exec form to avoid the shell munging strings or in cases where the image doesn't have `/bin/sh`.

The following instructions are available in Dockerfiles:

ADD

Copies files from the build context or remote URLs into the image. If an archive file is added from a local path, it will automatically be unpacked. As the range of functionality covered by ADD is quite large, it's generally best to prefer the simpler COPY command for copying files and directories in the build context and RUN instructions with curl or wget to download remote resources (which retains the possibility of processing and deleting the download in the same instruction).

CMD

Runs the given instruction when the container is started. If an ENTRYPOINT has been defined, the instruction will be interpreted as an argument to the ENTRY POINT (in this case, make sure you use the exec format). The CMD instruction is overridden by any arguments to docker run after the image name. Only the last CMD instruction will have an effect, and any previous CMD instructions will be overridden (including those in base images).

COPY

Used to copy files from the build context into the image. It has two forms, COPY *src* dest_ and COPY ["*src*", "*dest*"], both of which copy the file or directory at *src* in the build context to *dest* inside the container. The JSON array format is required if the paths have spaces in them. Wildcards can be used to specify multiple files or directories. Note that you cannot specify *src* paths outside the build context (e.g., *../another_dir/myfile* will not work).

ENTRYPOINT

Sets an executable (and default arguments) to be run when the container starts. Any CMD instructions or arguments to docker run after the image name will be passed as parameters to the executable. ENTRYPOINT instructions are often used to provide "starter" scripts that initialize variables and services before interpreting any given arguments.

ENV

Sets environment variables inside the image. These can be referred to in subsequent instructions. For example:

```
...
ENV MY_VERSION 1.3
RUN apt-get install -y mypackage=$MY_VERSION
...
```

The variables will also be available inside the image.

EXPOSE

Indicates to Docker that the container will have a process listening on the given port or ports. This information is used by Docker when linking containers (see

"Linking Containers") or publishing ports by supplying the -P argument to docker run; by itself the EXPOSE instruction will not affect networking.

FROM
> Sets the base image for the Dockerfile; subsequent instructions build on top of this image. The base image is specified as IMAGE:TAG (e.g., debian:wheezy). If the tag is omitted, it is assumed to be latest, but I strongly recommend you always set the tag to a specific version to avoid surprises. Must be the first instruction in a Dockerfile.

MAINTAINER
> Sets the "Author" metadata on the image to the given string. You can retrieve this with docker inspect -f {{.Author}} IMAGE. Normally used to set the name and contact details of the maintainer of the image.

ONBUILD
> Specifies an instruction to be executed later, when the image is used as the base layer to another image. This can be useful for processing data that will be added in a child image (e.g., the instruction may copy in code from a chosen directory and run a build script on the data).

RUN
> Runs the given instruction inside the container and commits the result.

USER
> Sets the user (by name or UID) to use in any subsequent RUN, CMD, or ENTRYPOINT instructions. Note that UIDs are the same between the host and container, but usernames may be assigned to different UIDs, which can make things tricky when setting permissions.

VOLUME
> Declares the specified file or directory to be a volume. If the file or directory already exists in the image, it will copied into the volume when the container is started. If multiple arguments are given, they are interpreted as multiple volume statements. You cannot specify the host directory for a volume inside a Dockerfile for portability and security reasons. For more information, see "Managing Data with Volumes and Data Containers".

WORKDIR
> Sets the working directory for any subsequent RUN, CMD, ENTRYPOINT, ADD, or COPY instructions. Can be used multiple times. Relative paths may be used and are resolved relative to the previous WORKDIR.

Connecting Containers to the World

Say you're running a web server inside a container. How do you provide the outside world with access? The answer is to "publish" ports with the -p or -P commands. This command forwards ports on the host to the container. For example:

```
$ docker run -d -p 8000:80 nginx
af9038e18360002ef3f3658f16094dadd4928c4b3e88e347c9a746b131db5444
$ curl localhost:8000
<!DOCTYPE html>
<html>
<head>
<title>Welcome to nginx!</title>
...
```

The -p 8000:80 argument has told Docker to forward port 8000 on the host to port 80 in the container. Alternatively, the -P argument can be used to tell Docker to automatically select a free port to forward to on the host. For example:

```
$ ID=$(docker run -d -P nginx)
$ docker port $ID 80
0.0.0.0:32771
$ curl localhost:32771
<!DOCTYPE html>
<html>
<head>
<title>Welcome to nginx!</title>
...
```

The primary advantage of the -P command is that you are no longer responsible for keeping track of allocated ports, which becomes important if you have several containers publishing ports. In these cases, you can use the docker port command to discover the port allocated by Docker.

Linking Containers

Docker *links* are the simplest way to allow containers on the same host to talk to each other. When using the default Docker networking model, communication between containers will be over an internal Docker network, meaning communications are not exposed to the host network.

Docker Networking Changes

In future versions of Docker (likely 1.9 and up), the idiomatic way to network containers will be to "publish services," rather than link containers. However, links will continue to be supported for the foreseeable future, and the examples in this book should work without changes.

For more information on the upcoming changes to networking, see "New Docker Networking".

Links are initialized by giving the argument `--link CONTAINER:ALIAS` to `docker run`, where `CONTAINER` is the name of the link container[3] and `ALIAS` is a local name used inside the master container to refer to the link container.

Using Docker links will also add the alias and the link container ID to */etc/hosts* on the master container, allowing the link container to be addressed by name from the master container.

In addition, Docker will set a bunch of environment variables inside the master container that are designed to make it easy to talk to the link container. For example, if we create and link to a Redis container:

```
$ docker run -d --name myredis redis
c9148dee046a6fefac48806cd8ec0ce85492b71f25e97aae9a1a75027b1c8423
$ docker run --link myredis:redis debian env
PATH=/usr/local/sbin:/usr/local/bin:/usr/sbin:/usr/bin:/sbin:/bin
HOSTNAME=f015d58d53b5
REDIS_PORT=tcp://172.17.0.22:6379
REDIS_PORT_6379_TCP=tcp://172.17.0.22:6379
REDIS_PORT_6379_TCP_ADDR=172.17.0.22
REDIS_PORT_6379_TCP_PORT=6379
REDIS_PORT_6379_TCP_PROTO=tcp
REDIS_NAME=/distracted_rosalind/redis
REDIS_ENV_REDIS_VERSION=3.0.3
REDIS_ENV_REDIS_DOWNLOAD_URL=http://download.redis.io/releases/redis-3.0.3.tar.gz
REDIS_ENV_REDIS_DOWNLOAD_SHA1=0e2d7707327986ae652df717059354b358b83358
HOME=/root
```

We can see that Docker has set up environment variables prefixed with `REDIS_PORT` that contain information on how to connect to the container. Most of these seem somewhat redundant, as the information in the value is already contained in the variable name. Nevertheless, they are useful as a form of documentation if nothing else.

---

3 In this discussion and throughout the book, I will refer to the container being linked as the *link container* and the container being launched as the *master container* (as it is responsible for initiating the link).

Docker has also imported environment variables from the linked container, which it has prefixed with REDIS_ENV. While this functionality can be very useful, it's important to be aware that this happens if you use environment variables to store secrets such as API tokens or database passwords.

By default, containers will be able to talk to each other whether or not they have been explicitly linked. If you want to prevent containers that haven't been linked from communicating, use the arguments --icc=false and --iptables when starting the Docker daemon. Now when containers are linked, Docker will set up iptables rules to allow the containers to communicate on any ports that have been declared as exposed.

Unfortunately, Docker links as they stand have several shortcomings. Perhaps most significantly, they are static—although links should survive container restarts, they aren't updated if the linked container is replaced. Also, the link container must be started before the master container, meaning you can't have bidirectional links.

For further information on networking containers, see Chapter 11.

Managing Data with Volumes and Data Containers

To recap, Docker volumes are directories[4] that are not part of the container's UFS (see "Images, Containers, and the Union File System")—they are just normal directories on the host that are *bind mounted* (see Bind Mounting) into the container.

There are three[5] different ways to initialize volumes, and it's important to understand the differences between the methods. First, we can declare a volume at runtime with the -v flag:

```
$ docker run -it --name container-test -h CONTAINER -v /data debian /bin/bash
root@CONTAINER:/# ls /data
root@CONTAINER:/#
```

This will make the directory */data* inside the container into a volume. Any files the image held inside the */data* directory will be copied into the volume. We can find out where the volume lives on the host by running docker inspect on the host from a new shell:

```
$ docker inspect -f {{.Mounts}} container-test
[{5cad... /mnt/sda1/var/lib/docker/volumes/5cad.../_data /data local  true}]
```

---

4 Technically, directories or files, as a volume may be a single file.

5 OK, two-and-a-half, depending on how you want to count.

In this case, the volume */data/* in the container is simply a link to the directory */var/lib/docker/volumes/5cad.../_data* on the host. To prove this, we can add a file into the directory on the host:[6]

```
$ sudo touch /var/lib/docker/volumes/5cad.../_data/test-file
```

And you should immediately be able to see from inside the container:

```
root@CONTAINER:/# ls /data
test-file
```

The second way to set up a volume is by using the VOLUME instruction in a Dockerfile:

```
FROM debian:wheezy
VOLUME /data
```

This has exactly the same effect as specifying -v /data to docker run.

Setting Volume Permissions in Dockerfiles

You will often need to set the permissions and ownership on a volume or initialize a volume with some default data or configuration files. The key point to be aware of here is that any instruction *after* the VOLUME instruction in a Dockerfile will *not* be able to make changes to that volume. For example, the following Dockerfile will not work as expected:

```
FROM debian:wheezy
RUN useradd foo
VOLUME /data
RUN touch /data/x
RUN chown -R foo:foo /data
```

We want the touch and chown commands to run on the image's filesystem, but they will actually run inside the volume of a temporary container used to create the layer (refer back to "How Images Get Built" for more details). This volume will be removed once the commands complete, rendering the instruction pointless.

The following Dockerfile will work:

```
FROM debian:wheezy
RUN useradd foo
RUN mkdir /data && touch /data/x
RUN chown -R foo:foo /data
VOLUME /data
```

When a container is started from this image, Docker will copy any files from the volume directory in the image into the container's volume. This won't happen if you

---

6 If you're connected to a remote Docker daemon, you'll need to run this on the remote host via SSH. If you're using Docker Machine (which you will be if you installed Docker via the Docker Toolbox), you can do this via `docker-machine ssh default`.

---

specify a host directory for the volume (so that host files aren't accidentally overwritten).

If, for some reason, you can't set permissions and ownership in a RUN instruction, you will have to do so using a CMD or ENTRYPOINT script that runs after container creation.

The third[7] way is to extend the -v argument to docker run with an explicit directory to bind to on the host using the format -v HOST_DIR:CONTAINER_DIR. This can't be done from a Dockerfile (it would be nonportable and a security risk). For example:

```
$ docker run -v /home/adrian/data:/data debian ls /data
```

This will mount the directory /home/adrian/data on the host as /data inside the container. Any files already existing in the /home/adrian/data directory will be available inside the container. If the /data directory already exists in the container, its contents will be hidden by the volume. Unlike the other invocations, no files from the image will be copied into the volume, and the volume won't be deleted by Docker (i.e., docker rm -v will not remove a volume that is mounted at a user-chosen directory).

Bind Mounting

When a specific host directory is used in a volume (the -v HOST_DIR:CONTAINER_DIR syntax), it is often referred to as *bind mounting*. This is somewhat misleading, as all volumes are technically bind mounted—the difference is that the mount point is made explicit rather than hidden in a directory owned by Docker.

Sharing Data

The -v HOST_DIR:CONTAINER_DIR syntax is very useful for sharing files between the host and one or more containers. For example, configuration files can be kept on the host and mounted into containers built from generic images.

We can also share data between containers by using the --volumes-from CONTAINER argument with docker run. For example, we can create a new container that has access to the volumes from the container in our previous example like so:

```
$ docker run -it -h NEWCONTAINER --volumes-from container-test debian /bin/bash
root@NEWCONTAINER:/# ls /data
test-file
root@NEWCONTAINER:/#
```

---

7 Second equal?

It's important to note that this works whether or not the container holding the volumes (container-test, in this case) is currently running. As long as at least one existing container links to a volume, it won't be deleted.

Data Containers

A common practice is to create *data containers*—containers whose sole purpose is to share data between other containers. The main benefit of this approach is that it provides a handy namespace for volumes that can be easily loaded using the --volumes-from command.

For example, we can create a data container for a PostgreSQL database with the following command:

```
$ docker run --name dbdata postgres echo "Data-only container for postgres"
```

This will create a container from the postgres image and initialize any volumes defined in the image before running the echo command and exiting.[8] There's no need to leave data containers running, as doing so would just be a waste of resources.

We can then use this volume from other containers with the --volumes-from argument. For example:

```
$ docker run -d --volumes-from dbdata --name db1 postgres
```

Images for Data Containers

There's normally no need to use a "minimal image" such as busy box or scratch for the data container. Just use the same image that is used for the container consuming the data. For example, use the postgres image to create a data container to be used with the Postgres database.

Using the same image doesn't take up any extra space—you must already have downloaded or created the image for the consumer. It also gives the image a chance to seed the container with any initial data and ensures permissions are set up correctly.

Deleting volumes

Volumes are deleted only if:

- The container was deleted with docker rm -v, *or*

---

8 We could have used any command that exits immediately here, but the echo message will serve to remind us of the purpose of the container when we run docker ps -a. Another option is not to start the container at all by using the docker create command instead of docker run.

- The `--rm` flag was provided to `docker run`

and:

- No existing container links to the volume
- No host directory was specified for the volume (the `-v HOST_DIR:CON TAINER_DIR` syntax was not used)

At the moment, this means that unless you are very careful about always running your containers like this, you are likely to have orphan files and directories in your Docker installation directory and no easy way of telling what they represent. Docker is working on a top-level "volume" command that will allow you to list, create, inspect, and remove volumes independent of containers. This is expected to land in 1.9, which should be out by the time this book is published.

Common Docker Commands

This section gives a brief (at least in comparison to the official documentation) and nonexhaustive overview of the various Docker commands, focusing on the commands commonly used on a day-to-day basis. Because Docker is rapidly changing and evolving, refer to the official documentation (*http://docs.docker.com*) on the Docker website for full and up-to-date details on a given command. I have not specified in detail the arguments and syntax of the various commands (with the exception of `docker run`). Refer to the built-in help for this, which can be accessed by giving the `--help` argument to any command or via the `docker help` command.

Docker Boolean Flags

In most Unix command-line tools, you will find flags that don't take a value, such as -l in ls -l. Because these flags are either set or not set, Docker considers these to be *boolean* flags and—unlike most other tools—supports explicitly supplying a boolean value flag (i.e., it will accept both -f=true and -f). In addition (and this is where things get confusing), you can have both *default true* and *default false* flags. Unlike default false, default true flags are considered to be set if unspecified. Specifying a flag without an argument has the same effect as setting it to true—a default true flag is *not* unset by an argument with a value; the only way a default true flag can be unset is by explicitly setting it to false (e.g., -f=false).

To find out if a flag is default true or default false, refer to docker help for the command. For example:

```
$ docker logs --help
...
  -f, --follow=false      Follow log output
  --help=false            Print usage
  -t, --timestamps=false  Show timestamps
...
```

shows that the -f, --help, and -t arguments are all default false.

To give a couple of concrete examples, consider the default true --sig-proxy argument to docker run. The only way to turn this argument off is by explicitly setting it false. For example:

```
$ docker run --sig-proxy=false ...
```

All of the following are equivalent:

```
$ docker run --sig-proxy=true ...
$ docker run --sig-proxy ...
$ docker run ...
```

In the case of a default false argument, such as --read-only, the following will set it to true:

```
$ docker run --read-only=true
$ docker run --read-only
```

Leaving it unspecified or explicitly setting to false are equivalent.

This also leads to some quirky behavior with flags that normally short-circuit logic (e.g., docker ps --help=false will work as normal without printing the help message).

The run Command

We've already seen docker run in action; it's the go-to command for launching new containers. As such, it is by far the most complex command and supports a large list of potential arguments. The arguments allow users to configure how the image is run, override Dockerfile settings, configure networking, and set privileges and resources for the container.

The following options control the lifecycle of the container and its basic mode of operation:

`-a, --attach`
    Attaches the given stream (`STDOUT`, etc.) to the terminal. If unspecified, both `stdout` and `stderr` are attached. If unspecified and the container is started in interactive mode (`-i`), `stdin` is also attached.

    Incompatible with `-d`

`-d, --detach`
    Runs the container in "detached" mode. The command will run the container in the background and return the container ID.

`-i, --interactive`
    Keeps `stdin` open (even when it's not attached). Generally used with `-t` to start an interactive container session. For example:

```
$ docker run -it debian /bin/bash
root@bd0f26f928bb:/# ls
...snip...
```

`--restart`
    Configures when Docker will attempt to restart an exited container. The argument no will never attempt to restart a container, and `always` will always try to restart, regardless of exit status. The `on-failure` argument will attempt to restart containers that *exit with a nonzero status* and can take an optional argument specifying the number of times to attempt to restart before giving up (if not specified, it will retry forever). For example, `docker run --restart on-failure:10 postgres` will launch the postgres container and attempt to restart it 10 times if it exits with a nonzero code.

`--rm`
    Automatically removes the container when it exits. Cannot be used with `-d`.

`-t, --tty`
    Allocates a pseudo-TTY. Normally used with `-i` to start an interactive container.

The following options allow setting of container names and variables:

`-e, --env`
    Sets environment variables inside the container. For example:

```
$ docker run -e var1=val -e var2="val 2" debian env
PATH=/usr/local/sbin:/usr/local/bin:/usr/sbin:/usr/bin:/sbin:/bin
HOSTNAME=b15f833d65d8
var1=val
var2=val 2
HOME=/root
```

Also note the `--env-file` option for passing variables in via a file.

`-h, --hostname`

Sets the container's Unix hostname to `NAME`. For example:

```
$ docker run -h "myhost" debian hostname
myhost
```

`--name NAME`

Assigns the name `NAME` to the container. The name can then be used to address the container in other Docker commands.

The following options allow the user to set up volumes (see "Managing Data with Volumes and Data Containers" for more details):

`-v, --volume`

There are two forms of the argument to set up a volume (a file or directory within a container that is part of the native host filesystem, not the container's union filesystem). The first form only specifies the directory within the container and will bind to a host directory of Docker's choosing. The second form specifies the host directory to bind to.

`--volumes-from`

Mounts volumes from the specified container. Often used in association with data containers (see "Data Containers").

There are several options affecting networking. The basic commands you can expect to frequently use are:

`--expose`

Equivalent of Dockerfile `EXPOSE` instruction. Identifies the port or port range as being used in the container but does not open the port. Only really makes sense in association with `-P` and when linking containers.

`--link`

Sets up a private network interface to the specified container. See "Linking Containers" for more information.

`-p, --publish`

"Publishes" a port on the container, making it accessible from the host. If the host port is not defined, a random high-numbered port will chosen, which can be discovered by using the docker port command. The host interface on which to expose the port may also be specified.

-P, --publish-all
> Publish all *exposed* ports on the container to the host. A random high-numbered port will be chosen for each exposed port. The docker port command can be used to see the mapping.

There are several more advanced options you may find useful if you need to do more advanced networking. Be aware that several of these options will require you to have some understanding of networking and how it is implemented in Docker. For more information, refer to Chapter 11.

The docker run command also has a large set of options for controlling the privileges and capabilities of containers. See Chapter 13 for details on these.

The following options directly override Dockerfile settings:

--entrypoint
> Sets the entrypoint for the container to the given argument, overriding any ENTRY POINT instruction in the Dockerfile.

-u, --user
> Sets the user that commands are run under. May be specified as a username or UID. Overrides USER instruction in Dockerfile.

-w, --workdir
> Sets the working directory in the container to the provided path. Overrides any value in the Dockerfile.

Managing Containers

In addition to docker run, the following docker commands are used to manage containers during their lifecycle:

docker attach [OPTIONS] CONTAINER
> The attach command allows the user to view or interact with the main process inside the container. For example:

```
$ ID=$(docker run -d debian sh -c "while true; do echo 'tick'; sleep 1; done;")
$ docker attach $ID
tick
tick
tick
tick
```

Note that using Ctrl-C to quit will end the process and cause the container to exit.

docker create
> Creates a container from an image but does not start it. Takes most of the same arguments as docker run. To start the container, use docker start.

docker cp
> Copies files and directories between a container and the host.

docker exec
> Runs a command inside a container. Can be used to perform maintenance tasks or as a replacement for ssh to log in to a container.

> For example:

```
$ ID=$(docker run -d debian sh -c "while true; do sleep 1; done;")
$ docker exec $ID echo "Hello"
Hello
$ docker exec -it $ID /bin/bash
root@5c6c32041d68:/# ls
bin   dev  home  lib64  mnt  proc  run   selinux  sys  usr
boot  etc  lib   media  opt  root  sbin  srv      tmp  var
root@5c6c32041d68:/# exit
exit
```

docker kill
> Sends a signal to the main process (PID 1) in a container. By default, sends a SIGKILL, which will cause the container to exit immediately. Alternatively, the signal can be specified with the -s argument. The container ID is returned.

> For example:

```
$ ID=$(docker run -d debian bash -c \
    "trap 'echo caught' SIGTRAP; while true; do sleep 1; done;")
$ docker kill -s SIGTRAP $ID
e33da73c275b56e734a4bbbefc0b41f6ba84967d09ba08314edd860ebd2da86c
$ docker logs $ID
caught
$ docker kill $ID
e33da73c275b56e734a4bbbefc0b41f6ba84967d09ba08314edd860ebd2da86c
```

docker pause
> Suspends all processes inside the given container. The processes do not receive any signal that they are being suspended and consequently cannot shut down or clean up. The processes can be restarted with docker unpause. docker pause uses the Linux cgroups freezer functionality internally. This command contrasts with docker stop, which stops the processes and sends signals observable by the processes.

`docker restart`

Restarts one or more containers. Roughly equivalent to calling `docker stop` followed by `docker start` on the containers. Takes an optional argument -t that specifies the amount of time to wait for the container to shut down before it is killed with a SIGTERM.

`docker rm`

Removes one or more containers. Returns the names or IDs of successfully deleted containers. By default, `docker rm` will not remove any volumes. The -f argument can be used to remove running containers, and the -v argument will remove volumes created by the container (as long as they aren't bind mounted or in use by another container).

For example, to delete all stopped containers:

```
$ docker rm $(docker ps -aq)
b7a4e94253b3
e33da73c275b
f47074b60757
```

`docker start`

Starts a stopped container (or containers). Can be used to restart a container that has exited or to start a container that has been created with `docker create` but never launched.

`docker stop`

Stops (but does not remove) one or more containers. After calling `docker stop` on a container, it will transition to the "exited" state. Takes an optional argument -t which specifies the amount of time to wait for the container to shutdown before it is killed with a SIGTERM.

`docker unpause`

Restarts a container previously paused with `docker pause`.

 Detaching from Containers

When attached to a Docker container, either by starting it in interactive mode or attaching to it with `docker attach`, you will stop the container if you try to disconnect with Ctrl-C. Instead, if you use Ctrl-P Ctrl-Q you can detach from the container without stopping it.

This code will only work when attached in interactive mode with a TTY (i.e., using both the -i and -t flags).

Docker Info

The following subcommands can be used to get more information on the Docker installation and usage:

docker info
> Prints various information on the Docker system and host.

docker help
> Prints usage and help information for the given subcommand. Identical to running a command with the --help flag.

docker version
> Prints Docker version information for client and server as well as the version of Go used in compilation.

Container Info

The following commands provide more information on running and stopped containers:

docker diff
> Shows changes made to the containers filesystem compared to the image it was launched from. For example:
>
> ```
> $ ID=$(docker run -d debian touch /NEW-FILE)
> $ docker diff $ID
> A /NEW-FILE
> ```

docker events
> Prints real-time events from the daemon. Use Ctrl-C to quit. For more information on this, see Chapter 10.

docker inspect
> Provides detailed information on given containers or images. The information includes most configuration information and covers network settings and volume mappings. The command can take one argument, -f, which is used to supply a Go template that can be used to format and filter the output.

docker logs
> Outputs the "logs" for a container. This is simply everything that has been written to STDERR or STDOUT inside the container. For more information on logging in Docker, see Chapter 10.

`docker port`

Lists the exposed port mappings for the given container. Can optionally be given the internal container port and protocol to look up. Often used after `docker run -P <image>` to discover the assigned ports.

For example:

```
$ ID=$(docker run -P -d redis)
$ docker port $ID
6379/tcp -> 0.0.0.0:32768
$ docker port $ID 6379
0.0.0.0:32768
$ docker port $ID 6379/tcp
0.0.0.0:32768
```

`docker ps`

Provides high-level information on current containers, such as the name, ID, and status. Takes a lot of different arguments, notably `-a` for getting all containers, not just running ones. Also note the `-q` argument, which only returns the container IDs and is very useful as input to other commands such as `docker rm`.

`docker top`

Provides information on the running processes inside a given container. In effect, this command runs the Unix `ps` utility on the host and filters for processes in the given container. The command can be given the same arguments the `ps` utility and defaults to `-ef` (but be careful to make sure the PID field is still in the output).

For example:

```
$ ID=$(docker run -d redis)
$ docker top $ID
UID    PID   PPID  C  STIME  TTY  TIME      CMD
999    9243  1836  0  15:44  ?    00:00:00  redis-server *:6379
$ ps -f -u 999
UID  PID   PPID  C  STIME  TTY      TIME      CMD
999  9243  1836  0  15:44  ?        00:00:00  redis-server *:6379
$ docker top $ID -axZ
LABEL           PID   TTY  STAT  TIME  COMMAND
docker-default  9243  ?    Ssl   0:00  redis-server *:6379
```

Dealing with Images

The following commands provide tools for creating and working with images:

`docker build`

Builds an image from a Dockerfile. See "Building Images from Dockerfiles" and "How Images Get Built" for details on usage.

docker commit

Creates an image from the specified container. While `docker commit` can be useful, it is generally preferable to create images using `docker build`, which is easily repeatable. By default, containers are paused prior to commit, but this can be turned off with the `--pause=false` argument. Takes `-a` and `-m` arguments for setting metadata.

For example:

```
$ ID=$(docker run -d redis touch /new-file)
$ docker commit -a "Joe Bloggs" -m "Comment" $ID commit:test
ac479108b0fa9a02a7fb290a22dacd5e20c867ec512d6813ed42e3517711a0cf
$ docker images commit
REPOSITORY   TAG    IMAGE ID      CREATED           VIRTUAL SIZE
commit       test   ac479108b0fa  About a minute ago  111 MB
$ docker run commit:test ls /new-file
/new-file
```

docker export

Exports the contents of the container's filesystem as a tar archive on STDOUT. The resulting archive can be loaded with `docker import`. Note that only the filesystem is exported; any metadata such as exported ports, CMD, and ENTRYPOINT settings will be lost. Also note that any volumes are not included in the export. Contrast with `docker save`.

docker history

Outputs information on each of the layers in an image.

docker images

Provides a list of local images, including information such as repository name, tag name, and size. By default, intermediate images (used in the creation of top-level images) are not shown. The VIRTUAL SIZE is the total size of the image including all underlying layers. As these layers may be shared with other images, simply adding up the size of all images does not provide an accurate estimate of disk usage. Also, images will appear multiple times if they have more than one tag; different images can be discerned by comparing the ID. Takes several arguments; in particular, note `-q`, which only returns the image IDs and is useful as input to other commands such as `docker rmi`.

For example:

```
$ docker images | head -4
REPOSITORY                TAG     IMAGE ID      CREATED       VIRTUAL SIZE
identidock_identidock     latest  9fc66b46a2e6  26 hours ago  839.8 MB
redis                     latest  868be653dea3  6 days ago    110.8 MB
containersol/pres-base    latest  13919d434c95  2 weeks ago   401.8 MB
```

To remove all dangling images:

```
$ docker rmi $(docker images -q -f dangling=true)
Deleted: a9979d5ace9af55a562b8436ba66a1538357bc2e0e43765b406f2cf0388fe062
```

docker import

Creates an image from an archive file containing a filesystem, such as that created by docker export. The archive may be identified by a file path or URL or streamed through STDIN (by using the - flag). Returns the ID of the newly created image. The image can be tagged by supplying a repository and tag name. Note that an image built from import will only consist of a single layer and will lose Docker configuration settings such as exposed ports and CMD values. Contrast with docker load.

Example of "flattening" an image by exporting and importing:

```
$ docker export 35d171091d78 | docker import - flatten:test
5a9bc529af25e2cf6411c6d87442e0805c066b96e561fbd1935122f988086009
$ docker history flatten:test
IMAGE           CREATED          CREATED BY    SIZE      COMMENT
981804b0c2b2    59 seconds ago                 317.7 MB  Imported from -
```

docker load

Loads a repository from a tar archive passed via STDIN. The repository may contain several images and tags. Unlike docker import, the images will include history and metadata. Suitable archive files are created by docker save, making save and load a viable alternative to registries for distributing images and producing backups. See docker save for an example.

docker rmi

Deletes the given image or images. Images are specified by ID or repository and tag name. If a repository name is supplied but no tag name, the tag is assumed to be latest. To delete images that exist in multiple repositories, specify that image by ID and use the -f argument. You will need to run this once per repository.

docker save

Saves the named images or repositories to a tar archive, which is streamed to STDOUT (use -o to write to a file). Images can be specified by ID or as repository:tag. If only a repository name is given, all images in that repository will be saved to the archive, not just the latest tag. Can be used in conjunction with docker load to distribute or back up images.

For example:

```
$ docker save -o /tmp/redis.tar redis:latest
$ docker rmi redis:latest
Untagged: redis:latest
Deleted: 868be653dea3ff6082b043c0f34b95bb180cc82ab14a18d9d6b8e27b7929762c
...
```

```
$ docker load -i /tmp/redis.tar
$ docker images redis
REPOSITORY          TAG                 IMAGE ID            CREATED
VIRTUAL SIZE
redis               latest              0f3059144681        3 months ago
111 MB
```

docker tag

> Associates a repository and tag name with an image. The image can identified by
> ID or repository and tag (the latest tag is assumed if none is given). If no tag is
> given for the new name, latest is assumed.

> For example:

```
$ docker tag faa2b75ce09a newname ❶
$ docker tag newname:latest amouat/newname ❷
$ docker tag newname:latest amouat/newname:newtag ❸
$ docker tag newname:latest myregistry.com:5000/newname:newtag ❹
```

> ❶ Adds the image with ID faa2b75ce09a to the repository newname, using the
> tag latest, as none was specified.

> ❷ Adds the newname:latest image to the amouat/newname repository, again
> using the tag latest. This label is in a format suitable for pushing to the
> Docker Hub, assuming the user is amouat.

> ❸ As above, except using the tag newtag instead of latest.

> ❹ Adds the newname:latest image to the repository myregistry.com/newname
> with the tag newtag. This label is in a format suitable for pushing to a registry
> at *http://myregistry.com:5000*.

Using the Registry

The following commands relate to using registries, including the Docker Hub. Be
aware that Docker saves credentials to the file *.dockercfg* in your home directory:

docker login

> Register with, or log in to, the given registry server. If no server is specified, it is
> assumed to be the Docker Hub. The process will interactively ask for details if
> required, or they can be supplied as arguments.

docker logout

> Logs out from a Docker registry. If no server is specified, it is assumed to be the
> Docker Hub.

`docker pull`
> Downloads the given image from a registry. The registry is determined by the image name and defaults to the Docker Hub. If no tag name is given, the image tagged `latest` will be downloaded (if available). Use the `-a` argument to download all images from a repository.

`docker push`
> Pushes an image or repository to the registry. If no tag is given, this will push *all* images in the repository to the registry, not just the one marked `latest`.

`docker search`
> Prints a list of public repositories on the Docker Hub matching the search term. Limits results to 25 repositories. You can also filter by stars and automated builds. In general, it's easiest to use the website.

Conclusion

There has been a lot of information in this chapter! If you even just managed to skim the main points, you should have a reasonably broad understanding of how Docker works and the main commands. In Part II, we will see how to apply this knowledge to a software project, from development through to production. You may find it easier to understand some of the material in this chapter after seeing it in practice.

PART II

The Software Lifecycle with Docker

In Part I, we introduced the philosophy behind containers and got familiar with their basic use. In Part II, we go into more depth, using Docker to build, test, and deploy a web application. We will see how Docker containers can be used in development, testing, and production. The chapters in this part will focus on a single-host system (see Part III for information on deploying and orchestrating containers on multiple hosts).

By the end of Part II, you will understand how to integrate Docker into the software development process and be comfortable with everyday use of Docker. To make the most of Docker, it is important to adopt a DevOps approach. In particular, during development, we will be thinking about how to run software in production, which will ease the pain of deployment to a variety of environments.

While the application we will build over the course of the chapters is necessarily very small, we will also cover technology and practices required for running large-scale applications maintained by large teams of developers.

Containers are not suited to building enterprise software monoliths with a release cycle measured in weeks or months. Instead, we will naturally find ourselves taking a microservices approach and exploring techniques such as continuous deployment where it is possible to safely push to production multiple times a day.

The advantage of containers, DevOps, microservices, and continuous delivery essentially comes down to the idea of a fast feedback loop. By iterating quicker, we can develop, test, and validate systems of higher quality in shorter time periods.

CHAPTER 5

Using Docker in Development

Throughout Part II, we are going to develop a simple web application that returns a unique image for a given string, similar to the identicons used on GitHub and Stack Overflow for users with no set image. We will write the application using the Python programming and the Flask web framework. Python was chosen for this example because it is commonly used and succinct and readable. Don't worry if you don't program in Python. We will focus on how to interact with Docker, not on details of the Python code.[1] Similarly, Flask was chosen because it is lightweight and easy to understand. We will be using Docker to manage all our dependencies, so there is no need install Python or Flask on your host computer.

This chapter will focus on setting up a container-based workflow and getting tools in place before we begin development in the next chapter.

Say "Hello World!"

Let's begin by creating a web server that just returns "Hello World!" First, create a new directory called *identidock* to hold our project. Inside this directory, create a subdirectory *app* that will hold our Python code. Inside the *app* directory, create a file called *identidock.py*:

```
$ tree identidock/
identidock/
└── app
    └── identidock.py

1 directory, 1 file
```

---

1 If you want to learn more about Python and Flask, have a look at *Flask Web Development* by Miguel Grinberg (O'Reilly), especially if you're going to be creating web apps.

Put the following code in *identidock.py*:

```
from flask import Flask
app = Flask(__name__) ❶


@app.route('/') ❷
def hello_world():
    return 'Hello World!\n'

if __name__ == '__main__':
    app.run(debug=True, host='0.0.0.0') ❸
```

To briefly explain this code:

❶ Initializes Flask and sets up the application object.

❷ Creates a route associated with the URL. Whenever this URL is requested, it will result in a call to the hello_world function.

❸ Initializes the Python web server. The use of 0.0.0.0 (instead of localhost or 127.0.0.1) as host argument binds to all network interfaces, which is needed to allow the container to be accessed from the host or other containers. The if statement on the line above ensures this line only executes when the file is called as a standalone program and not when running as part of a larger application.

Source Code

The source code for this chapter can be found on GitHub (*https://github.com/using-docker/using_docker_in_dev*). There are tags for the various stages of the code through the chapter.

I've been told that code doesn't copy/paste well from the ebook release, so use the GitHub repo if you're having issues.

Now we need a container to put this code in and run it. In the *identidock* directory, create a file called *Dockerfile* with the following contents:

```
FROM python:3.4

RUN pip install Flask==0.10.1
WORKDIR /app
COPY app /app

CMD ["python", "identidock.py"]
```

This Dockerfile uses an official Python image as a base, which contains a Python 3 installation. On top of this, it installs Flask and copies in our code. The CMD instruction simply runs our identidock code.

Official Image Variants

Many of the official repositories for popular programming languages such as Python, Go, and Ruby contain multiple images for different purposes. In addition to images for different version numbers, you are likely to find one or both of the following:

slim

> These images are cut-down versions of the standard images. Many common packages and libraries will be missing. These are essential when you need to reduce on image size for distribution but often require extra work installing and maintaining packages already available in the standard image.

onbuild

> These images use the Dockerfile ONBUILD instruction to delay execution of certain commands until a new "child" image is built that inherits the onbuild image. These commands are processed as part of the FROM instruction of the child image and typically do things like copy over code and run a compile step. These images can make it quicker and easier to get started with a language, but in the long run, they tend to be limiting and confusing. I would generally only recommend using onbuild images when first exploring a repository.

For our example application, we are using a standard base image for Python 3 and not one of these variants.

Now we can build and run our simple application:

```
$ cd identidock
$ docker build -t identidock .
...
$ docker run -d -p 5000:5000 identidock
0c75444e8f5f16dfe5aceb0aae074cc33dfc06f2d2fb6adb773ac51f20605aa4
```

Here I've passed the -d flag to docker run in order to start the container in the background, but you can also omit it if you want to see output from the web server. The -p 5000:5000 argument tells Docker we want to forward port 5000 in the container to port 5000 on the host.

Now let's test it out:

```
$ curl localhost:5000
Hello World!
```

Docker Machine IPs

If you're running Docker using Docker machine (which you will be if you installed Docker using the Docker Toolbox on Mac or Windows), you won't be able to use `localhost` as the URL. Instead, you'll need to use the IP address of the VM running Docker. Using Docker machine's `ip` command can help automate this. For example:

```
$ curl $(docker-machine ip default):5000
Hello World!
```

This book assumes Docker is running locally; be sure to replace `localhost` with the appropriate IP where appropriate.

Excellent! But there's a pretty major problem with the workflow as it stands: every little change to the code means we need to rebuild the image and restart the container. Thankfully, there is a simple solution. We can *bind mount* the source code folder on the host over the top of the one inside the container. The following code stops and removes the last run container (if the previous example wasn't the last run container, you'll need to look up its ID in docker ps) before starting a new one with the code directory mounted to */app*:

```
$ docker stop $(docker ps -lq)
0c75444e8f5f
$ docker rm $(docker ps -lq)
$ docker run -d -p 5000:5000 -v "$PWD"/app:/app identidock
```

The -v "$PWD"/app:/app argument mounts the app directory at */app* inside the container. It will override the contents of */app* inside the container and also be writable inside the container (you can mount a volume as read-only if you don't want this). Arguments to -v must be absolute paths, so here we've used "$PWD" to prepend the current directory, which saves us some typing and keeps things portable (note that the quotes are only necessary if the path includes spaces).

Bind Mounts

When a host directory is specified for a volume using the `-v HOST_DIR:CONTAINER_DIR` argument to `docker run`, it is commonly referred to as a "bind mount," as it binds a folder (or file) on the host to a folder (or file) inside the container. This is a little confusing, as all volumes are technically bind mounts, but we have to do a little more work to find the folder on the host when it isn't specified explicitly.

Note that the `HOST_DIR` always refers to the machine running the Docker engine. If you are connected to a remote Docker daemon, the path must exist on the remote machine. If you're using a local VM provisioned by Docker machine (which you will be if you installed Docker via Toolbox), it will cross-mount your home directory to make things easier during development.

Verify that it's still working:

```
$ curl localhost:5000
Hello World!
```

Although we have just mounted the same directory that was added using the `COPY` command inside the image, it is now using exactly the same directory on the host and inside the container, rather than its own copy from the image. Because of this, we can now edit *identidock.py* and see our changes immediately:

```
$ sed -i '' s/World/Docker/ app/identidock.py
$ curl localhost:5000
Hello Docker!
```

Here I've used the sed utility to make a quick in-place change to the *identidock.py* file. If sed isn't available, or you're not familiar with it, you can always use a normal text editor to change the text "World" to "Docker."

So now we have a fairly normal development environment, except all our dependencies—the Python compiler and libraries—are encapsulated inside a Docker container. However, there is still a key problem. There is no way we could use this container in production, mainly because it is running the default Flask web server, which is only intended for development and too inefficient and insecure for production use. A crucial point in adopting Docker is to reduce the differences between development and production, so let's look at how we can do that now.

Wot, no virtualenv?

If you're an experienced Python developer, you may be surprised that we're not using virtualenv (*https://virtualenv.pypa.io/en/latest/*) to develop our application. virtualenv is an extremely useful tool for isolating Python environments. It allows developers to have separate versions of Python and supporting libraries for each application. Normally, it is essential and ubiquitous in Python development.

When using containers, however, it is less useful, as we are already provided with an isolated environment. If you're accustomed to working with virtualenv, you can certainly still use it inside a container, but you are unlikely to see much benefit, unless you experience clashes with other applications or libraries installed in the container.

---

uWSGI (*https://uwsgi-docs.readthedocs.org/en/latest/*) is a production-ready application server that can also sit behind a web server such as nginx. Using uWSGI instead of the default Flask web server will provide us with a flexible container we can use in a range of settings. We can transition the container to use uWSGI by just modifying two lines in the Dockerfile:

```
FROM python:3.4

RUN pip install Flask==0.10.1 uWSGI==2.0.8 ❶
WORKDIR /app
COPY app /app

CMD ["uwsgi", "--http", "0.0.0.0:9090", "--wsgi-file", "/app/identidock.py", \
    "--callable", "app", "--stats", "0.0.0.0:9191"] ❷
```

❶   Add uWSGI to the list of Python packages to install.

❷   Create a new command to run uWSGI. Here we tell uWSGI to start an http server listening on port 9090, running the app application from */app/identidock.py*. It also starts a stats server on port 9191. We could alternatively have overridden the CMD via the docker run command.

Build it and run it so that we can see the difference:

```
$ docker build -t identidock .
...
Successfully built 3133f91af597
$ docker run -d -p 9090:9090 -p 9191:9191 identidock
00d6fa65092cbd91a97b512334d8d4be624bf730fcb482d6e8aecc83b272f130
$ curl localhost:9090
Hello Docker!
```

If you now run `docker logs` with the container ID, you will see the logging information for uWSGI, confirming we are indeed using the uWSGI server. Also, we've asked uWSGI to expose some stats, which you can see at *http://localhost:9191*. The Python code that normally starts the default web server hasn't been executed as it wasn't run directly from the command line.

The server is working correctly now, but there is still some housekeeping we should do. If you examine the uWSGI logs, you'll notice that the server is rightly complaining about being run as root. This is a pointless security leak we can easily fix in the Dockerfile by specifying a user to run under. At the same time, we will explicitly declare the ports the container listens on:

```
FROM python:3.4

RUN groupadd -r uwsgi && useradd -r -g uwsgi uwsgi  ❶
RUN pip install Flask==0.10.1 uWSGI==2.0.8
WORKDIR /app
COPY app /app

EXPOSE 9090 9191  ❷
USER uwsgi  ❸

CMD ["uwsgi", "--http", "0.0.0.0:9090", "--wsgi-file", "/app/identidock.py", \
    "--callable", "app", "--stats", "0.0.0.0:9191"]
```

To explain the new lines:

❶ Creates the `uwsgi` user and group in a normal Unix fashion.

❷ Uses the `EXPOSE` instruction to declare the ports accessible to the host and other containers.

❸ Sets the user for all the following lines (including `CMD` and `ENTRYPOINT`) to be `uwsgi`.

Users and Groups Inside Containers

The Linux kernel uses *UID*s and *GID*s to identify users and determine their access rights. Mapping UIDs and GIDs to identifiers is handled in userspace by the OS. Because of this, UIDs in the container are the same as UIDs on the host, but users and groups created inside containers do not propagate to the host. A side effect of this is that access permissions can get confusing; files can appear to be owned by different users inside and outside of containers. For example, note the changing owner of the following file:

```
$ ls -l test-file
-rw-r--r--   1 docker   staff 0 Dec 28 18:26 test-file
$ docker run -it -v $PWD/test-file:/test-file
debian bash
root@e877f924ea27:/# ls -l test-file
-rw-r--r-- 1 1000 staff 0 Dec 28 18:26 test-file
root@e877f924ea27:/# useradd -r test-user
root@e877f924ea27:/# chown test-user test-file
root@e877f924ea27:/# ls -l /test-file
-rw-r--r-- 1 test-user staff 0 Dec 28 18:26 /test-file
root@e877f924ea27:/# exit
exit
docker@boot2docker:~$ ls -l test-file
-rw-r--r--   1 999      staff 0 Dec 28 18:26 test-file
```

Build this image as normal and test the new user setting:

```
$ docker build -t identidock .
...
$ docker run identidock whoami
uwsgi
```

Note we've overridden the default CMD instruction that calls the web server with the `whoami` command, which returns the name of the running user inside the container.

Always Set a USER

It's important to set the USER statement in all your Dockerfiles (or change the user within an ENTRYPOINT or CMD script). If you don't do this, your processes will be running as root within the container. As UIDs are the same within a container and on the host, should attackers manage to break the container, they will have root access to the host machine.

There is work ongoing to automatically map the root user inside a container to a high-numbered user on the host, but at the time of writing (Docker version 1.8), this hasn't landed yet.

Great, now commands inside the container are no longer running as root. Let's launch the container again, but with a slightly different set of arguments:

```
$ docker run -d -P --name port-test identidock
```

This time we haven't specified specific ports on the host to bind to. Instead, we've used the -P argument, which makes Docker automatically map a random high-numbered port on the host to each "exposed" port on the container. We have to ask Docker what these ports are before we can access the service:

```
$ docker port port-test
9090/tcp -> 0.0.0.0:32769
9191/tcp -> 0.0.0.0:32768
```

Here we can see that it has bound 9090 to 32769 on the host and 9191 to 32768, so we can now access the service (note that the port numbers are likely to be different for you):

```
$ curl localhost:32769
Hello Docker!
```

At first, this might seem a pointless extra step—and it is, in this case—but when you have multiple containers running on a single host, it's a lot easier to ask Docker to automatically map free ports than it is keep track of unused ports yourself.

So now we have a web service running that is pretty close to how it would look in production. There are still a lot of things you would want to tweak in production—such as the uWSGI options for processes and threads—but we have closed the gap enormously from the default Python debug web server.

We now have a new problem: we've lost access to the development tools such as debugging output and live code-reloading provided by the default Python web server. While we can drastically reduce the differences between the development and production environments, they still have fundamentally different needs that will always require some changes. Ideally, we want to use the same image for both development and production but enable a slightly different set of features depending on where it is running. We can achieve this by using an environment variable and a simple script to switch features depending on context.

Create a file called *cmd.sh* in the same directory as the Dockerfile with the following contents:

```
#!/bin/bash
set -e

if [ "$ENV" = 'DEV' ]; then
  echo "Running Development Server"
  exec python "identidock.py"
else
  echo "Running Production Server"
```

```
        exec uwsgi --http 0.0.0.0:9090 --wsgi-file /app/identidock.py \
               --callable app --stats 0.0.0.0:9191
    fi
```

The intent of this script should be fairly clear. If the variable ENV is set to DEV, it will
run the debug web server; otherwise it will use the production server.[2] The exec command is used in order to avoid creating a new process, which ensures any signals
(such as SIGTERM) are received by our uWSGI process rather than being swallowed by
the parent process.

 Use Configuration Files and Helper Scripts

To keep things simple, I've included everything inside the Dockerfile. However, as the application grows, it makes sense to move
things out into supporting files and scripts where possible. In particular, the pip dependencies should be moved to a *requirements.txt*
file, and the uWSGI configuration can move to a *.ini* file.

Next, we need to update the Dockerfile to use the script:

```
FROM python:3.4

RUN groupadd -r uwsgi && useradd -r -g uwsgi uwsgi
RUN pip install Flask==0.10.1 uWSGI==2.0.8
WORKDIR /app
COPY app /app
COPY cmd.sh /    ❶

EXPOSE 9090 9191
USER uwsgi

CMD ["/cmd.sh"]   ❷
```

❶ Adds the script to the container.

❷ Calls it from the CMD instruction.

Before we try out the new version, it's time to stop any old containers we have running. The following will stop and remove all containers from the host (*do not* run this
if you have containers you want to keep):

```
$ docker stop $(docker ps -q)
c4b3d240f187
9be42abaf902
78af7d12d3bb
```

---

2 We now have variables such as port numbers duplicated across files. We could fix this by using arguments or
   environment variables.

```
$ docker rm $(docker ps -aq)
1198f8486390
c4b3d240f187
9be42abaf902
78af7d12d3bb
```

Now we can rebuild the image with the script and test it out:

```
$ chmod +x cmd.sh
$ docker build -t identidock .
...
$ docker run -e "ENV=DEV" -p 5000:5000 identidock
Running Development Server
 * Running on http://0.0.0.0:5000/ (Press CTRL+C to quit)
 * Restarting with stat
```

Good. Now when we run with -e "ENV=DEV", we get a development server; otherwise, we get the production server.

Development Servers

You may find that the default Python server doesn't meet your needs during development, especially when linking several containers together. In this case, you can run uWSGI in development as well. You will still want the ability to switch environments so that you can turn on uWSGI features such as live code-reloading, which shouldn't be run in production.

Automating with Compose

There's a final bit of automation we can add to make things a bit simpler. Docker Compose (*http://docs.docker.com/compose/*) is designed to quickly get Docker development environments up and running. Essentially, it uses YAML files to store the configuration for sets of containers, saving developers from repetitive and error-prone typing or rolling their own solution. Our application is so basic that it doesn't buy us much at the moment, but it will quickly come into its own as things get more complicated. Compose will free us from the need to maintain our own scripts for orchestration, including starting, linking, updating, and stopping our containers.

If you installed Docker using the Docker Toolbox, you should already have Compose available. If not, follow the instructions at the Docker website (*http://docs.docker.com/compose/install/*). I used version 1.4.0 of Compose in this chapter, but as we're only using basic functionality, anything after 1.2 should be good.

Create a file called *docker-compose.yml* in the *identidock* directory with the following contents:

```
identidock:  ❶
  build: .  ❷
  ports:    ❸
   - "5000:5000"
  environment:  ❹
    ENV: DEV
  volumes:  ❺
   - ./app:/app
```

❶ The first line declares the name of the container to build. Multiple containers (often called services in Compose lingo) can be defined in a single YAML file.

❷ The build key tells Compose that the image for this container is to be built from a Dockerfile that exists in the current directory (.). Every container definition needs to include *either* a build or image key. image keys take the tag or ID of an image to use for the container, the same as image argument to docker run.

❸ The ports key is directly analogous to the -p argument to docker run for exposing ports. Here we map port 5000 in the container to port 5000 on the host. Ports can be specified without quotes, but this is best avoided as it can cause confusion when YAML parses statements such as 56:56 as a base 60 number.

❹ The environment key is directly analogous to the -e argument to docker run, which sets environment variables in the container. Here we are setting ENV to DEV in order to run the Flask development web server.

❺ The volumes key is directly analogous to the -v argument to docker run for setting volumes. Here we are bind mounting the app directory into the container as before in order to allow us to make changes to the code from the host.

Many more keys can be set in Compose YAML files, normally mapping directly to the equivalent docker run arguments.

If you now run docker-compose up, you will get almost exactly the same result as the previous docker run command:

```
$ docker-compose up
Creating identidock_identidock_1...
Attaching to identidock_identidock_1
identidock_1 | Running Development Server
identidock_1 |  * Running on http://0.0.0.0:5000/
identidock_1 |  * Restarting with reloader
```

From another terminal:

```
$ curl localhost:5000
Hello Docker!
```

When you're finished running the application, you can just hit Ctrl-C to stop the container.

To switch to the uWSGI server, we would need to change the `environment` and `ports` keys in the YAML. This can either be done by editing the existing *docker-compose.yml* or by creating a new YAML file for production and pointing `docker-compose` at using the `-f` flag or the `COMPOSE_FILE` environment variable.

The Compose Workflow

The following commands are commonly used when working with Compose. Most are self-explanatory and have direct Docker equivalents, but it's worth being aware of them:

up
: Starts all the containers defined in the Compose file and aggregates the log output. Normally you will want to use the `-d` argument to run Compose in the background.

build
: Rebuilds any images created from Dockerfiles. The `up` command will not build an image unless it doesn't exist, so use this command whenever you need to update an image.

ps
: Provides information on the status of containers managed by Compose.

run
: Spins up a container to run a one-off command. This will also spin up any linked containers unless the `--no-deps` argument is given.

logs
: Outputs colored and aggregated logs for the Compose-managed containers.

stop
: Stops containers without removing them.

rm
: Removes stopped containers. Remember to use the `-v` argument to remove any Docker-managed volumes.

A normal workflow begins with calling `docker-compose up -d` to start the application. The `docker-compose logs` and `ps` commands can be used to verify the status of the application and help debugging.

After changes to the code, call `docker-compose build` followed by `docker-compose up -d`. This will build the new image and replace the running container. Note that Compose will preserve any old volumes from the original containers, which means that databases and caches persist over containers (this can be confusing, so be careful). If you don't need a new image but have modified the Compose YAML, calling `up -d` will cause Compose to replace the container with one with the new settings. If you want to force Compose to stop and re-create all the containers, use the `--force-recreate` flag.

When you're finished with the application, calling `docker-compose stop` will halt the application. The same containers will be restarted if `docker-compose start` or `up` is called, assuming no code has changed. Use `docker-compose rm` to get rid of them completely.

For a full overview of all the commands, see the Docker reference page (*https://docs.docker.com/compose/reference/*).

Conclusion

We're now at the stage where we have a working environment and we can begin to develop our application. We've seen:

- How to leverage the official images to quickly create a portable and re-creatable development suite, without installing any tools on the host
- How to use volumes to make dynamic changes to code running in containers
- How to maintain both a production and development environment in a single container
- How to use Compose to automate the development workflow

Docker has given us a familiar development environment, with all the tools we need; yet at the same time, we can quickly test things out in an environment that mirrors production.

There's still a lot of things we need to do, especially with regard to testing and continuous integration/delivery, but we'll come to those in the next few chapters as we progress with development.

CHAPTER 6

Creating a Simple Web App

In this chapter, we'll turn our "Hello World!" program into a simple web app that generates a unique image for users when they enter some text. These images are sometimes known as *identicons* and can be used to identify users by providing a unique image generated from their username or IP address. At the end of this chapter, you'll have a basic working application that we will extend and play with in the following chapters. By creating this application, we'll see how to compose Docker containers to build a fully functioning system and how this naturally leads to a microservice approach.

Identicons

Identicons are images that are automatically generated from a value, normally the hash of an IP address or username. They provide a visual representation of the object so that it can be readily identified. Use cases include providing identifying images for users on a website by hashing their username or IP address and providing automatic favicons for websites.

They were originally developed by Don Park in early 2007 to identify commenters on his blog; the code is still available on his GitHub project page (*https://github.com/donpark/identicon*).

Since then, there have been several further implementations with different graphical styles. Two large adopters of identicons are Stack Overflow and GitHub, both of which use them for users who haven't set their own. Stack Overflow uses ones generated by the Gravatar service, which in turn uses the WP_Identicon project (*http://scott.sherrillmix.com/blog/blogger/wp_identicon/*), among others. GitHub generates its own identicons. See Figure 6-1.

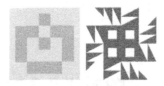

Figure 6-1. A typical GitHub identicon (left) and a typical Gravatar identicon (right)

If you've followed along with the previous chapter, you should have a project with the following structure:

```
identidock/
├── Dockerfile
├── app
│   └── identidock.py
├── cmd.sh
└── docker-compose.yml
```

Don't worry if you haven't been following along. You can grab the code so far from this book's GitHub page (*https://github.com/using-docker/creating-a-simple-web-app*). For example:

```
$ git clone -b v0 https://github.com/using-docker/creating-a-simple-web-app/
...
```

Alternatively, go to the releases page on the GitHub project to download the files.

The tag v0 is the code as it was at the end of the last chapter; later tags provide the updates as we work through the chapter.

Version Control

This book assumes knowledge of Git for pushing and cloning repositories. In a later chapter, we'll also look at the Docker Hub integration with GitHub and BitBucket. If you're not up to speed with Git, check out *https://try.github.io* for a free tutorial.

Creating a Basic Web Page

As a first step, let's get a very basic web page working for our application. For simplicity, we will just return the HTML as a string.[1] Replace *identidock.py* with the following:

---

[1] A better solution would be to use a templating engine such as Jinja2, which comes bundled with Flask.

```
from flask import Flask

app = Flask(__name__)
default_name = 'Joe Bloggs'


@app.route('/')
def mainpage():

    name = default_name

    header = '<html><head><title>Identidock</title></head><body>'
    body = '''<form method="POST">
            Hello <input type="text" name="name" value="{}">
            <input type="submit" value="submit">
            </form>
            <p>You look like a:
            <img src="/monster/monster.png"/>
            '''.format(name)
    footer = '</body></html>'

    return header + body + footer

if __name__ == '__main__':
    app.run(debug=True, host='0.0.0.0')
```

We're really not doing much more than the "Hello World!" program here. We've just modified the returned text to be a small HTML page including a form for the user to type in a name. The format function replaces the substring "{}" with the value of the name variable, which we've hardcoded to "Joe Bloggs" for the time being.

Run docker-compose up -d and open a browser to *http://localhost:5000* to see the page shown in Figure 6-2.

Figure 6-2. First look at identidock

The broken image is expected, as we haven't added any code for image generation yet. Similarly, the submit button is also broken.

At this point in development, it would be a wise idea to put in place automated tests and perhaps even continuous integration/delivery. However, for the sake of narrative, we'll continue to develop the application a bit more before introducing testing and continuous integration in the following chapters.

Taking Advantage of Existing Images

It's time to actually make this program do something. What we need is a function or service that takes a string and returns a unique image. We can then call it with the name the user supplies in the web page and use it to replace the broken image.

In this case, we are going to use dnmonster, an existing Docker image that exposes a (roughly) RESTful API we can use. We could easily substitute other identicon services for dnmonster, especially if they expose a RESTful API and are packaged into a container.

To call it from our existing code, we need to make a few changes, primarily adding a new get_identicon function:

```python
from flask import Flask, Response  ❶
import requests  ❷

app = Flask(__name__)
default_name = 'Joe Bloggs'


@app.route('/')
def mainpage():

    name = default_name

    header = '<html><head><title>Identidock</title></head><body>'
    body = '''<form method="POST">
            Hello <input type="text" name="name" value="{}">
            <input type="submit" value="submit">
            </form>
            <p>You look like a:
            <img src="/monster/monster.png"/>
            '''.format(name)
    footer = '</body></html>'

    return header + body + footer


@app.route('/monster/<name>')
def get_identicon(name):

    r = requests.get('http://dnmonster:8080/monster/' + name + '?size=80')  ❸
    image = r.content

    return Response(image, mimetype='image/png')  ❹

if __name__ == '__main__':
    app.run(debug=True, host='0.0.0.0')
```

❶ Import the Response module from Flask, which we use to return images.

---

❷ Import the requests library (*http://docs.python-requests.org/en/latest/*), which we will use to talk to the dnmonster service.

❸ Make an HTTP GET request to the dnmonster service. We ask for an identicon for the value of the name variable with a size of 80 pixels.

❹ Our return statement is a little more complicated because we need to use the Response function to tell Flask we are returning a PNG image rather than HTML or text.

Next, we need to make a small change to our Dockerfile so that our new code has the correct libraries:

```
FROM python:3.4

RUN groupadd -r uwsgi && useradd -r -g uwsgi uwsgi
RUN pip install Flask==0.10.1 uWSGI==2.0.8 requests==2.5.1 ❶
WORKDIR /app
COPY app /app
COPY cmd.sh /

EXPOSE 9090 9191
USER uwsgi

CMD ["/cmd.sh"]
```

❶ We've added the requests library used in the preceding Python code.

We're now ready to launch the dnmonster container and link it to our application container. In order to make it clear what is happening under the surface, we'll do this with plain Docker commands before moving to Compose later. As this is the first time we've used the dnmonster image, it will be downloaded from the Docker Hub:

```
$ docker build -t identidock .
...
$ docker run -d --name dnmonster amouat/dnmonster:1.0
Unable to find image 'amouat/dnmonster:1.0' locally
1.0: Pulling from amouat/dnmonster
...
Status: Downloaded newer image for amouat/dnmonster:1.0
e695026b14f7d0c48f9f4b110c7c06ab747188c33fc80ad407b3ead6902feb2d
```

Now we start the application container in almost the same way as the previous chapter, except we add the argument --link dnmonster:dnmonster to connect the containers. This is the magic that makes the URL *http://dnmonster:8080* addressable in the Python code:

```
$ docker run -d -p 5000:5000 -e "ENV=DEV" --link dnmonster:dnmonster identidock
16ae698a9c705587f6316a6b53dd0268cfc3d263f2ce70eada024ddb56916e36
```

For more information on links, refer back to "Linking Containers".

If you open your browser to *http://localhost:5000* again, you should see something like Figure 6-3.

Figure 6-3. The first identicon!

It doesn't look like much, but we've just generated our first identicon. The submit button is still broken, so we're not actually using any user input, but we'll fix that in a minute. First, let's get Compose running again so we don't have to remember all those docker run commands. Update *docker-compose.yml*:

```
identidock:
  build: .
  ports:
   - "5000:5000"
  environment:
    ENV: DEV
  volumes:
   - ./app:/app
  links: ❶
   - dnmonster

dnmonster: ❷
  image: amouat/dnmonster:1.0
```

❶ Declares a link from the identidock container to the dnmonster container. Compose will take care of starting containers in the correct order for this to happen.

❷ Defines the new dnmonster container. All we need to tell Compose is to use the amouat/dnmonster:1.0 image from the Docker Hub.

Before starting the application again, we need to stop and remove any old containers:

```
$ docker rm $(docker stop $(docker ps -q))
...
```

Note that this command will stop all running containers, not just the identidock ones. We can then rebuild and run the application with Compose:

```
$ docker-compose build
...
```

```
$ docker-compose up -d
...
```

The app should now be running again, and changes to the code will no longer require the containers to be restarted before taking effect.

To enable the button, we need to handle a POST request to the server and use the form variable (which holds the username) to generate the image. We're also going to be a bit clever and hash the user input. This anonymizes any sensitive input such as email addresses and also makes sure the input is in a form suitable for a URL (we won't need to escape characters such as spaces). In our application, the hashing isn't important because we're only dealing with names, but it shows how to use the service in other scenarios and protects anyone that does happen to enter sensitive information.

Update *identidock.py* so that it looks like:

```
from flask import Flask, Response, request
import requests
import hashlib   ❶

app = Flask(__name__)
salt = "UNIQUE_SALT"   ❷
default_name = 'Joe Bloggs'


@app.route('/', methods=['GET', 'POST'])   ❸
def mainpage():

    name = default_name
    if request.method == 'POST':   ❹
        name = request.form['name']

    salted_name = salt + name
    name_hash = hashlib.sha256(salted_name.encode()).hexdigest()   ❺

    header = '<html><head><title>Identidock</title></head><body>'
    body = '''<form method="POST">
            Hello <input type="text" name="name" value="{0}">
            <input type="submit" value="submit">
            </form>
            <p>You look like a:
            <img src="/monster/{1}"/>
            '''.format(name, name_hash)   ❻
    footer = '</body></html>'

    return header + body + footer


@app.route('/monster/<name>')
def get_identicon(name):
```

```
    r = requests.get('http://dnmonster:8080/monster/' + name + '?size=80')
    image = r.content

    return Response(image, mimetype='image/png')

if __name__ == '__main__':
    app.run(debug=True, host='0.0.0.0')
```

❶ Imports the library we will use to hash user input. As it's a standard library, we don't need to update the Dockerfile to install it.

❷ Defines the salt value to use with our hash function. By changing this value, different sites can produce different identicons for the same input.

❸ By default, Flask routes only respond to HTTP GET requests. Our form submits an HTTP POST request, so we need to add the named argument methods to the route declaration and explicitly announce that the route will handle both POST and GET requests.

❹ If the request.method equals "POST", the request is a result of clicking the submit button. In this case, we want to update the name variable to the value of the text entered by the user.

❺ Gets the hash for our input using the SHA256 algorithm.

❻ Modify the image URL to take our hashed value. This will cause the browser to call the get_identicon route with our hashed value when it tries to load the image.

Once you've saved the new version of this file, the debug Python web server should pick up the changes and automatically restart. You can now view the fully working version of our web app and find out what your identicon is (Figure 6-4).

Figure 6-4. Gordon the Turtle's identicon!

---

dnmonster

The dnmonster image is a Node.js application wrapped in a Docker container. The application is a port of Kevin Guadin's monsterid.js (*https://github.com/KevinGaudin/monsterid.js*) from in-browser JavaScript to Node.js. Monsterid.js is itself based on MonsterID (*http://www.splitbrain.org/projects/monsterid*) by Andreas Gohr, which creates monsters in the 8-bit computing style of RetroAvatar (*http://retroava tar.appspot.com/*). You can find dnmonster on GitHub (*https://github.com/amouat/dnmonster*).

Unlike monsterid.js, dnmonster does not do any hashing of inputs, instead leaving this up to the caller (Figure 6-5).

Figure 6-5. Monsters!

Add Some Caching

So far, so good. But there's one horrible thing about this application at the moment (apart from the monsters)—every time a monster is requested, we make a computationally expensive call to the dnmonster service. There's no need for this—the whole point of an identicon is that the image remains the same for a given input, so we should be caching the result.

To achieve this, we'll use Redis, which is an in-memory key-value data store. Redis is great for tasks like this where there's not a huge amount of information and we're not worried about durability (if an entry is lost or deleted, we can just regenerate the image). We could add the Redis server into our identidock container, but it's easier and more idiomatic to spin up a new container. This way we can take advantage of the official Redis image already available on the Docker Hub and avoid dealing with the extra hassle of running multiple processes in a container.

Running Multiple Process in a Container

The majority of containers only run a single process. Where multiple processes are needed, it's best to run multiple containers and link them together, as we have done in this example.

However, sometimes you really do need to run multiple processes in a single container. In these cases, it's best to use a process manager such as supervisord (*http://supervisord.org/*) or runit (*http://smarden.org/runit/*) to handle starting and monitoring the processes. It is possible to write a simple script to start your processes, but be aware that you will then be responsible for cleaning up the processes and forwarding any signals.

For more information on using supervisord inside containers, see this Docker article (*https://docs.docker.com/articles/using_supervisord/*).

First, we need to update our Python code to use the cache:

```
from flask import Flask, Response, request
import requests
import hashlib
import redis ❶

app = Flask(__name__)
cache = redis.StrictRedis(host='redis', port=6379, db=0) ❷
salt = "UNIQUE_SALT"
default_name = 'Joe Bloggs'


@app.route('/', methods=['GET', 'POST'])
def mainpage():

    name = default_name
    if request.method == 'POST':
        name = request.form['name']

    salted_name = salt + name
    name_hash = hashlib.sha256(salted_name.encode()).hexdigest()
    header = '<html><head><title>Identidock</title></head><body>'
    body = '''<form method="POST">
                Hello <input type="text" name="name" value="{0}">
                <input type="submit" value="submit">
                </form>
                <p>You look like a:
                <img src="/monster/{1}"/>
                '''.format(name, name_hash)
```

```
        footer = '</body></html>'

        return header + body + footer


@app.route('/monster/<name>')
def get_identicon(name):

    image = cache.get(name) ❸
    if image is None: ❹
        print ("Cache miss", flush=True) ❺
        r = requests.get('http://dnmonster:8080/monster/' + name + '?size=80')
        image = r.content
        cache.set(name, image) ❻

    return Response(image, mimetype='image/png')

if __name__ == '__main__':
    app.run(debug=True, host='0.0.0.0')
```

❶   Import the Redis module.

❷   Set up the Redis cache. We will use Docker links to make the `redis` hostname resolvable.

❸   Check to see if the name is already in the cache.

❹   Redis will return `None` if we have a cache miss. In this case, we just get the identicon as usual except we also...

❺   Output some debug information to say we didn't find a cached version and...

❻   Add the image into the cache and associate it with the given name.

We're using a new module and a new container, so unfortunately we need to update both the Dockerfile and our *docker-compose.yml*. First the Dockerfile:

```
FROM python:3.4

RUN groupadd -r uwsgi && useradd -r -g uwsgi uwsgi
RUN pip install Flask==0.10.1 uWSGI==2.0.8 requests==2.5.1 redis==2.10.3 ❶
WORKDIR /app
COPY app /app
COPY cmd.sh /

EXPOSE 9090 9191
USER uwsgi

CMD ["/cmd.sh"]
```

❶ We just need to install the Redis client library for Python.

And the updated *docker-compose.yml*:

```
identidock:
  build: .
  ports:
    - "5000:5000"
  environment:
    ENV: DEV
  volumes:
    - ./app:/app
  links:
    - dnmonster
    - redis ❶

dnmonster:
  image: amouat/dnmonster:1.0

redis:
  image: redis:3.0 ❷
```

❶ Sets up a link to the Redis container.

❷ Creates a Redis container based on the official image.

Now if you first stop identidock with `docker-compose stop`, you can do a `docker-compose build` and `docker-compose up` to launch the new version. As we haven't made any functional changes, you shouldn't notice any differences with the new version of the app. If you want to convince yourself that the new code is working, you can check the debug output; or if you're really keen, try hooking up a monitoring solution such as Prometheus (described in Chapter 10) and seeing what happens when you generate load against the application.

Microservices

We've developed identidock according to a *microservice* architecture, where systems are composed of multiple small and independent services. The style is often contrasted with *monolithic* architectures where the system is contained within a single large service. Even though identidock is just a toy application, it still highlights various characteristics of the style.

If we had instead used a monolithic architecture, we would have equivalents of dnmonster, Redis, and identidock all written in a single language and running as a single component in a single container. A well-designed monolith would factor these components into separate libraries and use existing libraries where possible.

In contrast, our identidock application has a Python web application talking to a Java-Script service and a C key-value store across three containers. Later on in the book, we will see how to plug in more microservices to identidock with very little work, including a reverse proxy in Chapter 9 and a monitoring and logging solution in Chapter 10.

There are several advantages to this approach. It is much easier to scale-out a microservice framework to multiple machines. Microservices can be quickly and easily swapped out for more efficient equivalents, or rolled back in the case of unexpected problems without bringing down the rest of the system. Different languages can be used in separate microservices, allowing developers to choose languages appropriate to the task at hand.

There are disadvantages as well, primarily in the overhead of all the distributed components. Communication occurs over the network rather than being a library call. We have to use tools like Compose to ensure all the components are started together and linked properly. Orchestration and service discovery become significant issues that need to be addressed.

Modern Internet applications can derive enormous benefits from the increased scaling and dynamic options provided by microservices, as proven by companies such as Netflix, Amazon, and SoundCloud. For this reason, microservices will be a significant and important architecture going forward, but—as usual—they are no silver bullet.[2]

Conclusion

We've now got a basic working version of our application. While it's still very simple, it has enough functionality to use several containers and highlight various aspects of developing with containers. We've seen how we can reuse existing images, both as foundations to build on (as with the Python base image) and as black boxes that provide a service (as with the dnmonster image).

Most importantly, we've seen how containers naturally lead to groups of small, well-defined services that interact to form a larger system—the microservices approach.

---

2 For more information on the advantages and disadvantages of microservices, take a look a Martin Fowler's articles on the subject, including "Microservices" (*http://martinfowler.com/articles/microservices.html*).

CHAPTER 7

Image Distribution

Once you've created your images, you'll want to make them available, be it to coworkers, continuous integration servers, or end users. There are several ways to distribute images: you can rebuild them from Dockerfiles, pull from a registry, or use the `docker load` command to install from an archive file.

In this chapter, we'll take a deeper look at the differences between these methods and explore the best ways to handle image distribution both internally in a team and externally to users. We'll see how we can tag and upload our identidock image so that it can be used in other parts of our workflow and downloaded by others.

 The code for this chapter is available at this book's GitHub (*http:// bit.ly/1IaHmJE*). The tag v0 is the code as it was at the end of the last chapter, with later tags representing the progression of the code through this chapter. To get this version of the code:

```
$ git clone -b v0 \
https://github.com/using-docker/image-dist/
 . . .
```

Alternatively, you can download the code for any tag from the Releases page on the GitHub project (*http://bit.ly/1IaHitw*).

Image and Repository Naming

We saw in "Working with Registries" how to tag images appropriately and upload them to remote repositories. When distributing images, it's very important to use descriptive and accurate names and tags. To recap, image names and tags are set when building the image or by using the `docker tag` command:

```
$ cd identidock
$ docker build -t "identidock:0.1" .  ❶
$ docker tag "identidock:0.1" "amouat/identidock:0.1"  ❷
```

❶ Sets the repository name to identidock and the tag to 0.1.

❷ Associates the name amouat/identidock with the image, which refers to the username amouat on the Docker Hub.

Beware of the latest Tag

Do not let the latest tag mislead you! Docker will use the tag as a default when none is given, but beyond this, it carries no special meaning. Many repositories use it as an alias for the most up-to-date stable image, but this is only a convention and is entirely unenforced.

Images tagged latest, as with all other images, will not be updated automatically when a new version is pushed to the registry—you still need to explicitly run docker pull to retrieve updated versions.

When a docker run or docker pull refers to an image name with no tag, Docker will use the image tagged latest if it exists or throw an error if it doesn't.

Because of the amount of user confusion surrounding the latest tag, it is worth considering avoiding it completely, especially for public-facing repositories.

Tag names have to follow a few rules. Tags must be made up of upper- or lowercase letters, numbers, or the symbols . and -. They must be between 1 and 128 characters in length. The first character cannot be . or -.

Repository names and tags are critically important when building a development workflow. Docker places very few restrictions on legal names and allows the creation and deletion of names at any time. This means it is up to the development team to come up with and enforce a workable naming scheme.

The Docker Hub

The most straightforward solution to making your images available is to use the Docker Hub. The Docker Hub is the online registry provided by Docker, Inc. The Hub provides free repositories for public images, or users can pay for private repositories.

Alternative Private Hosting

The Docker Hub isn't the only game in town if you're looking to host your private repositories in the cloud. At the time of writing, the leading competitor is Quay.io, which offers a few more features than the Docker Hub at a competitive price.

We can easily upload our identidock image. Assuming you already have an account on the Docker Hub,[1] we can do this directly from the command line:

```
$ docker tag identidock:latest amouat/identidock:0.1  ❶
$ docker push amouat/identidock:0.1  ❷
The push refers to a repository [docker.io/amouat/identidock] (len: 1)
76899e56d187: Image successfully pushed
...
0.1: digest: sha256:8aecd14cb97cc4333fdffe903aec1435a1883a44ea9f25b45513d4c2...
```

❶ The first thing we need to do is create an alias for the image in the Docker Hub user namespace. This means it must be in the form *<username>/<repository name>* where *<username>* is your username on the Docker Hub (in my case, amouat) and *<repositoryname>* is the name you want the repository to have on the Hub. We also take the opportunity to set the tag to 0.1 for this image.

❷ Pushes the image using the alias we just created. This will create the repository if it doesn't exist and upload the image under the appropriate tag.

At this point, identidock is publicly available, and anyone can retrieve it by doing a docker pull.

If you go to the Docker Hub website, you will be able to find your repository under a URL such as *https://registry.hub.docker.com/u/amouat/identidock/*. If you're logged in, you will also be able to perform various admin tasks, such as setting a description for the repository, marking other users as collaborators, and setting up webhooks.

---

1 If not, go and sign up at *https://hub.docker.com*.

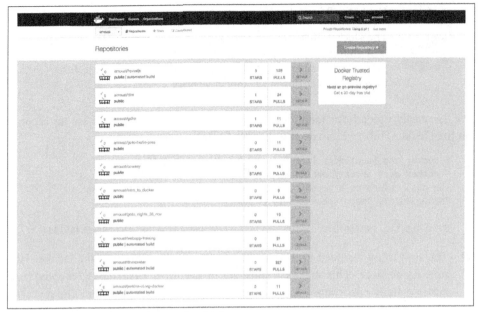

Figure 7-1. Homepage on the Docker Hub

Whenever we want to update the repository, we just repeat the tag and push steps using whichever image we want. If we use an existing tag, the previous image will be overwritten. This is great, but what if we simply want our images to be updated whenever our code is? This is a very common use case; and for that reason, the Docker Hub introduced the concept of *automated builds*.

Automated Builds

Let's set up an automated build on the Docker Hub for identidock. Once we've done this, the Hub will build the identidock image and save it to our repository whenever we push changes to the source code. To do this, you'll need to set up a GitHub or Bitbucket repository. You can either push up the code you have so far, or "fork" the official code, which can be found on this book's GitHub (*https://github.com/using-docker/image-dist*).

Automated builds are configured via the Hub's website interface rather than on the command line. If you are logged in to the website, you should see a drop-down menu on the top right titled "Create." From here, select "Create Automated Build" and locate the repository with the identidock code.[2] Once you've selected the repository, you will be taken to the configuration page for the automated build. The repository

---

2 You will first need to link your GitHub or Bitbucket account if you haven't already done so.

---

name defaults to the name of the source code repository, which you should change to something meaningful like `identidock_auto`. Give the repository a short description such as "Automatic build for identidock." Leave the first "Tag" field as `Branch` and name as `master` to track the code from the master branch. Set "Dockerfile Location" to */identidock/Dockerfile* if you've forked from my repository. The final "Tag" field determines the name assigned to the image on the Docker Hub. You can leave this as `latest`, or change it to something more meaningful such as `auto`. Once you're done, click "Create." Docker will take you to the build page for this new repository. You can kick off the first build by clicking "Trigger a Build." Once the build has completed, you will be able to download the image (assuming the build succeeds).

We can test the build automation by making a small change to source code. In this case, we'll add a README file the Docker Hub will also use to display some information on the repository. Create a file *README.md* in the identidock directory with a short description such as the following:[3]

```
identidock
==========

Simple identicon server based on monsterid from Kevin Gaudin.

From "Using Docker" by Adrian Mouat published by O'Reilly Media.
```

Check this file in and push it:

```
$ git add README.md
$ git commit -m "Added README"
[master d8f3317] Added README
 1 file changed, 6 insertions(+)
 create mode 100644 identidock/README.md
$ git push
Counting objects: 4, done.
Delta compression using up to 4 threads.
Compressing objects: 100% (4/4), done.
Writing objects: 100% (4/4), 456 bytes | 0 bytes/s, done.
Total 4 (delta 2), reused 0 (delta 0)
To git@github.com:using-docker/image-dist.git
   c81ff68..d8f3317  master -> master
```

If you wait a moment and then visit the build page for the repository, you should see it building a new version of the image.

Should a build fail for whatever reason, you can get the logs by clicking on "Build Code" on the "Build Details" tab. You can also kick off a new build at any time by clicking the "Trigger a Build" button.

---

3 If you forked the repo, this file will already exist; just change some of the text instead.

This approach to building and distributing images isn't a great fit for all projects. Your images are public unless you pay for private repositories, and you're at the mercy of the Docker Hub—should the Hub go down, you won't be able to update your images, and users won't be able to download them. There's also the simple matter of efficiency; if you need to quickly build and move images through a pipeline, you are not going to want the overhead of transferring files from the Hub and waiting on queued builds. For open source projects and small side projects, the Hub is perfect. But for anything larger or more serious, you will want to replace or augment it with other solutions.

Private Distribution

There are a few options outside of the Docker Hub. You could do things manually, by exporting and importing images or simply rebuilding images from Dockerfiles on each Docker Host. Both these solutions are suboptimal: building from Dockerfiles each time is slow and may result in differences between images across hosts; exporting and importing images is somewhat tricky and error prone. The remaining option is to use a different registry, which can be hosted either by yourself or a third party.

We'll start by looking at the free solution—running your own registry—before taking a look at some of the commercial offerings.

Running Your Own Registry

The Docker registry is not the same as the Docker Hub. Both implement the registry API, allowing users to push, pull, and search images, but the Docker Hub is a closed source remote service, whereas the registry is an open source application that be run locally. The Docker Hub also contains support for user accounts, statistics, and a web interface that are not present in the Docker registry.

Work in Progress

While registry v2 is stable, several important features are still being developed. For this reason, I have focused on the main use cases in this section and avoided going into detail on advanced features. Full, up-to-date documentation on the registry can be found on the Docker distribution GitHub project page (*https://github.com/docker/distribution*).

In this chapter, we're only going to look at version 2 of the registry, which will only work with Docker daemons version 1.6 and later. If you need to support older versions of Docker, you'll need to run the previous version of the registry (it's also possible to run both versions of the registry in tandem for a transitionary period). Version

2 of the registry represents a major advance in security, reliability, and efficiency over version 1, so I strongly recommend using version 2 if at all possible.

The easiest way to run a local registry is by using the official image. We can quickly get started by running:

```
$ docker run -d -p 5000:5000 registry:2
...
75fafd23711482bbee7be50b304b795a40b7b0858064473b88e3ddcae3847c37
```

Now that we have a running registry, we can tag an image appropriately and push it. If you're using docker-machine, you can still use the localhost address, as it will be interpreted by the Docker engine (rather than the client), which is running on the same host as the registry:

```
$ docker tag amouat/identidock:0.1 localhost:5000/identidock:0.1
$ docker push localhost:5000/identidock:0.1
The push refers to a repository [localhost:5000/identidock] (len: 1)
...
0.1: digest: sha256:d20affe522a3c6ef1f8293de69fea5a8621d695619955262f3fc2885...
```

If we now remove the local version, we can pull it again:

```
$ docker rmi localhost:5000/identidock:0.1
Untagged: localhost:5000/identidock:0.1
$ docker pull localhost:5000/identidock:0.1
0.1: Pulling from identidock
...
76899e56d187: Already exists
Digest: sha256:d20affe522a3c6ef1f8293de69fea5a8621d695619955262f3fc28852e173108
Status: Downloaded newer image for localhost:5000/identidock:0.1
```

Docker sees that we already have an image with the same content, so all that really happens is the tag is added back. You may have noticed that the registry generated a *digest* for the image. This is a unique hash based on the content on the image and its metadata. You can pull images using the digest like so:

```
$ docker pull localhost:5000/identidock@sha256:\
d20affe522a3c6ef1f8293de69fea5a8621d695619955262f3fc28852e173108
sha256:d20affe522a3c6ef1f8293de69fea5a8621d695619955262f3fc28852e173108: Pul...
...
76899e56d187: Already exists
Digest: sha256:d20affe522a3c6ef1f8293de69fea5a8621d695619955262f3fc28852e173108
Status: Downloaded newer image for localhost:5000/identidock@sha256:d20affe5...
```

The primary advantage of using a digest is that it guarantees you are pulling exactly the image you think you are. When pulling by tag, the underlying image may change at any time without you knowing. Also, using digests ensures the integrity of the image; you can be sure it hasn't been tampered with during transit or in storage. For details on how to securely handle images and establish their provenance, see "Image Provenance".

The main reason you want a registry is to act as a central store for your team or organization. That means you will need to be able to pull from the registry from a remote Docker daemon. But if we try that with the registry we just launched, we'll get the following error:

```
$ docker pull 192.168.1.100:5000/identidock:0.1 ❶
Error response from daemon: unable to ping registry endpoint
https://192.168.99.100:5000/v0/
v2 ping attempt failed with error: Get https://192.168.99.100:5000/v2/:
tls: oversized record received with length 20527
 v1 ping attempt failed with error: Get https://192.168.99.100:5000/v1/_ping:
tls: oversized record received with length 20527
```

❶ Here I've substituted the IP address of the server for "localhost." You will get this error whether you pull from a daemon on another machine or on the same machine as the registry.

So what happened? The Docker daemon is refusing to connect to the remote host because it doesn't have a valid Transport Layer Security (TLS) certificate. The only reason it worked before is because Docker has a special exception for pulling from "localhost" servers. We can fix this issue in one of three ways:

- Restart each Docker daemon that accesses the registry with the following argument and port as appropriate for your server:

  `--insecure-registry 192.168.1.100:5000`

- Install a signed certificate from a trusted certificate authority on the host, as you would for hosting a website accessed over HTTPS.

- Install a self-signed certificate on the host and a copy on every Docker daemon that needs to access the registry.

The first option is the easiest, but we won't consider it here due to the security concerns. The second option is the best, but requires you to obtain a certificate from a trusted certificate authority, which normally has an associated cost. The third option is secure, but requires the manual step of copying the certificate to each daemon.

If you want to create your own self-signed certificate, you can use the OpenSSL tool. These steps should be carried out on a machine you want to keep running long term as a registry server (they were tested on an Ubuntu 14.04 VM running on Digital Ocean; there are likely to be differences on other operating systems):

```
root@reginald:~# mkdir registry_certs
root@reginald:~# openssl req -newkey rsa:4096 -nodes -sha256 \
>     -keyout registry_certs/domain.key -x509 -days 365 \
      -out registry_certs/domain.crt ❶
Generating a 4096 bit RSA private key
.....................................................++
.....................................................++
```

```
writing new private key to 'registry_certs/domain.key'
-----
You are about to be asked to enter information that will be incorporated
into your certificate request.
What you are about to enter is what is called a Distinguished Name or a DN.
There are quite a few fields but you can leave some blank
For some fields there will be a default value,
If you enter '.', the field will be left blank.
-----
Country Name (2 letter code) [AU]:
State or Province Name (full name) [Some-State]:
Locality Name (eg, city) []:
Organization Name (eg, company) [Internet Widgits Pty Ltd]:
Organizational Unit Name (eg, section) []:
Common Name (e.g. server FQDN or YOUR name) []:reginald ❷
Email Address []:
root@reginald:~# ls registry_certs/
domain.crt  domain.key ❸
```

❶ Creates a x509 self-signed certificate and a 4096-bit RSA private key. The certificate is signed with a SHA256 digest and is valid for 365 days. OpenSSL will ask for information—you can input or leave at the default values.

❷ The common name is important; it must match the name you want to access the server on and should not be an IP address ("reginald" is the name of my server).

❸ At the end of this process, we have a certificate file called *domain.crt* that will be shared with clients and a private key *domain.key* that *must be kept secure and not shared.*

Addressing the Registry by IP Address

If you want to use an IP address to reach your registry, things are a little more complicated. You can't simply use the IP address as the common name. You need to set up Subject Alternative Names (or SANs) for the IP address or addresses you want to use.

In general, I would advise against this approach. It's better just to pick a name for your server and make it addressable by the name internally (in the worst case, you can always manually add the server name to */etc/hosts*). This is generally easier to set up and doesn't require retagging of all images should you want to change the IP address.

Next, we need to copy the certificate to each Docker daemon that will access the registry.[4] It should be copied to the file */etc/docker/certs.d/<registry_address>/ca.crt* where *<registry_address>* is the address and port of your registry server. You will also need to restart the Docker daemon. For example:

```
root@reginald:~# sudo mkdir -p /etc/docker/certs.d/reginald:5000
root@reginald:~# sudo cp registry_certs/domain.crt \
                 /etc/docker/certs.d/reginald:5000/ca.crt ❶
root@reginald:~# sudo service docker restart
docker stop/waiting
docker start/running, process 3906
```

❶ To run on a remote host, you will need to transfer the CA certificate to the Docker host, using scp or a similar tool. If you used a public, trusted CA, you can skip this step.

Now we can start the registry:[5]

```
root@reginald:~# docker run -d -p 5000:5000 \
                 -v $PWD/registry_certs:/certs \ ❶
                 -e REGISTRY_HTTP_TLS_CERTIFICATE=/certs/domain.crt \
                 -e REGISTRY_HTTP_TLS_KEY=/certs/domain.key \ ❷
                 --restart=always --name registry registry:2
...
b79cb734d8778c0e36934514c0a1ed13d42c342c7b8d7d4d75f84497cc6f45f4
```

❶ Places the certificates in the container as a volume.

❷ We can use environment variables to configure the registry to use our certificates.

Pull an image, retag it, and push it, just to prove things are working:

```
root@reginald:~# docker pull debian:wheezy
wheezy: Pulling from library/debian
ba249489d0b6: Pull complete
19de96c112fc: Pull complete
library/debian:wheezy: The image you are pulling has been verified.
Important: image verification is a tech preview feature and should not be
relied on to provide security.
Digest: sha256:90de9d4ecb9c954bdacd9fbcc58b431864e8023e42f8cc21782f2107054344e1
Status: Downloaded newer image for debian:wheezy
root@reginald:~# docker tag debian:wheezy reginald:5000/debian:local ❶
root@reginald:~# docker push reginald:5000/debian:local
The push refers to a repository [reginald:5000/debian] (len: 1)
19de96c112fc: Image successfully pushed
ba249489d0b6: Image successfully pushed
local: digest: sha256:3569aa2244f895ee6be52ed5339bc83e19fafd713fb1138007b987...
```

---

4 You can skip this step if you have a certificate signed by a trusted certificate authority.

5 You may need to remove any previously launched registry instances.

❶ You'll need to replace "reginald" with the name of your server.

Finally, we have a remotely accessible registry working securely and storing images. When testing from other machines, remember to copy the certificate file to */etc/docker/certs.d/<registry_address>/ca.crt* on the Docker engine, and make sure the Docker engine can resolve the address of the registry.[6]

There are plenty of configuration options for Docker that you can use to set up and tweak the registry for particular use cases. The registry options are configured by a YAML file in the image, which you can replace with a volume. Values can also be overridden at runtime by specifying environment variables, as we did in the previous example with `REGISTRY_HTTP_TLS_KEY` and `REGISTRY_HTTP_TLS_CERTIFICATE`. At the time of writing, the configuration file lives at */go/src/github.com/docker/distribution/cmd/registry/config.yml*, but this is likely to change to an easier path. The default configuration is designed for development use and will need significant changes for production usage. You can find full details on how to configure the registry as well as example configuration files on the distribution GitHub project.

The following sections describe the major features and customizations you'll need to consider when setting up a registry.

Storage

By default, the registry image uses the filesystem driver, which will unsurprisingly save all data and images to the filesystem. This is a great choice for development and probably appropriate for many setups. You will need to declare a volume at the defined root directory and point it to a reliable filestore. For example, including the following code in *config.yml* will configure the registry to use the filesystem driver and save data under */var/lib/registry*, which should be declared as a volume:

```
storage:
    filesystem:
        rootdirectory: /var/lib/registry
```

To save data to the cloud, you can use either the Amazon S3 or Microsoft Azure storage drivers.

There is also support for the Ceph distributed object store and using Redis as an in-memory cache to speed up layer access.

---

6 You can't swap the registry name for an IP address, as it will fail to match the certificate. Instead, edit */etc/hosts* or set up the DNS to allow the name to resolve.

Authentication

So far, we've seen how to access the registry with TLS, but we've not done anything about authenticating users. This is probably reasonable if you are only using public images or your registry is only accessible on a private network, but most organizations will want to restrict access to only authenticated users.

There are two ways to achieve this:

- Set up a proxy, such as nginx, in front of the registry that is responsible for authenticating users. An example of this is given in the official documentation (*https://docs.docker.com/registry/nginx/*) on the GitHub project, which uses nginx's user/password authentication. Once set up, the docker login command can be used to authenticate to the registry.

- Token-based authentication using JSON Web Tokens. When using this method, the registry will refuse to serve clients that do not present a valid token but will redirect them to the authentication server. Tokens can be obtained from the authentication server after which the client will be able to access the registry. The authentication server is not provided by Docker, and at the time of writing, there is only a single open source solution by Cesanta Software (*https://github.com/cesanta/docker_auth*). Currently, the only other option is to roll your own based on a JSON Web Token library or pay for one of the commercial solutions described in "Commercial Registries". Although this is clearly more complex and difficult to set up, it will be essential for many large or distributed organizations.

HTTP

This section is used to configure the HTTP interface for the registry. It's essential that this is set correctly for the registry to function. In particular, you will need to set the location of the TLS certificate and key for the registry; in the previous example, we accomplished this by using the environment variables REGISTRY_HTTP_TLS_KEY and REGISTRY_HTTP_TLS_CERTIFICATE.

A typical configuration might look like:

```
http:
    addr: reginald:5000 ❶
    secret: DD100CC4-1356-11E5-A926-33C19330F945 ❷
    tls: ❸
        certificate: /certs/domain.crt
        key: /certs/domain.key
```

❶   Address of the registry.

❷ A random string used to sign state information stored by clients. Intended to protect against tampering. Ideally should be randomly generated.

❸ Sets up the certificates as we saw before. The files must be accessible to the container, either by mounting a volume or copying into the container.

Other settings

Note that there are various other settings that can be used to set up middleware, notifications, logging, and caching. For full information, see the Docker distribution GitHub project.

Commercial Registries

If you're looking for a more complete solution with web-based management, both the Docker Trusted Registry (*https://www.docker.com/docker-trusted-registry*) and the CoreOS Enterprise Registry (*https://coreos.com/products/enterprise-registry/*) are available. These are on-premise commercial solutions that will sit behind your firewall.

Both offerings come with significant features beyond the simple storing of images. They both offer tools for working with Docker images in teams such as fine-grained permission controls and GUIs for installation and administration tasks.

Reducing Image Size

By this point, you've probably noticed that Docker images can be on the large side; most images seem to be hundreds of megabytes in size, which means a lot of time spent waiting for images to be transferred back and forth. This is mitigated to a large degree by the hierarchical structure of images; if you already have a parent layer of an image, you only need to download the new child layers.

However, there is still a lot to be said for trying to reduce the size of images, and it's not quite as easy as it sounds. The naive answer is to start deleting unneeded files from the image. Unfortunately, this doesn't work. Remember that an image is made up of multiple layers, one for each of the commands in the corresponding Dockerfile and its parent Dockerfiles. The total size of the image is the sum of all its layers. If you remove a file in one layer, it will still be present in the parent layers. To give a concrete example, consider the following Dockerfile:

```
FROM debian:wheezy

RUN dd if=/dev/zero of=/bigfile count=1 bs=50MB ❶
RUN rm /bigfile
```

❶ This is just a quick way to create a file.

If we now build and inspect the image:

```
$ docker build -t filetest .
...
$ docker images filetest ❶
REPOSITORY   TAG      IMAGE ID      CREATED        VIRTUAL SIZE
filetest     latest   e2a98279a101  8 seconds ago  135 MB
$ docker history filetest ❷
IMAGE            ...  CREATED BY                                 SIZE      ...
e2a98279a101          /bin/sh -c rm /bigfile                     0 B
5d0f04380012          /bin/sh -c dd if=/dev/zero of=/bigfile count=  50 MB
c90d655b99b2          /bin/sh -c #(nop) CMD [/bin/bash]          0 B
30d39e59ffe2          /bin/sh -c #(nop) ADD file:3f1a40df75bc5673ce  85.01 MB
511136ea3c5a                                                     0 B
```

❶ We can see here the total size of the image is 135 MB, exactly 50 MB larger than the base image.

❷ The docker history command gives us the full picture. The top two lines describe the layers created by our Dockerfile. We can see the dd command has created a layer 50 MB in size, and the rm command has just created a new layer on top.

In contrast, if we have the following Dockerfile:

```
FROM debian:wheezy

RUN dd if=/dev/zero of=/bigfile count=1 bs=50MB && rm /bigfile
```

And we build and inspect it:

```
$ docker build -t filetest .
...
$ docker images filetest
REPOSITORY   TAG      IMAGE ID      CREATED        VIRTUAL SIZE
filetest     latest   40a9350a4fa2  34 seconds ago  85.01 MB
$ docker history filetest
IMAGE            ...  CREATED BY                                 SIZE      ...
40a9350a4fa2          /bin/sh -c dd if=/dev/zero of=/bigfile count=  0 B
c90d655b99b2          /bin/sh -c #(nop) CMD [/bin/bash]          0 B
30d39e59ffe2          /bin/sh -c #(nop) ADD file:3f1a40df75bc5673ce  85.01 MB
511136ea3c5a                                                     0 B
```

We haven't increased the size of the base image. If we delete the file in the same layer that it's created, it won't be included in the image. Because of this, you will often find Dockerfiles that download tarballs or other archive files, unpack them, and immediately remove the archive file in one RUN instruction. For example, the official MongoDB image includes the following instruction (URL truncated for formatting):

```
RUN curl -SL "https://$MONGO_VERSION.tgz" -o mongo.tgz \
    && curl -SL "https://$MONGO_VERSION.tgz.sig" -o mongo.tgz.sig \
```

```
    && gpg --verify mongo.tgz.sig \
    && tar -xvf mongo.tgz -C /usr/local --strip-components=1 \
    && rm mongo.tgz*
```

A similar technique can applied to source code—you will sometimes see it downloaded, compiled to a binary, and deleted all in the same line.

For the same reason, there is no point in attempting to clean up after the package manager like this:

```
RUN rm -rf /var/lib/apt/lists/*
```

But you can do this (again from the official MongoDB Dockerfile):

```
RUN apt-get update \
    && apt-get install -y curl numactl \
    && rm -rf /var/lib/apt/lists/*
```

Also see the previous discussion in "Base Images" about choosing base images wisely to keep image size down.

There is another option you can use for reducing image size if you're really in a pinch. If you run docker export on a container then docker import the result, you end up with an image containing only a single layer. For example:

```
$ docker create identidock:latest
fe165be64117612c94160c6a194a0d8791f4c6cb30702a61d4b3ac1d9271e3bf
$ docker export $(docker ps -lq) | docker import -
146880a742cbd0e92cd9a79f75a281f0fed46f6b5ece0219f5e1594ff8c18302
$ docker tag 146880a identidock:import
$ docker images identidock
REPOSITORY   TAG      IMAGE ID       CREATED        VIRTUAL SIZE
identidock   import   146880a742cb   5 minutes ago  730.9 MB
identidock   0.1      76899e56d187   23 hours ago   839.5 MB
identidock   latest   1432cc6c20e5   4 days ago     839 MB
$ docker history identidock:import
IMAGE          CREATED          CREATED BY  SIZE       COMMENT
146880a742cb   11 minutes ago               730.9 MB   Imported from -
```

This has cut down the image size, but at a cost:

- We need to redo all the Dockerfile instructions such as EXPOSE, CMD, PORTS, which are not reflected in the filesystem.

- We have lost all the metadata associated with the image.

- We can no longer share space with other images that have the same parent.

Image Provenance

When distributing and consuming images, it is important to consider how to establish the *provenance* of images-that is, where and who they came from. If you download an image, you want to be sure that it was really created by who it claims to be, that it hasn't been tampered with, and that it is exactly the same image the creator of the image tested.

The Docker solution for this is known as Docker content trust (*https://docs.docker.com/security/trust/content_trust/*), which at the time of writing is undergoing testing and not enabled by default. See "Image Provenance" for more details.

Conclusion

The effective distribution of images is a crucial component in any Docker workflow. This chapter has taken a look at the primary solutions to accomplish this: the Docker Hub and private registries. We also looked at some of the issues surrounding image distribution, including the need to name and tag images appropriately and how to reduce the size of images.

In the following chapter, we'll see how to push the images to the next step in the workflow—the continuous integration server.

CHAPTER 8

Continuous Integration and Testing with Docker

In this chapter, we're going to look into how Docker and Jenkins can be used to create a continuous integration (CI) workflow for building and testing our application. We'll also take a look at other aspects of testing with Docker and a brief look at how to test a microservices architecture.

Testing containers and microservices brings a few different challenges to testing. Microservices make for easy unit tests but difficult system and integration tests due to the increased number of services and network links. Mocking of network services becomes more relevant than the traditional mocking of classes in a monolithic Java or C# codebase. Keeping test code in images maintains the portability and consistency benefits of containers, but increases their size.

 The code for this chapter is available from this book's GitHub (*https://github.com/using-docker/ci-testing*). The tag v0 is the identi-dock code as it was at the end of the last chapter, with later tags representing the progression of the code through this chapter. To get this version of the code:

```
$ git clone -b v0 \
https://github.com/using-docker/ci-testing/
...
```

Alternatively, you can download the code for any tag from the Releases page on the GitHub project (*https://github.com/using-docker/ci-testing/releases*).

Adding Unit Tests to Identidock

The first thing we should do is add some unit tests to our identidock codebase. These will test some basic functionality of our identidock code, with no reliance on external services.[1]

Start by creating the file *identidock/app/tests.py* with the following contents:

```
import unittest
import identidock


class TestCase(unittest.TestCase):

    def setUp(self):
        identidock.app.config["TESTING"] = True
        self.app = identidock.app.test_client()

    def test_get_mainpage(self):
        page = self.app.post("/", data=dict(name="Moby Dock"))
        assert page.status_code == 200
        assert 'Hello' in str(page.data)
        assert 'Moby Dock' in str(page.data)

    def test_html_escaping(self):
        page = self.app.post("/", data=dict(name='"><b>TEST</b><!--'))
        assert '<b>' not in str(page.data)


if __name__ == '__main__':
    unittest.main()
```

This is just a very simple test file with three methods:

setUp
> Initializes a test version of our Flask web application.

test_get_mainpage
> Test method that calls the URL / with the input "Moby Dock" for the name field. The test then checks that the method returns a 200 status code and the data contains the strings "Hello" and "Moby Dock."

test_html_escaping
> Tests that HTML entities are properly escaped in input.

Let's run these tests:

---

[1] Many developers advocate a test-driven development (TDD) approach, where tests are written before the code that makes them pass. This book hasn't followed this approach, mainly for the sake of narrative.

```
$ docker build -t identidock .
...
$ docker run identidock python tests.py
.F
=====================================================================
FAIL: test_html_escaping (__main__.TestCase)
---------------------------------------------------------------------
Traceback (most recent call last):
  File "tests.py", line 19, in test_html_escaping
    assert '<b>' not in str(page.data)
AssertionError


---------------------------------------------------------------------
Ran 2 tests in 0.010s

FAILED (failures=1)
```

Hmm, that's not good. The first test passed, but the second one has failed, because we're not escaping user input properly. This is a serious security issue that in a larger application can lead to data leaks and cross-site scripting attacks (XSS). To see the effect on the application, launch identidock and try inputing a name such as ">pwned!<!--", including the quotes. An attacker could potentially inject malicious JavaScript into our application and trick users into running it.

Thankfully, the fix is easy. We just need to update our Python application to *sanitize* the user input by replacing HTML entities and quotes with escape codes. Update *identidock.py* so that it looks like:

```
from flask import Flask, Response, request
import requests
import hashlib
import redis
import html

app = Flask(__name__)
cache = redis.StrictRedis(host='redis', port=6379, db=0)
salt = "UNIQUE_SALT"
default_name = 'Joe Bloggs'


@app.route('/', methods=['GET', 'POST'])
def mainpage():

    name = default_name
    if request.method == 'POST':
        name = html.escape(request.form['name'], quote=True) ❶

    salted_name = salt + name
    name_hash = hashlib.sha256(salted_name.encode()).hexdigest()
    header = '<html><head><title>Identidock</title></head><body>'
    body = '''<form method="POST">
```

Adding Unit Tests to Identidock | 117

```
                  Hello <input type="text" name="name" value="{0}">
                  <input type="submit" value="submit">
                  </form>
                  <p>You look like a:
                  <img src="/monster/{1}"/>
                  '''.format(name, name_hash)
        footer = '</body></html>'

        return header + body + footer


    @app.route('/monster/<name>')
    def get_identicon(name):

        name = html.escape(name, quote=True)  ❶
        image = cache.get(name)
        if image is None:
            print ("Cache miss", flush=True)
            r = requests.get('http://dnmonster:8080/monster/' + name + '?size=80')
            image = r.content
            cache.set(name, image)

        return Response(image, mimetype='image/png')

    if __name__ == '__main__':
        app.run(debug=True, host='0.0.0.0')
```

❶ Use the html.escape method to sanitize the user input.

Now if we build and test our application again:

```
$ docker build -t identidock .
...
$ docker run identidock python tests.py
..
----------------------------------------------------------------
Ran 2 tests in 0.009s

OK
```

Great—problem solved. You can verify this by restarting identidock with the new containers (remember to run docker-compose build to ensure Compose uses the new code) and trying to enter malicious input.[2] If we had used a real templating engine rather than simple string concatenation, the escaping would have been handled for us, avoiding this issue.

---

2 Embarrassingly, I never noticed this problem until the review stages of the book. I again learned the lesson that it is important to test even trivial-looking code and that it's best to use preexisting, proven code and tools where possible.

Now that we have some tests, we should extend our *cmd.sh* file to support automatically executing them. Replace *cmd.sh* with the following:

```
#!/bin/bash
set -e

if [ "$ENV" = 'DEV' ]; then
  echo "Running Development Server"
  exec python "identidock.py"
elif [ "$ENV" = 'UNIT' ]; then
  echo "Running Unit Tests"
  exec python "tests.py"
else
  echo "Running Production Server"
  exec uwsgi --http 0.0.0.0:9090 --wsgi-file /app/identidock.py \
          --callable app --stats 0.0.0.0:9191
fi
```

Now we can rebuild and run the tests by just changing the environment variable:

```
$ docker build -t identidock .
...
$ docker run -e ENV=UNIT identidock
Running Unit Tests
..
----------------------------------------------------------------
Ran 2 tests in 0.010s

OK
```

There are more unit tests we could write. In particular, there are no tests for the get_identicon method. To test this method in a unit test, we would need to either bring up test versions of the dnmonster and Redis services, or use a *test double*. A test double stands in for the real service, and is commonly either a *stub*, which simply returns a canned answer (e.g., the stub for a stock price service might always return "42") or a *mock* that can be programmed with expectations for how it expects to be called (such as being called exactly once for a given transaction). For more information on test doubles, see the Python mock module (*https://docs.python.org/3/library/unittest.mock.html*) as well as specialist HTTP tools such as Pact (*https://github.com/realestate-com-au/pact*), Mountebank (*http://www.mbtest.org/*), and Mirage (*https://mirage.readthedocs.org*).

Including Tests in Images

In this chapter, we bundle the tests for identidock into the identidock image, which is in line with the Docker philosophy of using a single image through development, testing, and production. This also means we can easily check the tests on images running in different environments, which can be useful to rule out issues when debugging.

The disadvantage is that it creates a larger image—you have to include the test code plus any dependencies such as testing libraries. In turn, this also means there is a greater *attack surface*; it's possible, if unlikely, that an attacker could use test utilities or code to break the system in production.

In most cases, the advantages of the simplicity and reliability of using a single image will outweigh the disadvantages of the slightly increased size and theoretical security risk.

The next step is to get our tests automatically run in a CI server so we can see how our code could be automatically tested when code is checked in to source control and before moving to staging or production.

Using Containers for Fast Testing

All tests, and in particular unit tests, need to run quickly in order to encourage developers to run them often without getting stuck waiting on results. Containers represent a fast way to boot a clean and isolated environment, which can be useful when dealing with tests that mutate their environment. For example, imagine you have a suite of tests that make use of a service[3] that has been prepopulated with some test data. Each test that uses the service is likely to mutate the data in some way, either adding, removing, or modifying data. One way to write the tests is to have each test attempt to clean up the data after running, but this is problematic; if a test (or the cleanup) fails, it will pollute the test data for all following tests, making the source of the failure difficult to diagnose and requiring knowledge of the service being tested (it is no longer a black box). An alternative is to destroy the service after each test and start with a fresh one for each test. Using VMs for this purpose would be far too slow, but it is achievable with containers.

Another area of testing where containers shine is running services in different environments/configurations. If your software has to run across a range of Linux distribu-

---

3 Tests like these are likely to be system or integration tests rather than unit tests, or they could be unit tests in a nonmockist test configuration. Many unit test experts will advise that components such as databases should be replaced with mocks, but in situations where the component is stable and reliable, it is often easiest and sensible to use the component directly.

---

tions with different databases installed, set up an image for each configuration and you can fly through your tests. The caveat of this approach is that it won't take into account kernel differences between distributions.

Creating a Jenkins Container

Jenkins is a popular open source CI server. There are other options for CI servers and hosted solutions, but we'll use Jenkins for our web app, simply because of its popularity. We want to set up Jenkins so that whenever we push changes to our identidock project, Jenkins will automatically check out the changes, build the new images, and run some tests against them—both our unit tests and some system tests. It will then create a report on the results of the tests.

We'll base our solution on an image from the official Jenkins repository. I've used version 1.609.3, but new Jenkins releases are constantly appearing—feel free to try using a newer version, but I can't guarantee it will work without modification.

In order to allow our Jenkins container to build images, we're going to mount the Docker socket[4] from the host into the container, effectively allowing Jenkins to create "sibling" containers. An alternative to this is to use Docker-in-Docker (DinD), where the Docker container can create its own "child" containers. The two approaches are contrasted in Figure 8-1.

---

4 The Docker socket is the endpoint used for communicating between the client and the daemon. By default, this is an IPC socket accessed via the file /var/run/docker.sock, but Docker also supports TCP sockets exposed via a network address and systemd-style sockets. This chapter assumes you are using the default socket at /var/run/docker.sock. As the socket is accessed via a file descriptor, we can simply mount this endpoint as a volume in the container.

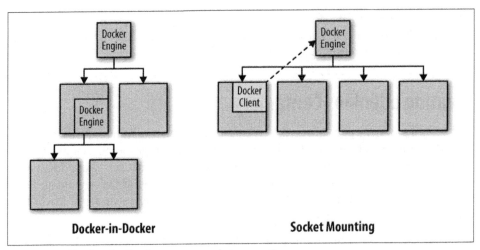

Docker-in-Docker   **Socket Mounting**

Figure 8-1. Docker-In-Docker versus socket mounting

Docker-in-Docker

Docker-in-Docker (or DinD) is simply running Docker itself inside a Docker container. There is some special configuration necessary to get this to work, primarily running the container in privileged mode and dealing with some filesystem issues. Rather than work this out yourself, it's easiest to use Jérôme Petazzoni's DinD project, which is available at *https://github.com/jpetazzo/dind* and describes all the required steps. You can quickly get started by using Jérôme's DinD image from the Docker Hub:

```
$ docker run --rm --privileged -t -i -e LOG=file jpetazzo/dind
ln: failed to create symbolic link '/sys/fs/cgroup/systemd/name=systemd':
Operation not permitted
root@02306db64f6a:/# docker run busybox echo "Hello New World!"
Unable to find image 'busybox:latest' locally
Pulling repository busybox
d7057cb02084: Download complete
cfa753dfea5e: Download complete
Status: Downloaded newer image for busybox:latest
Hello New World!
```

The major difference between DinD and the socket-mounting approach is that the containers created by DinD are isolated from the host containers; running docker ps in the DinD container will only show the containers created by the DinD Docker daemon. In contrast, running docker ps under the socket-mounting approach will show all the containers, regardless of where the command is run from.

In general, I prefer the simplicity of the socket-mounting approach, but in certain circumstances, you may want the extra isolation of DinD. If you do choose to run DinD, be aware of the following:

- You will have your own cache, so builds will be slower at first, and you will have to pull all your images again. This can be mitigated by using a local registry or mirror. Don't try mounting the build cache from the host; the Docker engine assumes exclusive access to this, so bad things can happen when shared between two instances.

- The container has to run in privileged mode, so it's not any more secure than the socket-mounting technique (if an attacker gains access, she can mount any device, including drives). This should get better in the future as Docker adds support for finer-grained privileges, which will allow users to choose the devices DinD has access to.

- DinD uses a volume for the */var/lib/docker* directory, which will quickly eat up your disk space if you forget to delete the volume when removing the container.

For more information on why you should be careful with DinD, see jpetazzo's GitHub article (*http://bit.ly/1WtECmm*).

In order to mount the socket from the host, we need to make sure that the Jenkins user inside the container has sufficient access privileges. In a new directory called *identijenk*, create a Dockerfile with the following contents:

```
FROM jenkins:1.609.3

USER root
RUN echo "deb http://apt.dockerproject.org/repo debian-jessie main" \
        > /etc/apt/sources.list.d/docker.list \
    && apt-key adv --keyserver hkp://p80.pool.sks-keyservers.net:80 \
        --recv-keys 58118E89F3A912897C070ADBF76221572C52609D \
    && apt-get update \
    && apt-get install -y apt-transport-https \
    && apt-get install -y sudo \
    && apt-get install -y docker-engine \
    && rm -rf /var/lib/apt/lists/*
RUN echo "jenkins ALL=NOPASSWD: ALL" >> /etc/sudoers

USER jenkins
```

This Dockerfile takes the Jenkins base image, installs the Docker binary, and adds password-less sudo rights to the jenkins user. We intentionally haven't added jenkins to the docker group, so we will have to prefix all our Docker commands with sudo.

Don't Use the Docker Group

Instead of using sudo, we could have added the jenkins user to the host's docker group. The problem is that this requires us to find and use the GID of the docker group on the CI host and hardcode it into the Dockerfile. This makes our Dockerfile nonportable, as different hosts will have different GIDs for the docker group. To avoid the confusion and pain this can cause, it is preferable to use sudo.

Build the image:

```
$ docker build -t identijenk .
...
Successfully built d0c716682562
```

Test it:

```
$ docker run -v /var/run/docker.sock:/var/run/docker.sock \
      identijenk sudo docker ps
CONTAINER ID   IMAGE        COMMAND          CREATED       STATUS   ...
a36b75062e06   identijenk   "/bin/tini -- /usr/lo"  1 seconds ago  Up Less tha...
```

In the docker run command, we have mounted the Docker socket in order to connect to the host's Docker daemon. In older versions of Docker, it was common to also mount the Docker binary, rather than install Docker inside the container. This had the advantage of keeping the version of Docker on the host and in the container in sync. However, from version 1.7.1, Docker began using dynamic libraries, which means any dependencies also need to be mounted in the container. Rather than deal with the problems of finding and updating the correct libraries to mount, it is easier to simply install Docker in the image.

Now that we've got Docker working inside the container, we can install some other stuff we need to get our Jenkins' build working. Update the Dockerfile like so:

```
FROM jenkins:1.609.3

USER root
RUN echo "deb http://apt.dockerproject.org/repo debian-jessie main" \
       > /etc/apt/sources.list.d/docker.list \
    && apt-key adv --keyserver hkp://p80.pool.sks-keyservers.net:80 \
       --recv-keys 58118E89F3A912897C070ADBF76221572C52609D \
    && apt-get update \
    && apt-get install -y apt-transport-https \
    && apt-get install -y sudo \
    && apt-get install -y docker-engine \
    && rm -rf /var/lib/apt/lists/*
RUN echo "jenkins ALL=NOPASSWD: ALL" >> /etc/sudoers

RUN curl -L https://github.com/docker/compose/releases/download/1.4.1/\
docker-compose-`uname -s`-`uname -m` > /usr/local/bin/docker-compose; \
```

```
    chmod +x /usr/local/bin/docker-compose ❶
USER jenkins
COPY plugins.txt /usr/share/jenkins/plugins.txt ❷
RUN /usr/local/bin/plugins.sh /usr/share/jenkins/plugins.txt
```

❶ Install Docker Compose, which we will use to build and run our images.

❷ Copy in and process a *plugins.txt* file, which defines a list of plugins to install in Jenkins.

Create the file *plugins.txt* in the same directory as the Dockerfile with the following contents:

```
scm-api:0.2
git-client:1.16.1
git:2.3.5
greenballs:1.14
```

The first three plugins set up an interface we can use to set up access to the Identidock project in Git. The "greenballs" plugin replaces the default Jenkins blue balls for successful builds with green ones.

We're now just about ready to launch our Jenkins container and start configuring our build, but first we should create a data container to persist our configuration:

```
$ docker build -t identijenk .
...
$ docker run --name jenkins-data identijenk echo "Jenkins Data Container"
Jenkins Data Container
```

We've used the Jenkins image for data container so we can be sure the permissions are set correctly. The container exits once the echo command completes, but as long as it's not deleted, it can be used in --volumes-from arguments. For more details on data containers, see "Managing Data with Volumes and Data Containers".

Now we're ready to launch the Jenkins container:

```
$ docker run -d --name jenkins -p 8080:8080 \
    --volumes-from jenkins-data \
    -v /var/run/docker.sock:/var/run/docker.sock \
    identijenk
75c4b300ade6a62394a328153b918c1dd58c5f6b9ac0288d46e02d5c593929dc
```

If you open a browser at *http://localhost:8080*, you should see Jenkins initializing. In a moment, we'll set it up with a build and test for our identidock project. But first we need to make a minor change to the identidock project itself. Currently, the *docker-compose.yml* file for our project initializes a development version of identidock, but we are about to develop some system tests we want to run on something much closer to production. For this reason, we need to create a new file *jenkins.yml* that we will use to start the production version of identidock inside Jenkins:

```
identidock:
  build: .
  expose:
    - "9090"  ❶
  environment:
    ENV: PROD  ❷
  links:
    - dnmonster
    - redis

dnmonster:
  image: amouat/dnmonster:1.0

redis:
  image: redis:3.0
```

❶ As Jenkins lives in a sibling container, we don't need to publish ports on the host in order to connect to it. I've included the expose command mainly as documentation; you will still be able to access the identidock container from Jenkins without it, assuming you haven't played with the default networking settings.

❷ Set the environment to production.

This file needs to be added to the identidock repository that Jenkins will retrieve the source code from. You can either add it to your own repository if you configured one earlier or use the existing repository (*https://github.com/using-docker/identidock*).

We're now ready to start configuring our Jenkins build. Open the Jenkins web interface running at *http://localhost:8080* and follow these instructions:

1. Click the Create new jobs link.

2. Enter **identidock** for the Item name, select Freestyle project, and click OK.

3. Configure the Source Code Management settings. If you used a public GitHub repository, you just need to select Git and enter the repository URL. If you used a private repository, you will need to set up credentials of some sort (several repositories, including BitBucket, have *deployment keys* that can be used to set up read-only access for this purpose). Alternatively, you can use the version available on GitHub (*https://github.com/using-docker/identidock*).

4. Click "Add build step" and select "Execute shell." In the Command box, enter the following:

```
#Default compose args
COMPOSE_ARGS=" -f jenkins.yml -p jenkins "

#Make sure old containers are gone
sudo docker-compose $COMPOSE_ARGS stop  ❶
sudo docker-compose $COMPOSE_ARGS rm --force -v
```

```
#build the system
sudo docker-compose $COMPOSE_ARGS build --no-cache
sudo docker-compose $COMPOSE_ARGS up -d

#Run unit tests
sudo docker-compose $COMPOSE_ARGS run --no-deps --rm -e ENV=UNIT identidock
ERR=$?

#Run system test if unit tests passed
if [ $ERR -eq 0 ]; then
  IP=$(sudo docker inspect -f {{.NetworkSettings.IPAddress}} \
        jenkins_identidock_1) ❷
  CODE=$(curl -sL -w "%{http_code}" $IP:9090/monster/bla -o /dev/null) || true ❸
  if [ $CODE -ne 200 ]; then
    echo "Site returned " $CODE
    ERR=1
  fi
fi

#Pull down the system
sudo docker-compose $COMPOSE_ARGS stop
sudo docker-compose $COMPOSE_ARGS rm --force -v

return $ERR
```

❶ Note that sudo is used to call Docker Compose, again because the Jenkins user isn't in the docker group.

❷ We use docker inspect to discover the IP address of the identidock container.

❸ We use curl to access the identidock service and check that it returns an HTTP 200 code indicating it is functioning correctly. Note that we are using the path /monster/bla to ensure that identidock can connect to the dnmonster service.

You can also get this code from GitHub (*https://github.com/using-docker/ci-testing*). Normally, scripts like this would be checked into source control with other code, but for our example, simply pasting into Jenkins is enough.

Now, you should be able to test this out by clicking Save followed by Build Now. You can view the details of the build by clicking on the build ID and selecting Console Output. You should see something similar to Figure 8-2.

Figure 8-2. Successful Jenkins build

This is pretty good in as far as it goes; we've successfully got Docker running and managed to execute our unit tests, plus a simple "smoke test" on our application. However, if this was a real application, we would be looking to have a full suite of tests that ensure the application is functioning correctly and can handle a range of inputs, but this is all we need for our simple demo.

Triggering Builds

At the moment, builds are triggered manually by clicking Build Now. A major improvement to this is to have builds happen automatically on check-in to the GitHub project. To do this, enable the Poll SCM method in the identidock configuration and enter *H/5 * * * ** into the text box. This will cause Jenkins to check the repository every five minutes for any changes and schedule a build if any changes have occurred.

This is a simple solution and it works well enough, but it is somewhat wasteful and means builds are constantly lagging by up to five minutes. A better solution is to configure the repository to notify Jenkins of updates. This can be done using Web Hooks from either BitBucket or GitHub but requires that the Jenkins server is accessible on the public Internet.

Using the Docker Hub Image

At this point, some of you may be asking, "Why are we building an image at all?" If you followed the previous section, you should have an automated build set up on the Docker Hub that is firing on check-ins to the source repository. It is possible to take advantage of this by using the Webhooks feature on Docker Hub to automatically kick off a Jenkins build after a successful build on the Docker Hub repository. We can then pull, rather than build, the image in our script. This also requires the Jenkins server to be accessible on the public Internet.

This solution may be useful for small projects that are creating standalone Docker images, but larger projects will probably want the extra speed and security of controlling their own build.

Pushing the Image

Now that we've tested our identidock image, we need to push it through the rest of our pipeline somehow. The first step in this is to tag it and push it to a registry. From here it can be picked up by the next stage in the pipeline and pushed to staging or production.

Responsible Tagging

Tagging images correctly is essential for maintaining control and provenance over a container-based pipeline. Get it wrong and you will have images running in production that are difficult—if not impossible—to relate back to builds, making debugging and maintenance unnecessarily tricky. For any given image, we should be able to point to the exact Dockerfile and build context that was used to create it.[5]

Tags can be overwritten and changed at any time. Because of this, *it is up to you to create and enforce a reliable process for tagging and versioning images.*

For our example application, we will add two tags to the image: the Git hash of the repository and newest. This way the newest tag will always refer to the newest build that has passed our tests, and we can use the Git hash to recover the build files for any image. I've intentionally avoided using the latest tag due to the issues discussed in Beware of the latest Tag. Update the build script in Jenkins to:

```
#Default compose args
COMPOSE_ARGS=" -f jenkins.yml -p jenkins "
```

---

5 Note that this doesn't guarantee you will be able to re-create an identical container, as dependencies may have changed. See "Reproducible and Trustworthy Dockerfiles" for details on how to mitigate this.

```
#Make sure old containers are gone
sudo docker-compose $COMPOSE_ARGS stop
sudo docker-compose $COMPOSE_ARGS rm --force -v

#build the system
sudo docker-compose $COMPOSE_ARGS build --no-cache
sudo docker-compose $COMPOSE_ARGS up -d

#Run unit tests
sudo docker-compose $COMPOSE_ARGS run --no-deps --rm -e ENV=UNIT identidock
ERR=$?

#Run system test if unit tests passed
if [ $ERR -eq 0 ]; then
  IP=$(sudo docker inspect -f {{.NetworkSettings.IPAddress}} \
        jenkins_identidock_1)
  CODE=$(curl -sL -w "%{http_code}" $IP:9090/monster/bla -o /dev/null) || true
  if [ $CODE -eq 200 ]; then
    echo "Test passed - Tagging"
    HASH=$(git rev-parse --short HEAD) ❶
    sudo docker tag -f jenkins_identidock amouat/identidock:$HASH ❷
    sudo docker tag -f jenkins_identidock amouat/identidock:newest ❷
    echo "Pushing"
    sudo docker login -e joe@bloggs.com -u jbloggs -p jbloggs123❸
    sudo docker push amouat/identidock:$HASH ❹
    sudo docker push amouat/identidock:newest ❹
  else
    echo "Site returned " $CODE
    ERR=1
  fi
fi

#Pull down the system
sudo docker-compose $COMPOSE_ARGS stop
sudo docker-compose $COMPOSE_ARGS rm --force -v

return $ERR
```

❶ Get the short version of the Git hash.

❷ Add the tags.

❸ Log in to the registry.

❹ Push the images to the registry.

Note that you will need to rename the tag appropriately for the repository you wish to push to. For example, if your repository is running at myhost:5000, you will need to use myhost:5000/identidock:newest. Similarly, you will need to change the docker login credentials to match.

If you start a new build, you should find that the script now tags and pushes the images to the registry, ready for the next stage in the pipeline. This is great for our example application and is probably a good start for most projects. But as things get more complex, you are likely to want to use more tags and more descriptive names. The git describe command can be put to good use in generating more meaningful names based on tags.

Finding All Tags for an Image

Each tag for an image is stored separately. This means that in order to discover all the tags for an image, you need to filter the full image list based on the image ID. For example, to find all tags for the image with tag amouat/identidock:newest:

```
$ docker images --no-trunc | grep \
    $(docker inspect -f {{.Id}} amouat/identidock:newest)
amouat/identidock   51f6152  96c7b4c094c8f76ca82b6206f...
amouat/identidock   newest   96c7b4c094c8f76ca82b6206f...
jenkins_identidock  latest   96c7b4c094c8f76ca82b6206f...
```

And we can see that the same image is also tagged 51f6152.

Remember that you will only see a tag if it exists in your image cache. For example, if I pull debian:latest, I don't get the debian: 7 tag even though (at the time of writing) it has the image ID. Similarly, if I have both the debian:latest and debian:7 images, and I pull a new version of debian:latest, the debian:7 tagged image will not be affected and will remain linked to the previous image ID.

Staging and Production

Once an image has been tested, tagged, and pushed to a registry, it needs to be passed on to the next stage in the pipeline, probably *staging* or *production*. This can be triggered in several ways, including by using Registry webhook notifications (*https://docs.docker.com/registry/notifications/*), or by using Jenkins to call the next step.

Image Sprawl

In a production system, you will need to address the problem of *image sprawl*. The Jenkins server should be periodically purged of images, and you will also need to control the number of images in the Registry, or it will rapidly fill with old and obsolete images. One solution is to remove all images older than a given date, possibly saving them to a backup store if space allows.[6] Alternatively, you may want to look at more advanced tooling such as the CoreOS Enterprise Registry or Docker Trusted Registry, both of which include advanced features for managing repositories.

Test the Right Thing

It is important to make sure you test the same container image that is run in production. Don't build the image from a Dockerfile in testing and build again for production—you want to be certain that you are running the same thing you tested and no differences have crept in. For this reason, it is essential to run some form of registry or store for your images that can be shared between testing, staging, and production.

Using Docker to Provision Jenkins Slaves

As your build requirements grow, you will require more and more resources to run your tests. Jenkins uses the concept of "build slaves," which essentially form a task farm Jenkins can use to outsource builds.

If you would like to use Docker to dynamically provision these slaves, take a look at the Docker plugin for Jenkins (*https://wiki.jenkins-ci.org/display/JENKINS/Docker +Plugin*).

Backing Up Jenkins

Because we used a data container for our Jenkins service, backing up Jenkins should be as simple as:

```
$ docker run --volumes-from jenkins-data -v $PWD:/backup \
        debian tar -zcvf /backup/jenkins-data.tar.gz /var/jenkins_home
```

This should result in the file *jenkins-data.tar.gz* appearing in your *$PWD/backup* directory. You may want to stop or pause the Jenkins container prior to running this command. You can then run something like the following command to create a new data container and extract the backup into it:

```
$ docker run --name jenkins-data2 identijenk echo "New Jenkins Data Container"
$ docker run --volumes-from jenkins-data2 -v $PWD:/backup \
        debian tar -xzvf /backup/backup.tar
```

---

6 At the time of writing, this is easier said than done with locally hosted Docker registries, as the remove function hasn't been implemented. There are several issues to be overcome, which are described in detail on the distribution roadmap (*https://github.com/docker/distribution/blob/master/ROADMAP.md*).

Unfortunately, this approach does require you to be aware of the mount points of your container. This can be automated by inspecting the container, so you can also use tools like docker-backup (*https://github.com/discordianfish/docker-backup*) to do this for you, and I expect to see more support for workflows like this in future versions of Docker.

Hosted CI Solutions

There are also numerous hosted solutions for CI, from companies that will maintain a Jenkins installation in the cloud for you, to more specialized solutions such as Travis (*https://travis-ci.org*), Wercker (*http://wercker.com/*), CircleCI (*https://circleci.com*), and Drone (*https://drone.io*). Most of these solutions seem to be targeted at running unit tests for predefined language stacks rather than running tests against systems of containers. There does seem to be some movement in this area, and I expect to see offerings aimed at testing Docker containers soon.

Testing and Microservices

If you're using Docker, there's a good chance you've also adopted a microservice architecture. When testing a microservice architecture, you will find that there are more levels of testing that are possible, and it is up to you to decide how and what to test. A basic framework might consist of:

Unit tests
> Each service[7] should have a comprehensive set of unit tests associated with it. Unit tests should only test small, isolated pieces of functionality. You may use test doubles to replace dependencies on other services. Due to the number of tests, it is important that they run as quickly as possible to encourage frequent testing and avoid developers waiting on results. Unit tests should make up the largest proportion of tests in your system.

Component tests
> These can be on the level of testing the external interface of individual services, or on the level of subsystem testing of groups of services. In both cases, you are likely to find you have dependencies on other services, which you may need to replace with test doubles as described earlier. You may also find it useful to expose metrics and logging via your service's API when testing, but make sure this is kept in a separate namespace (e.g., use a different URL prefix) to your functional API.

---

7 Normally, there will be one container per service, or multiple containers per service if more resources are needed.

End-to-end tests

Tests that ensure the entire system is working. Because these are quite expensive to run (in terms of both resources and time), there should only be a few of these —you really don't want a situation where it takes hours to run the tests, seriously delaying deployments and fixes (consider *scheduled runs*, which we describe shortly). Some parts of the system may be impossible or prohibitively expensive to run in testing and may still need to be replaced with test doubles (launching nuclear missiles in testing is probably a bad idea). Our identidock test falls under end-to-end testing; the test runs the full system from end to end with no use of test doubles.

In addition, you may want to consider:

Consumer contract tests

These tests, which are also called consumer-driven contracts, are written by the *consumer* of a service and primarily define the expected input and output data. They can also cover side effects (changing state) and performance expectations. There should be a separate contract for each consumer of the service. The primary benefit of such tests is that it allows the developers of a service to know when they risk breaking compatibility with consumers; if a contract test fails, they know they need to either change their service, or work with the developers of the consumer to change the contract.

Integration tests

These are tests to check that the communication channels between each component are working correctly. This sort of testing becomes important in a microservice architecture where the amount of plumbing and coordination between components is an order of magnitude greater than monolithic architectures. However, you are likely to find that most of your communication channels are covered by your component and end-to-end testing.

Scheduled runs

Because it's important to keep the CI build fast, there often isn't enough time to run extensive tests, such as testing against unusual configurations or different platforms. Instead, these tests can be scheduled to run overnight when there is spare capacity.

Many of these tests can be classified as *preregistry* and *postregistry*, depending on whether they occur prior to adding the image to the registry. For example, unit testing is preregistry: no image should be pushed to the registry if it fails a unit test. The same goes for some consumer contract tests and some component tests. On the other hand, an image will have already been pushed to a registry before it can be end-to-end tested. If a postregistry test fails, there is a question about what to do next. While any new images should not be pushed to production (or should be rolled back if they have already been deployed), the fault may actually be due to other, older images or the interaction between new images. These sort of failures may require a greater level of investigation and thought to handle correctly.

Testing in Production

Finally, you may want to think about testing in production. Don't worry, this isn't as crazy as it sounds. In particular, it can make a lot of sense when dealing with a large number of users with widely different environments and configurations that are hard to test for.

One common approach is sometimes called *blue/green deployment*. Say we want to update an existing production service (let's call it the "blue" version) to new a version (let's call it the "green" version). Rather than just replace the blue version with the green version, we can run them in tandem for a given time period. Once the green version is up and running, we flip the switch to start routing traffic to it. We then monitor the system for any unexpected changes in behavior, such as increased error rates or latency. If we're not happy with the new version, all we have to do is flip the switch back to return the blue version to production. Once we're satisfied things are working correctly, we can turn off the blue version.

Other methods follow a similar principle—both the old and new versions should run in tandem. In *A/B*, or *multivariate testing*, two (or more) versions of a service are run together for a test period, with users randomly split between two. Certain statistics are monitored, and based on the results at the end of testing, one of the versions is kept. In *ramped deployment*, the new version of a service is only made available to a small subset of users. If these users find no problems, the new version will be progressively made available to more and more users. In *shadowing*, both versions of the service are run for all requests, but only the results from the old, stable version are used. By comparing the results from the old version and the proposed new version, it is possible to ensure the new version has identical behavior to the old version (or differs in an expected and positive way). Shadowing is particularly useful when testing new versions that do not have functional changes such as performance improvements.

Conclusion

The key idea to take away is that containers fit naturally into a continuous integration/delivery workflow. There are a few things to bear in mind—primarily that you must push the same image through the pipeline rather than rebuilding at separate stages—but you should be able to adapt existing CI tooling to containers without too many problems, and the future is likely to bring further specialized tooling in this area.

If you're embracing a large microservice architecture, it's worth taking more time to think about how you are going to do testing and researching some of the techniques outlined in this chapter.

CHAPTER 9

Deploying Containers

Now it's time to start getting to the business end of things and thinking about how to actually run Docker in production. At the time of writing, everybody is talking about Docker, and many are experimenting with Docker, but comparatively few run Docker in production. While detractors sometimes point to this as a failing of Docker, they seem to miss a couple of key points. Given the relative youth of Docker, it is very encouraging that so many people are using it in production (including Spotify, Yelp, and Baidu) and that those who only use it in development and testing are still gaining many advantages.

That being said, it is perfectly possible and reasonable to use containers in production today. Larger projects and organizations may want to start small and build up over time, but it is already a feasible and straightforward solution for the majority of projects.

As things currently stand, the most common way of deploying containers is by first provisioning VMs and then starting containers on the VMs. This isn't an ideal solution—it creates a lot of overhead, slows down scaling, and forces users to provision on a multicontainer granularity. The main reason for running containers inside VMs is simply security. It's essential that customers cannot access other customers' data or network traffic, and containers by themselves only provide weak guarantees of isolation at the moment. Further, if one container monopolizes kernel resources, or causes a panic, it will affect all containers running on the same host. Even most of the specialist solutions—Google Container Engine (GKE) and the Amazon EC2 Container Service (ECS)—still use VMs internally. There are currently two exceptions to this rule, Giant Swarm and Triton from Joyent, both of which are discussed later.

Throughout this chapter, we will show how our simple web application can be deployed on a range of clouds, as well as specialized Docker hosting services. We will

137

also look at some of the issues and techniques for running containers in production, both in the cloud and using on-premise resources.

The code for this chapter is available at this book's GitHub (*https://github.com/using-docker/deploying-containers*). We won't build on the previous Python code anymore but will continue to use the images we have created. You can choose to use your own version of the identidock image or simply use the `amouat/identidock` repository.

You can check out the code for the start of the chapter using the `v0` tag:

```
$ git clone -b v0 \
  https://github.com/using-docker/deploying-containers/
  ...
```

Later tags represent the progression of the code throughout the chapter.

Alternatively, you can download the code for any tag from the Releases page on the GitHub project (*https://github.com/using-docker/deploying-containers/releases*).

Provisioning Resources with Docker Machine

The fastest and simplest way to provision new resources and run containers on them is via *Docker Machine*, which can create servers, install Docker on them, and configure the local Docker client to access them. Docker Machine comes with drivers for most of the major cloud providers (including AWS, Google Compute Engine, Microsoft Azure, and Digital Ocean) as well as VMWare and VirtualBox.

Beta Software Alert!

At the time of writing, Docker Machine is in beta (I tested Docker Machine version 0.4.1). This means you are likely to encounter bugs and missing functionality, but it should still be usable and reasonably stable. Unfortunately, it also means the commands and syntax are likely to change slightly from what you see here. For this reason, I don't recommend using Machine in production yet, although it is very useful for testing and experimentation.

(And yes, this warning is true for nearly everything in this book—it just felt like a good time to point that out again.)

Let's have a look at how to use Machine to get identidock up and running in the cloud. To begin with, you'll need to install Machine on your local computer. If you installed Docker via Docker Toolbox, it should already be available. If not, you can download a binary from GitHub (*https://github.com/docker/machine/releases*), which can then be placed on your path (e.g., */usr/local/bin/docker-machine*). Once you've done this, you should be able to start running commands:

```
$ docker-machine ls
NAME        ACTIVE   DRIVER       STATE     URL                          SWARM
default              virtualbox   Running   tcp://192.168.99.100:2376
```

You may or may not get any output here, depending on what hosts Machine has detected. In my case, it picked up my local boot2docker VM. What we want to do next is add a host somewhere in the cloud. I'll walk through this using Digital Ocean, but AWS and the other cloud providers should be very similar. In order to follow along, you'll need to have registered online and generated a personal access token; to do this, open the "Applications & API" page (*https://cloud.digitalocean.com/settings/applications*). You will be charged for resource usage, so make sure to remove the machine when you're finished with it:

```
$ docker-machine create --driver digitalocean \
    --digitalocean-access-token 4820... \
    identihost-do
Creating SSH key...
Creating Digital Ocean droplet...
To see how to connect Docker to this machine, run: docker-machine env identi...
```

We've now created a Docker host on Digital Ocean. The next thing to do is to point our local client at it, using the command given in the output:

```
$ docker-machine env identihost-do
export DOCKER_TLS_VERIFY="1"
export DOCKER_HOST="tcp://104.236.32.178:2376"
export DOCKER_CERT_PATH="/Users/amouat/.docker/machine/machines/identihost-do"
export DOCKER_MACHINE_NAME="identihost-do"
# Run this command to configure your shell:
# eval "$(docker-machine env identihost-do)"
$ eval "$(docker-machine env identihost-do)"
$ docker info
Containers: 0
Images: 0
Storage Driver: aufs
 Root Dir: /var/lib/docker/aufs
 Backing Filesystem: extfs
 Dirs: 0
 Dirperm1 Supported: false
Execution Driver: native-0.2
Logging Driver: json-file
Kernel Version: 3.13.0-57-generic
Operating System: Ubuntu 14.04.3 LTS
CPUs: 1
Total Memory: 490 MiB
Name: identihost-do
```

```
ID: PLDY:REFM:PU5B:PRJK:L4QD:TRKG:RWL6:5T6W:AVA3:2FXF:ESRC:6DCT
Username: amouat
Registry: https://index.docker.io/v1/
WARNING: No swap limit support
Labels:
 provider=digitalocean
```

And we can see that we're connected to an Ubuntu host running on Digital Ocean. If we now run docker run hello-world, it will execute on the remote server.

Now to run identidock, you can use the previous *docker-compose.yml* from the end of Chapter 6, or use the following *docker-compose.yml,* which uses an image from the Docker Hub for identidock:

```
identidock:
  image: amouat/identidock:1.0
  ports:
   - "5000:5000"
   - "9000:9000"
  environment:
    ENV: DEV
  links:
   - dnmonster
   - redis
dnmonster:
  image: amouat/dnmonster:1.0
redis:
  image: redis:3
```

Note that if the Compose file includes a build instruction, this build will occur on the remote server. Any volume mounts will need to be removed, as they will refer to the disk on the remote server, not your local computer.

Run Compose normally:

```
$ docker-compose up -d ❶
...
Creating identidock_identidock_1...
$ curl $(docker-machine ip identihost-do):5000 ❷
<html><head><title>Hello...
```

❶ This will take a while as it will need to first download and build the required images.

❷ We can use the docker-machine ip command to find where our Docker host is running.

So now identidock is running in the cloud and accessible to anyone.[1] It's fantastic that we were able to get something up and running so quickly, but there are a few things that aren't quite right. Notably, the application is running the development Python web server on port 5000. We should change to use the production version, but it would also be nice to put a reverse proxy or load balancer in front of the application, which would allow us to make changes to the identidock infrastructure without changing the external IP address. Nginx has support for load balancing, so it also makes it simple to bring up several identidock instances and share traffic between them.

Smoke Testing Identidock

Throughout this book, we curl the identidock service to make sure it works. However, simply grabbing the front page isn't a great test; it only proves that the identidock container is up and running. A better test is to retrieve an identicon, which proves both the identidock and dnmonster containers are active and communicating. You can do this with a test such as:

```
$ curl localhost:5000/monster/gordon | head -c 4
◆PNG
```

Here we've used the Unix head utility to grab the first four characters of the image, which avoids dumping binary data to our terminal.

Using a Proxy

Let's start by creating a reverse proxy using nginx that our identidock service can sit behind. Create a new folder *identiproxy* for this and create the following Dockerfile:

```
FROM nginx:1.7

COPY default.conf /etc/nginx/conf.d/default.conf
```

Also create a file *default.conf* with the following contents:

```
server {
    listen       80;
    server_name  45.55.251.164;  ❶

    location / {

        proxy_pass  http://identidock:9090;  ❷
        proxy_next_upstream error timeout invalid_header http_500 http_502
                            http_503 http_504;
```

---

1 Some providers, including AWS, may require you to open port 5000 in the firewall first.

```
        proxy_redirect off;
        proxy_buffering off;
        proxy_set_header        Host            45.55.251.164; ❶
        proxy_set_header        X-Real-IP       $remote_addr;
        proxy_set_header        X-Forwarded-For $proxy_add_x_forwarded_for;
    }
}
```

❶ Replace this with the IP address of your Docker host or a domain name that points to it.

❷ Redirect all traffic to the identidock container. We'll use links to make this work.

If you still have Machine running and pointed to the cloud server, we can now build our image on the remote server:

```
$ docker build --no-cache -t identiproxy:0.1 .
Sending build context to Docker daemon 3.072 kB
Sending build context to Docker daemon
Step 0 : FROM nginx:1.7
 ---> 637d3b2f5fb5
Step 1 : COPY default.conf /etc/nginx/conf.d/default.conf
 ---> 2e82d9a1f506
Removing intermediate container 5383f47e3d1e
Successfully built 2e82d9a1f506
```

It's easy to forget that we're speaking to a remote Docker engine, but the image now exists on the remote server, not your local development machine.

Now we can return to the *identidock* folder and create a new Compose configuration file to test it out. Create a *prod.yml* with the following contents:

```
proxy:
  image: identiproxy:0.1 ❶
  links:
    - identidock
  ports:
    - "80:80"
identidock:
  image: amouat/identidock:1.0
  links:
   - dnmonster
   - redis
  environment:
    ENV: PROD ❷
dnmonster:
  image: amouat/dnmonster:1.0 ❶
redis:
  image: redis:3 ❶
```

❶ Note that I've used tags for the all the images. In production, you should be careful about the versions of containers you are running. Using latest is particularly bad, as it can be difficult or impossible to figure out what version of the application the container is running.

❷ Note that we're no longer exposing ports on the identidock container (only the proxy container needs to do that) and we've updated the environment variable to start the production version of the web server.

Using extends in Compose

For more verbose YAML files, you can use the extends keyword to share config details between environments. For example, we could define a file *common.yml* with the following contents:

```
identidock:
  image: amouat/identidock:1.0
  environment:
    ENV: DEV
dnmonster:
  image: amouat/dnmonster:1.0
redis:
  image: redis:3
```

We can then rewrite our *prod.yml* file as:

```
proxy:
  image: identiproxy:0.1
  links:
    - identidock
  ports:
    - "80:80"
identidock:
  extends:
    file: common.yml
    service: identidock
  environment:
    ENV: PROD
dnmonster:
  extends:
    file: common.yml
    service: dnmonster
redis:
  extends:
    file: common.yml
    service: redis
```

Where the extends keyword pulls in the appropriate config from the common file. Settings in the *prod.yml* will override settings in the *common.yml*. Values in links and

---

volumes-from are *not* inherited to avoid unexpected breakages. Because of this, in our case, using extends actually results in a more verbose *prod.yml* file, although it would still have the important advantage of automatically inheriting any changes made to the base file. The main reason I've avoided using extends in the book is simply to keep the examples standalone.

Stop the old version and start the new:

```
$ docker-compose stop
Stopping identidock_identidock_1... done
Stopping identidock_redis_1... done
Stopping identidock_dnmonster_1... done
Starting identidock_dnmonster_1...
Starting identidock_redis_1...
Recreating identidock_identidock_1...
Creating identidock_proxy_1...
```

Now let's test it out; it should now answer on the default port 80 rather than port 9090:

```
$ curl $(docker-machine ip identihost-do)
<html><head><title>Hello...
```

Excellent! Now our container is sitting behind a proxy, which makes it possible to do things like load balance over a group of identidock instances or move identidock to a new host without breaking the IP address (as long as the proxy remains on the old host and is updated with the new value). In addition, security has increased because the application container can only be accessed via the proxy and is no longer exposing ports to the Internet at large.

We can do a bit better than this though. It's really annoying that the IP of the host and the container name are hardcoded into the proxy image; if we want to use a different name than "identidock" or use identiproxy for another service, we need to build a new image or overwrite the config with a volume. What we want is to have these parameters set as environment variables. We can't use environment variables directly in nginx, but we can write a script that will generate the config at runtime, then start nginx. We need to go back to our *identiproxy* folder and update the *default.conf* file so that we have placeholders instead of the hardcoded variables:

```
server {
    listen       80;
    server_name {{NGINX_HOST}};

    location / {

        proxy_pass  {{NGINX_PROXY}};
        proxy_next_upstream error timeout invalid_header http_500 http_502
                            http_503 http_504;
        proxy_redirect off;
```

```
        proxy_buffering off;
        proxy_set_header      Host            {{NGINX_HOST}};
        proxy_set_header      X-Real-IP       $remote_addr;
        proxy_set_header      X-Forwarded-For $proxy_add_x_forwarded_for;
    }
}
```

and create the following *entrypoint.sh*, which will do our replacement:

```
#!/bin/bash
set -e

sed -i "s|{{NGINX_HOST}}|$NGINX_HOST|;s|{{NGINX_PROXY}}|$NGINX_PROXY|" \
    /etc/nginx/conf.d/default.conf ❶
cat /etc/nginx/conf.d/default.conf ❷
exec "$@" ❸
```

❶ We're using the sed utility to do our replacement. This is a bit hacky, but it will be fine for our purposes. Note we've used bars (|) instead of slashes (/) to avoid confusion with slashes in URLs.

❷ Prints the final template into the logs, which is handy for debugging.

❸ Executes whatever CMD has been passed. By default, the Nginx container defines a CMD instruction that starts nginx in the foreground, but we could define a different CMD at runtime that runs different commands or starts a shell if required.

Now we just need to update our Dockerfile to include our new script:

```
FROM nginx:1.7

COPY default.conf /etc/nginx/conf.d/default.conf
COPY entrypoint.sh /entrypoint.sh

ENTRYPOINT ["/entrypoint.sh"]
CMD ["nginx", "-g", "daemon off;"] ❶
```

❶ This command starts our proxy and will be passed as an argument to our *entrypoint.sh* script if no command is specified in docker run.

Make it executable and rebuild. This time we'll just call it proxy, as we've abstracted out the identidock details:

```
$ chmod +x entrypoint.sh
$ docker build -t proxy:1.0 .
...
```

To use our new image, go back to the *identidock* folder and update our *prod.yml* to use the new image:

```
proxy:
  image: proxy:1.0
  links:
    - identidock
  ports:
    - "80:80"
  environment:
    - NGINX_HOST=45.55.251.164 ❶
    - NGINX_PROXY=http://identidock:9090
identidock:
  image: amouat/identidock:1.0
  links:
    - dnmonster
    - redis
  environment:
    ENV: PROD
dnmonster:
  image: amouat/dnmonster:1.0
redis:
  image: redis:3
```

❶ Set this variable to the IP or name of your host.

So now if you bring down the old version and restart the app, we'll be using the new, generic image. For our simple web app, this is all we need, but due to the use of Docker links, we are currently stuck with a single-host configuration—we can't move to a multihost architecture (which would be necessary for fault tolerance and scaling) without using more advanced networking and service discovery features that we will see in Chapters 11 and 12.

Once you've finished with the application, you can stop it as follows:

```
$ docker-compose -f prod.yml stop
...
$ docker-compose -f prod.yml rm
...
```

When you're ready to shut down the cloud resource, just do this:

```
$ docker-machine stop identihost-do
$ docker-machine rm identihost-do
```

It's worth making sure the resources have been correctly freed in the cloud provider's web interface.

Next, let's take a look at some of the alternatives to using Compose.

Setting the COMPOSE_FILE Variable

Rather than explicitly specifying `-f prod.yml` to compose each time, you can also set the `COMPOSE_FILE` environment variable. For example:

```
$ export COMPOSE_FILE=prod.yml
$ docker-compose up -d
...
```

This will use the file *prod.yml* rather than the default *docker-compose.yml*.

Supercharged Config File Generation

The technique of using templates to build configuration files for Docker containers is fairly common when Dockerizing applications, especially when they don't natively support environment variables. When moving beyond simple examples like the one here, you will want to use a proper template processor, such as Jinja2 or Go templates, in order to avoid strange errors due to regexp clashes.

The problem is common enough that there is now a utility to help automate this process: Jason Wilder's dockerize (*https://github.com/jwilder/dockerize*). Dockerize will generate configuration files from a template file and environment variables, then call the normal application. In this way, it can be used to wrap application startup scripts called from a `CMD` or `ENTRYPOINT` instruction.

However, Jason took this one step further with docker-gen (*https://github.com/jwilder/docker-gen*), which can use values from container metadata (such as IP address) as well as environment variables. It can also run continuously, responding to Docker events such as new container creation to update configuration files appropriately. A great example of this is his nginx-proxy container, which will automatically add containers with the `VIRTUAL_HOST` environment variable to a load-balanced group.

Execution Options

Now that we've got a production ready system,[2] how should we go about starting the system on the server?[3] So far we've looked at Compose and Machine, but because both these projects are relatively new and in rapid development, it's wise to be wary of

---

2 Well, not really. It's important to think about how to secure your application before inviting Joe Public to take a look. See Chapter 13 for more information.

3 Oh, and you'll want to think about how to handle monitoring and logging, too. Don't forget those. See Chapter 10.

using them in production for anything except small side projects (and, at the time of writing, there are warnings to this extent on the Docker website). Both the projects are quickly maturing and developing production features; to get an idea of where they are going, you can find roadmap documents in the GitHub repositories, which are great for feeling out how close the projects are to production-ready.

So, if Compose isn't an option, what is? Let's take a look at some of the other possibilities. All of the following code assumes that images are available on Docker Hub, rather than building them on the server. If you want to follow along, either push your own images to a registry or use my images from the Docker Hub (`amouat/identidock:1.0`, `amouat/dnmonster:1.0` and `amouat/proxy:1.0`).

Shell Scripts

The easiest answer to running without Compose is just to write a short shell script that executes Docker commands to bring up the containers. This will work well enough for a lot of simple use cases, and if you add in some monitoring, you can make sure you know about it if anything goes wrong that requires your attention. However, in the long run, it is far from perfect; you will likely end up maintaining a messy and unstructured script that evolves over time to grow features of other solutions.

We can ensure containers that exit prematurely are automatically restarted by using the `--restart` argument to `docker run`. The argument specifies the restart policy, which can be `no`, `on-failure`, or `always`. The default is `no`, which will never automatically restart containers. The `on-failure` policy will only restart containers that exit with a nonzero exit code and can also specify a maximum number of retries (e.g., `docker run --restart on-failure:5` will attempt to restart the container five times before giving up).

The following script (named *deploy.sh*) will get our identidock service up and running:

```
#!/bin/bash
set -e

echo "Starting identidock system"

docker run -d --restart=always --name redis redis:3
docker run -d --restart=always --name dnmonster amouat/dnmonster:1.0
docker run -d --restart=always \
  --link dnmonster:dnmonster \
  --link redis:redis \
  -e ENV=PROD \
  --name identidock amouat/identidock:1.0
docker run -d --restart=always \
  --name proxy \
```

```
--link identidock:identidock \
-p 80:80 \
-e NGINX_HOST=45.55.251.164 \
-e NGINX_PROXY=http://identidock:9090 \
amouat/proxy:1.0

echo "Started"
```

Note that we're really just converting our *docker-compose.yml* file into the equivalent shell commands. But unlike Compose, there is no logic for cleaning up after failures, or to check for already running containers.

In the case of Digital Ocean, I can now use the following `ssh` and `scp` commands to start identidock using the shell script:

```
$ docker-machine scp deploy.sh identihost-do:~/deploy.sh
deploy.sh                                          100%  575     0.6KB/s   00:00
$ docker-machine ssh identihost-do
...
$ chmod +x deploy.sh
$ ./deploy.sh
Starting identidock system
3b390441b16eaece94df7e0e07d1edcb4c11ce7232108849d691d153330c6dfb
57459e4c0c2a75d2fbcef978aca9344d445693d2ad6d9efe70fe87bf5721a8f4
5da04a34302b400ec08e9a1d59c3baeec14e3e65473533c165203c189ad58364
d1839d8de1952fca5c41e0825ebb27384f35114574c20dd57f8ce718ed67e3f5
Started
```

We could also have just run these commands directly in the shell. The main reason to prefer the script is for documentation and portability reasons—if I want to start identidock on a new host, I can easily find the instructions to bring up an identical version of the application.

When we need to update images or make changes, we can either use Machine to connect our local client to the remote Docker server or log directly into the remote server and use the client there. To perform a zero-downtime update of a container, you will need to have a load balancer or reverse proxy in front of the container and do something like:

1. Bring a up a new container with the updated image (it's best to avoid trying to update images in place).
2. Point the load balancer at the new image, for some or all of the traffic.
3. Test the new container is working.
4. Turn off the old container.

Also, refer to "Testing in Production", which describes various techniques for deploying updates without breaking services.

Breaking Links on Restart

Older versions of Docker had problems with links breaking when containers restarted. If you see similar issues, make sure you are running an up-to-date version of Docker. At the time of writing, I am using Docker version 1.8, which works correctly; any changes to a container's IP address are automatically propagated to linked containers. Also note that only *etc/hosts* is updated, and environment variables are *not* updated on changes to linked containers.

In the rest of this section, we'll look at how you can control the initialization and deployment of containers using existing technology you may already be familiar with. In Chapter 12, we will look at some of the newer, Docker-specific tooling that also addresses this issue.

Using a Process Manager (or systemd to Rule Them All)

Instead of relying on a shell script and the Docker restart functionality, you can use a process manager or init system such as systemd or upstart to bring up your containers. This can be particularly useful if you have host services that don't run in a container, but are dependent on one or more containers. If you want to do this, be aware that there are some issues:

- You will need to make sure you don't use Docker's automatic container restarting functionality-that is, don't use `--restart=always` in your docker run commands.

- Normally, your process manager will end up monitoring the docker client process, rather than the processes inside the container. This works most of the time, but if the network connection drops or something else goes wrong, the Docker client will exit but leave the container running, which can cause problems. Instead, it would be much better if the process manager monitored the main process inside the container. This situation may change in the future, but until then, be aware of the systemd-docker project (*https://github.com/ibuildthecloud/ systemd-docker*), which works around this by taking control of the container's cgroup. (For more information on the problem, see this GitHub issue (*https:// github.com/docker/docker/issues/6791*).)

To give you an example of how to manage containers with systemd, the following service files can be used to start our identidock service on a systemd host. For this example, I've used CentOS 7, but other systemd-based distributions should be very similar. I haven't included an upstart example, as all major distributions seem to be moving to systemd. All of the files should be stored under */etc/systemd/system/*.

Let's start by looking at the service file for the Redis container, *identidock.redis.service*, which isn't dependent on any other containers:

```
[Unit]
Description=Redis Container for Identidock
After=docker.service
Requires=docker.service ❶

[Service]
TimeoutStartSec=0 ❷
Restart=always
ExecStartPre=-/usr/bin/docker stop redis ❸
ExecStartPre=-/usr/bin/docker rm redis
ExecStartPre=/usr/bin/docker pull redis ❹
ExecStart=/usr/bin/docker run --rm --name redis redis

[Install]
WantedBy=multi-user.target
```

❶ We need to make sure Docker is running before starting the container.

❷ As the Docker commands may take some time to run, it's easiest to turn the timeout off.

❸ Before starting the container, we first remove any old container with the same name, which means we will destroy the Redis cache on restart. But in the case of identidock, it's not an issue. The use of - at the start of the command tells systemd not to abort if the command returns a nonzero return code.

❹ Doing a pull ensures we are running the newest version.

The identidock service *identidock.identidock.service* is similar but requires other services:

```
[Unit]
Description=identidock Container for Identidock
After=docker.service
Requires=docker.service
After=identidock.redis.service ❶
Requires=identidock.redis.service
After=identidock.dnmonster.service
Requires=identidock.dnmonster.service

[Service]
TimeoutStartSec=0
Restart=always
ExecStartPre=-/usr/bin/docker stop identidock
ExecStartPre=-/usr/bin/docker rm identidock
ExecStartPre=/usr/bin/docker pull amouat/identidock
ExecStart=/usr/bin/docker run --name identidock \
```

```
--link dnmonster:dnmonster \
--link redis:redis \
-e ENV=PROD \
amouat/identidock

[Install]
WantedBy=multi-user.target
```

❶ In addition to Docker, we need to declare that we are dependent on the other containers used in identidock-in this case, the Redis and dnmonster containers. Both `After` and `Requires` are needed to avoided race conditions.

The proxy service (called *identidock.proxy.service*) looks like:

```
[Unit]
Description=Proxy Container for Identidock
After=docker.service
Requires=docker.service
Requires=identidock.identidock.service

[Service]
TimeoutStartSec=0
Restart=always
ExecStartPre=-/usr/bin/docker stop proxy
ExecStartPre=-/usr/bin/docker rm proxy
ExecStartPre=/usr/bin/docker pull amouat/proxy
ExecStart=/usr/bin/docker run --name proxy \
  --link identidock:identidock \
  -p 80:80 \
  -e NGINX_HOST=0.0.0.0 \
  -e NGINX_PROXY=http://identidock:9090 \
  amouat/proxy

[Install]
WantedBy=multi-user.target
```

And finally, the dnmonster service (called *identidock.dnmonster.service*) looks like:

```
[Unit]
Description=dnmonster Container for Identidock
After=docker.service
Requires=docker.service

[Service]
TimeoutStartSec=0
Restart=always
ExecStartPre=-/usr/bin/docker stop dnmonster
ExecStartPre=-/usr/bin/docker rm dnmonster
ExecStartPre=/usr/bin/docker pull amouat/dnmonster
ExecStart=/usr/bin/docker run --name dnmonster amouat/dnmonster

[Install]
WantedBy=multi-user.target
```

We can now start identidock with `systemctl start identidock.*`. The major difference between using this system and the Docker restart functionality is that restarting a stopped container will kick off a chain of restarts in systemd; if the Redis container goes down, both the identidock and proxy containers will also be restarted. This isn't the case in Docker, as it knows how to update links without restarting the container completely.

Despite the previously mentioned issues, it is worth noting that both CoreOS and the Giant Swarm PaaS use systemd to control containers. At the moment, it seems fair to say that there is unresolved tension between Docker and systemd, both of which want to be in charge of the lifecycle of services running on the host.

Using a Configuration Management Tool

If your organization is responsible for more than a handful of hosts, chances are that you're using some sort of configuration management (CM) tool (and if not, you probably should be). All projects need to consider how they are going to ensure the operating system on the Docker host is up to date, especially with regard to security patches. In turn, you also want to make sure the Docker images you are running are up to date and you aren't mixing multiple versions of your software. CM solutions such as Puppet, Chef, Ansible, and Salt are designed to help manage these issues.

There are two main ways we can use CM tools with containers:

- We can treat our containers as VMs and use CM software to manage and update the software inside them.
- We can use the CM software to manage the Docker host and ensure containers are running the correct version of images, but view the containers themselves as black boxes that can be replaced, but not modified.

The first approach is feasible, but is not the Docker way. You'll be working against Dockerfiles and the small-container-with-a-single-process philosophy that Docker is built around. In the rest of this section, we'll focus on the second alternative, which is much more in line with the Docker philosophy and microservices approach.

In this approach, the containers themselves are similar to *golden images* in VM parlance and shouldn't be modified once running. When you need to update them, you replace the entire container with one running the new image rather than try to change anything running inside the image. This has the major advantage that you know exactly what is running in your container by just looking at the image tag (assuming you are using a proper tagging system and aren't reusing tags).

Let's look at an example of how you can do this.

Ansible

For this example, we'll use Ansible (*http://www.ansible.com*)—it's popular, easy to get started with, and open source. This isn't to say it is better or worse than other tools!

Unlike many other configuration management solutions, Ansible doesn't require the installation of agents on hosts. Instead, it mainly relies on SSH to configure hosts.

Ansible has a Docker module, which has functionality for both building and orchestrating containers. It is possible to use Ansible inside Dockerfiles to install and configure software, but here we will just consider using Ansible to set up a VM with our identidock image. We're only running on a single host so we're not really making the most the Ansible here, but it does demonstrate how well Ansible and Docker can be used together.

Rather than install the Ansible client, we can just use an Ansible client image from the Hub. There isn't an official image available, but the `generik/ansible` image will work for testing.

Start by creating a *hosts* file that contains a list of all the servers we want Ansible to manage (make sure to include the IP address of your remote host or VM here):

```
$ cat hosts
[identidock]
46.101.162.242
```

Now we need to create the "playbook" for installing identidock. Create a file *identidock.yml* with the following contents, replacing the image names if you want to use your own:

```
---
- hosts: identidock
  sudo: yes
  tasks:
  - name: easy_install
    apt: pkg=python-setuptools
  - name: pip
    easy_install: name=pip
  - name: docker-py
    pip: name=docker-py
  - name: redis container
    docker:
      name: redis
      image: redis:3
      pull: always
      state: reloaded
      restart_policy: always
  - name: dnmonster container
    docker:
      name: dnmonster
      image: amouat/dnmonster:1.0
```

```
          pull: always
          state: reloaded
          restart_policy: always
  - name: identidock container
    docker:
      name: identidock
      image: amouat/identidock:1.0
      pull: always
      state: reloaded
      links:
        - "dnmonster:dnmonster"
        - "redis:redis"
      env:
        ENV: PROD
      restart_policy: always
  - name: proxy container
    docker:
      name: proxy
      image: amouat/proxy:1.0
      pull: always
      state: reloaded
      links:
        - "identidock:identidock"
      ports:
        - "80:80"
      env:
        NGINX_HOST: www.identidock.com
        NGINX_PROXY: http://identidock:9090
      restart_policy: always
```

Most of the configuration is very similar to Docker Compose, but note that:

- We have to install docker-py on the host in order to use the Ansible Docker module. This in turn requires us to install some Python dependencies.

- The pull variable determines when Docker images are checked for updates. Setting it to always ensures Ansible will check for a new version of the image each time the task executes.

- The state variable determines what state the container should be in. Setting it to reloaded will restart the container whenever a change is made to the configuration.

There are many more configuration options available, but this config will get us something very similar to the other setups described in this chapter.

All that's left to do is to run the playbook:

```
$ docker run -it \
    -v ${HOME}/.ssh:/root/.ssh:ro \ ❶
    -v $PWD/identidock.yml:/ansible/identidock.yml \
    -v $PWD/hosts:/etc/ansible/hosts \
```

```
--rm=true generik/ansible ansible-playbook identidock.yml

PLAY [identidock] **************************************************************

GATHERING FACTS ***************************************************************
The authenticity of host '46.101.41.99 (46.101.41.99)' can't be established.
ECDSA key fingerprint is SHA256:R0LfM7Kf3OgRmQmgxINko7SonsGAC0VJb27LTotGEds.
Are you sure you want to continue connecting (yes/no)? yes
Enter passphrase for key '/root/.ssh/id_rsa':
ok: [46.101.41.99]

TASK: [easy_install] **********************************************************
changed: [46.101.41.99]

TASK: [pip] *******************************************************************
changed: [46.101.41.99]

TASK: [docker-py] *************************************************************
changed: [46.101.41.99]

TASK: [redis container] *******************************************************
changed: [46.101.41.99]

TASK: [dnmonster container] ***************************************************
changed: [46.101.41.99]

TASK: [identidock container] **************************************************
changed: [46.101.41.99]

TASK: [proxy container] *******************************************************
changed: [46.101.41.99]

PLAY RECAP ********************************************************************
46.101.41.99               : ok=8    changed=7    unreachable=0    failed=0
$ curl 46.101.41.99
<html><head><title>Hello...
```

❶ This command is needed to map in the SSH key pair used to access the remote server.

This will take some time, as Ansible will need to pull the images. But once it's finished, our identidock application should be running.

This brief example has merely scratched the surface of Ansible's full power. There are many more things you can do, especially in terms of defining processes to perform rolling updates of containers without breaking dependencies or significant downtime.

Host Configuration

So far, this chapter has assumed that containers are being run on the stock Docker droplet (Digital Ocean's term for preconfigured VMs) provided by Digital Ocean (which, at the time of writing, runs Ubuntu 14.04). But there are many other choices for the host operating system and infrastructure with different trade offs and advantages. In particular, if you are responsible for running an on-premise resource, you should consider your options carefully.

Although it is possible to provision bare-metal machines for running Docker hosts (both on-premise and in the cloud), currently the most practical option is to use VMs. Most organizations will already have some sort of VM service you can use to provision hosts for your containers and provides strong guarantees of isolation and security between users.

Choosing an OS

There are already a few choices in this space, with different advantages and disadvantages. If you want to run a small- to medium-sized application, you will probably find it easiest to stick to what you know—if you use Ubuntu or Fedora and you or your organization is familiar with it with that OS, use it (but be aware of the storage driver issues discussed shortly). If, on the other hand, you want to run a very large application or cluster (hundreds or thousands of containers across many hosts), you will want to look at more specialized options such as CoreOS, Project Atomic, or RancherOS, as well as the orchestration solutions we discuss in Chapter 12.

If you're running on a cloud host, most of them will already have a Docker image ready to use, which will have been tried and tested to work on their infrastructure.

Choosing a Storage Driver

There are currently several storage drivers supported by Docker, with more on the way. Choosing an appropriate storage driver is essential to ensuring reliability and efficiency in production. Which driver is best depends on your use case and operational experience. The current options are:

AUFS
> The first storage driver for Docker. To date, this is probably the most tested and commonly used driver. Along with Overlay, it has the major advantage of supporting sharing of memory pages between containers—if two containers load libraries or data from the same underlying layer, the OS will be able to use the same memory page for both containers. The major problem with AUFS is that it is not in the mainline kernel, although it has been used by Debian and Ubuntu for some time. Also, AUFS operates on the file level, so if you make a small change to a large file, the whole file will be copied into the container's read/write

layer. In contrast, BTRFS and Device mapper operate on the block level and are therefore more space efficient with large files. If you currently use an Ubuntu or Debian host, you will most likely be using the AUFS driver.

Overlay

Very similar to AUFS and was merged into the Linux kernel in version 3.18. Overlay is very likely to be the main storage driver going forward and should have slightly better performance than AUFS. Currently, the main drawbacks are the need to have an up-to-date kernel (which will require patching for most distros) and that it has seen less testing than AUFS and some of the other options.

BTRFS

A copy-on-write filesystem[4] focused on supporting fault tolerance and very large files sizes and volumes. Because BTRFS has several quirks and gotchas (especially regarding chunks), it's recommended only for organizations that have experience with BTRFS or require a particular feature of BTRFS that is not supported by the other drivers. It may be a good choice if your containers read and write to very large files due to the block-level support.

ZFS

This much-loved filesystem was originally developed by Sun Microsystems. Similar to BTRFS in many regards, but arguably with better performance and reliability. Running ZFS on Linux isn't trivial, as it can't be included in the kernel because of licensing issues. For this reason, it's only likely to be used by organizations with substantial existing experience with ZFS.

Device mapper

Used by default on Red Hat systems. Device mapper is a kernel driver that is used as a foundation to several other technologies, including RAID, device encryption, and snapshots. Docker uses Device mapper's thin provisioning[5] (sometimes called thinp) target to do copy-on-write on the level of blocks, rather than files. The "thin pool" is allocated from a sparse file that defaults to 100 GB. Containers are allocated a filesystem backed by the pool when created whose size defaults to 100 GB (as of Docker 1.8). As the files are sparse, the actual disk usage is much less, but a container won't be able to grow past 100 GB without changing the defaults. Device mapper is arguably the most complex of the Docker storage drivers and is a common source of problems and support requests. If possible, I would recommend using one of the alternatives. But if you do use device mapper,

---

4 Don't ask me how to pronounce BTRFS: some people say "ButterFS" and some say "BetterFS." I say "FSCK."

5 In thin provisioning, rather than allocating all the resources a client asks for immediately, resources are only allocated on demand. This contrasts with thick provisioning, where the requested resources are immediately set aside for the client, even though the client may only use a fraction of the resources.

be aware that there are a lot of options that can be tuned to provide better performance (in particular, it's a good idea to move storage off the default "loopback" device and onto a real device).

VFS

> The default Linux Virtual Filesystem. This does not implement CoW and requires making a full copy of the image when starting a container. This slows down starting containers significantly and massively increases the amount of disk space required. The advantages are that it is simple and doesn't require any special kernel features. VFS may be a reasonable choice if you have problems with other drivers and don't mind taking the performance hit (e.g., if you have a small number of long-lived containers).

Unless you have a specific reason to choose an alternative, I would suggest running either AUFS or Overlay, even if it means applying kernel updates.

Switching storage driver

Switching storage driver is pretty easy, assuming you have the requisite dependencies installed. Just restart the Docker daemon, passing the appropriate value for `--storage-driver` (`-s` for short). For example, use `docker daemon -s overlay` to start the daemon with the overlay storage driver if your kernel supports it. It's also important to note the `--graph` or `-g` argument, which sets the root of the Docker runtime—you may need to move this to a partition running the appropriate filesystem (e.g., `docker daemon -s btrfs -g /mnt/btrfs_partition` for the BTRFS driver).

To make the change permanent, you'll need to edit the startup script or config file for the docker service. On Ubuntu 14.04, this means editing the variable `DOCKER_OPTS` in the file */etc/default/docker*.

Moving Images Between Storage Drivers

When you switch storage driver, you will lose access to all your old containers and images. Switching back to the old storage driver will restore access. To move an image to a new storage driver, just save the image to a TAR file and then load in the new filesystem. For example:

```
$ docker save -o /tmp/debian.tar debian:wheezy
$ sudo stop docker
$ docker daemon -s vfs
...
```

From a new terminal:

```
$ docker images
REPOSITORY   TAG    IMAGE ID      CREATED     VIRTUAL SIZE
$ docker load -i /tmp/debian.tar
$ docker images
REPOSITORY   TAG     IMAGE ID      CREATED      VIRTUAL SIZE
debian       wheezy b3d362b23ec1  2 days ago   84.96 MB
```

Specialist Hosting Options

There are already some specialist container hosting options that don't require you to manage hosts directly, including Triton, Google Container Engine, Amazon EC2 Container Service, and Giant Swarm. The following subsections take a closer look at each of these options.

Triton

Triton from Joyent (*https://www.joyent.com*) is perhaps the most interesting of the options, as it doesn't use VMs internally. This gives Triton a significant performance benefit over VM-based solutions and allows for provisioning on a per-container basis.

Triton doesn't use the Docker engine but has its own container engine running on the SmartOS hypervisor (which has its roots in Solaris) using Linux Virtualization. By implementing the Docker remote API, Triton is fully compatible with the normal Docker client, which is used as the standard interface to Triton. Images from the Docker Hub work as normal.

Triton is open source and available in both a hosted version that runs on the Joyent cloud and an on-premise version. We can quickly get identidock running using the public Joyent public cloud. After setting up a Triton account and pointing the Docker client at Triton, try running a docker info:

```
$ docker info
Containers: 0
Images: 0
```

```
Storage Driver: sdc
 SDCAccount: amouat
Execution Driver: sdc-0.3.0
Logging Driver: json-file
Kernel Version: 3.12.0-1-amd64
Operating System: SmartDataCenter
CPUs: 0
Total Memory: 0 B
Name: us-east-1
ID: 92b0cf3a-82c8-4bf2-8b74-836d1dd61003
Username: amouat
Registry: https://index.docker.io/v1/
```

Note the values for the OS and execution driver, which indicate we aren't running on a normal Docker engine. We can use Compose and the following *triton.yml* file to launch identidock, as Triton supports the majority of the Docker engine API:

```
proxy:
  image: amouat/proxy:1.0
  links:
    - identidock
  ports:
  - "80:80"
  environment:
    - NGINX_HOST=www.identidock.com
    - NGINX_PROXY=http://identidock:9090
  mem_limit: "128M"
identidock:
  image: amouat/identidock:1.0
  links:
    - dnmonster
    - redis
  environment:
    ENV: PROD
  mem_limit: "128M"
dnmonster:
  image: amouat/dnmonster:1.0
  mem_limit: "128M"
redis:
  image: redis
  mem_limit: "128M"
```

This is almost the same as the *prod.yml* from before, with the addition of memory settings that tell Triton the size of container to launch. We're also using public images rather than building our own (Triton doesn't currently support docker build).

Launch the application:

```
$ docker-compose -f triton.yml up -d
...
Creating triton_proxy_1...
$ docker inspect -f {{.NetworkSettings.IPAddress}} triton_proxy_1
165.225.128.41
```

```
$ curl 165.225.128.41
<html><head><title>Hello...
```

Triton automatically uses a publicly accessible IP when it sees a published port.

After running containers on Triton, make sure to stop and remove them; Triton charges for stopped but not removed containers.

Using the native Docker tools to interact with Triton is a great experience, but there are some rough edges; not all API calls are supported, and there are some issues surrounding how Compose handles volumes, but these should be worked out in time.

Until mainstream cloud providers are convinced that the isolation guarantees of the Linux kernel are strong enough that containers can be run without security concerns, Triton is one of the most attractive solutions for running containerized systems.

Google Container Engine

Google Container Engine (GKE) (*https://cloud.google.com/container-engine/*) takes a more opinionated approach to running containers, building on top of the Kubernetes orchestration system.

Kubernetes is an open source project designed by Google, using some of the lessons learned from running containers internally with their Borg cluster manager.[6]

Deploying an application to GKE requires a basic understanding of Kubernetes and the creation of some Kubernetes-specific configuration files (this will be more fully discussed in "Kubernetes").

In return for this extra work in configuring your application, you get services such as automatic replication and load balancing. These may sound like services that are only needed for large services with high traffic and many distributed parts, but they quickly become important for any service that wants to have any guarantees about up-time.

I'd strongly recommend Kubernetes, and GKE in particular, for deploying container systems, but be aware that this will tie to you to the Kubernetes model, making it more difficult to move your system between providers.

Amazon EC2 Container Service

Amazon's EC2 Container Service (ECS) (*https://aws.amazon.com/ecs/*) helps you run containers on Amazon's EC2 infrastructure. ECS provides a web interface and an API for launching containers and managing the underlying EC2 cluster.

---

6 See the paper, "Large-Scale Cluster Management at Google with Borg" (*https://research.google.com/pubs/pub43438.html*), for a fascinating look at how to run a cluster handling hundreds of thousands of jobs.

On each node of the cluster, ECS will start a container agent, which communicates with the ECS service and is responsible for starting, stopping, and monitoring containers.

It's relatively quick to get identidock running on ECS, although it does involve a typical AWS interface with dozens of configuration options. Once you are registered with ECS and have created a cluster, we need to upload a "Task Definition" for identidock. The following JSON can be used as the definition for identidock:

```
{
  "family": "identidock",
  "containerDefinitions": [
    {
      "name": "proxy",
      "image": "amouat/proxy:1.0",
      "cpu": 100,
      "memory": 100,
      "environment": [
        {
          "name": "NGINX_HOST",
          "value": "www.identidock.com"
        },
        {
          "name": "NGINX_PROXY",
          "value": "http://identidock:9090"
        }
      ],
      "portMappings": [
        {
          "hostPort": 80,
          "containerPort": 80,
          "protocol": "tcp"
        }
      ],
      "links": [
        "identidock"
      ],
      "essential": true
    },
    {
      "name": "identidock",
      "image": "amouat/identidock:1.0",
      "cpu": 100,
      "memory": 100,
      "environment": [
        {
          "name": "ENV",
          "value": "PROD"
        }
      ],
      "links": [
        "dnmonster",
```

```
        "redis"
      ],
      "essential": true
    },
    {
      "name": "dnmonster",
      "image": "amouat/dnmonster:1.0",
      "cpu": 100,
      "memory": 100,
      "essential": true
    },
    {
      "name": "redis",
      "image": "redis:3",
      "cpu": 100,
      "memory": 100,
      "essential": false
    }
  ]
}
```

Each container needs to specify an amount of memory (in megabytes) and number of CPU units. The essential key defines whether or not the task should be stopped if that container fails. In our case, the Redis container can be considered as nonessential, as the application will still work without it. The other fields should be self-explanatory.

Once the task has been successfully created, it needs to be started on the cluster. Identidock should be started as a *service*, rather than a one-off task. Running as a service means that ECS will monitor the containers to ensure availability and provides the option to connect to Amazon's Elastic Load Balancer to spread traffic between instances. When creating the service, ECS will ask for a name and the number of task instances it should ensure are running. After creating the service and waiting for the task to start, you should be able to access identidock via the IP address of the EC2 instance. This can be found on the task instance details page, in the expanded information for the proxy container.

Stopping the service and associated resources takes several steps. First, the service needs to be updated and the number of tasks changed to 0, to avoid ECS trying to bring up replacement tasks when shutting down. At this point, the service can be deleted. Before the cluster can be deleted, you will also need to deregister the container instances. Be careful to also stop any associated resources you may have started, such as Elastic Load Balancers or EBS storage.

There is a lot of engineering work going on behind the scenes in ECS. It's easy to launch hundreds or thousands of containers with a few clicks, providing serious capabilities for scaling. The scheduling of containers onto hosts is highly configurable, allowing users to optimize for their own needs, such as maximum efficiency or maximum reliability. Users can replace the default ECS scheduler with their own or use a third-party solution such as Marathon (see "Mesos and Marathon").

ECS also integrates with existing Amazon features such as Elastic Load Balancer for spreading load over multiple instances and the Elastic Block Store for persistent storage.

Giant Swarm

Giant Swarm (*https://giantswarm.io*) bills itself as "an opinionated solution for microservice architectures," which really means it's a fast and easy way to launch a Docker-based system using a specialized configuration format. Giant Swarm offers a hosted version on a shared cluster as well as a dedicated offering (where Giant Swarm will provision and maintain bare-metal hosts for you) and an on-premise solution. At the time of writing, the shared offering is still in alpha, but the dedicated offering is production ready.

Giant Swarm is a rarity in that it makes minimal-to-no use of VMs. Users with strict security requirements have separate bare-metal hosts, but the shared cluster has containers from separate users running next to each other.

Let's see how to run identidock on the Giant Swarm shared cluster. Assuming you've got access to Giant Swarm and installed the Swarm CLI,[7] start by creating the following configuration file and saving it as *swarm.json*:

```
{
    "name": "identidock_svc",
    "components": {
        "proxy": {
            "image": "amouat/proxy:1.0",
            "ports": [80],
            "env": {
                "NGINX_HOST": "$domain",
                "NGINX_PROXY": "http://identidock:9090"
            },
            "links": [ {
                "component": "identidock",
                "target_port": 9090
            }],
            "domains": { "80": "$domain" }
        },
        "identidock": {
            "image": "amouat/identidock:1.0",
            "ports": [9090],
            "links": [
                {
```

---

7 No relation to Docker's clustering solution, which is also called Swarm.

```
                "component": "dnmonster",
                "target_port": 8080
            },
            {

                "component": "redis",
                "target_port": 6379
            }
            ]
        },
        "redis": {
            "image": "redis:3",
            "ports": [6379]
        },
        "dnmonster": {
            "image": "amouat/dnmonster:1.0",
            "ports": [8080]
        }
    }
}
```

Now it's time to kick identidock into action:

```
$ swarm up --var=domain=identidock-$(swarm user).gigantic.io
Starting service identidock_svc...
Service identidock_svc is up.
You can see all components using this command:

    swarm status identidock_svc

$ swarm status identidock_svc
Service identidock_svc is up

component    image                   instanceid     created               status
dnmonster    amouat/dnmonster:1.0    m6eyoilfiei1   2015-09-04 09:50:40   up
identidock   amouat/identidock:1.0   r22ut7h0vx39   2015-09-04 09:50:40   up
proxy        amouat/proxy:1.0        6dr38cmrg3nx   2015-09-04 09:50:40   up
redis        redis:3                 jvcf15d6lpz4   2015-09-04 09:50:40   up
$ curl identidock-amouat.gigantic.io
<html><head><title>Hello...
```

Here we've shown off one of the features that distinguishes Giant Swarm configuration files from Docker Compose—the ability use template variables. In this case, we've passed in the hostname we want on the command line, and Swarm has gone ahead and replaced the $domain in the *swarm.json* with this value. Other features provided by *swarm.json* include the ability to define *pods*—groups of containers that are scheduled together—as well as the ability to define how many instances of a container should be running.

Finally, in addition to the Swarm CLI, there is a web UI for monitoring services and viewing logs and a REST API for automating interaction with Giant Swarm.

Persistent Data and Production Containers

Arguably, the data storage story hasn't changed much under Docker, at least at the larger end of the scale. If you run your own databases, you have the choice of using Docker container, VMs, or raw metal. Whenever you have a large amount of data, your VM or container will end up effectively pinned to the host machine due to the difficulties of moving the data around. This means the portability benefits normally associated with containers won't be of help here, but you may still want to use containers to keep a consistent platform and for isolation benefits. If you have concerns about performance, using `--net=host` and `--privileged` will ensure the container is effectively as efficient as the host VM or box, but be aware of the security implications. If you don't run your own databases, but use a hosted service such as Amazon RDS, things continue much as before.

At the smaller end of the scale, where containers have configuration files and moderate amounts of data, you may find volumes limiting, as they tie you to a host machine, making scaling and migrating containers more difficult. You may want to consider moving such data to separate key-value stores or DBs, which you can also run in a container. An interesting alternative approach is to use Flocker (*https://github.com/ClusterHQ/flocker*) to manage your data volumes. Flocker leverages the features of the ZFS filesystem to support the migration of data with containers. If you're trying to take a microservices approach, you will find things a lot simpler if you strive to keep your containers stateless where possible.

Sharing Secrets

You will probably have some sensitive data, such as passwords and API keys, that needs to be securely shared with your containers. The following subsections describe the various approaches to doing this, along with their advantages and disadvantages.[8]

Saving Secrets in the Image

Never do this. It's a bad idea.™

It might be the easiest solution, but it means the secret is now available to anyone with access to the image. It can't be deleted because it will still exist in previous layers. Even if you're using a private registry or not using a registry at all, it would be far too easy for someone to accidentally share the image, and there is no need for everyone who can access the image to know the secret. Also, it ties your image to a specific deployment.

---

8 If you're using configuration management software such as Ansible to manage container deployment, it may come with or prescribe a solution to this problem.

You *could* store secrets encrypted in images, but then you still need a way of passing the decryption key, and you are unnecessarily giving attackers something to work with.

Just forget about this idea. I only included it here so I can point at this section when someone does it and it goes horribly wrong.

Passing Secrets in Environment Variables

Using environment variables to pass secrets is a very straightforward solution and is considerably better than baking secrets into the image. It's simple to do: just pass the secrets as arguments to docker run. For example:

```
$ docker run -d -e API_TOKEN=my_secret_token myimage
```

A better method is to pass the variables in via a file, which has the advantage of keeping them from appearing in shell history or the output of the ps command (which will be visible to other users on a shared host):

```
$ cat pass.txt
API_TOKEN=my_secret_token
$ docker run -d --env-file ./pass.txt myimage
```

Many applications and configuration files will support using environment variables directly. For the rest, you may need some scripting similar to what we did in "Using a Proxy".

This is the method recommended by The Twelve-Factor App (*http://12factor.net*), a popular and respected methodology for building software-as-a-service applications.[9] While I would strongly recommend reading this document and implementing most of the advice, storing secrets in the environment has some serious drawbacks, including:

- Environment variables are visible to all child processes, docker inspect, and any linked containers. None of these has a good reason for being able to see these secrets.

- The environment is often saved for logging and debugging purposes. There is a large risk of secrets appearing in debug logs and issue trackers.

- They can't be deleted. Ideally we would overwrite or wipe the secret after using it, but this isn't possible with Docker containers.

For these reasons, I would advise against using this method.

---

9 It's worth pointing out that the Twelve-Factor methodology predates Docker containers, so some advice needs to be adapted.

Passing Secrets in Volumes

A slightly better—but still far from perfect—solution is to use volumes to share secrets. For example:

```
$ docker run -d -v $PWD:/secret-file:/secret-file:ro myimage
```

Unless you map in whole configuration files with secrets, you will probably require some scripting to handle secrets passed this way. If you're feeling really clever, it is possible to create a temporary file with the secret and delete the file after reading it (be careful not to delete the original though!).

For configuration files that use environment variables, you can also create a script that sets up the environment variables and can be sourced prior to running the appropriate application. For example:

```
$ cat /secret/env.sh
export DB_PASSWORD=s3cr3t
$ source /secret/env.sh && run_my_app.sh
...
```

This has the important advantage of not exposing the variables to docker inspect or linked containers.

The major drawback with this approach is that it requires you to keep your secrets in files, which are all too easy to check into version control. It can also be a more fiddly solution that typically requires scripting.

Using a Key-Value Store

Arguably the best solution is to use a key-value store to keep secrets and retrieve them from the container at runtime. This allows a level of control over the secrets that isn't possible with the previous options, but also requires more set up and putting your trust in the key-value store.

Some solutions in this area include:

KeyWhiz (https://square.github.io/keywhiz/)
> Stores secrets encrypted in memory and provides access via a REST API and a CLI. Developed and used by Square (a payment-processing company).

Vault (https://hashicorp.com/blog/vault.html)
> Can store secrets encrypted in a variety of backends, including file and Consul. Also has a CLI and API. Has several features not currently present in KeyWhiz, but is arguably less mature. Developed by HashiCorp, which is also behind the Consul service discovery tool and the Terraform infrastructure configuration tool.

Crypt (https://xordataexchange.github.io/crypt/)

Stores values encrypted in the etcd or Consul key-value stores. The major advantage with this approach is that it allows a degree of control over the secrets that wasn't previously possible. It becomes easy to change and delete secrets, apply "leases" to secrets so they expire after a given time period, or to lock down access to secrets in case of a security alert.

However, there is still a problem here: how does the container authenticate itself to the store? Typically, you will still need to pass the container either a private key using a volume or a token via an environment variable. The previous objections to using an environment variable can be mitigated by creating a *one-use token* that is revoked immediately after use. Another solution currently in development is to use a volume plugin for the store that mounts secrets from the store as a file inside the container. GitHub (*https://github.com/calavera/docker-volume-keywhiz*) has more information on this approach with regard to the KeyWhiz store.

This type of solution will be the future. The level of control it provides over sensitive data is more than worth any complications in implementation, which should be reduced as tooling improves. However, you may wish to wait and see how the sector evolves before making a decision. In the meantime, use volumes to share your secrets, but be very careful not to check them into SCM.

Networking

Networking is discussed in depth in Chapter 11. However, it is worth noting that if you're using the stock Docker networking in production, you are taking a considerable performance hit—setting up the Docker bridge and using veth[10] means that a lot of network routing is happening in user space, which is a lot slower than being handled by routing hardware or the kernel.

Production Registry

With identidock, we've just been using the Docker Hub to retrieve our images. Most production setups will include a registry (or multiple registries) to provide fast access to images and avoid relying on a third party for crucial infrastructure (some organizations will also be uneasy about storing their code with a third party, whether it's in a private repository or not). For details on setting up a registry, refer back to "Running Your Own Registry".

---

10 Virtual Ethernet, or veth, is a virtual network device with its own MAC address that was developed for use in VMs.

Keeping the images inside the registry up to date and correct is important—you don't want hosts to be able to pull old and potentially vulnerable images. For this reason, it's a good idea to run regular audits on registries, as discussed in "Auditing". However, remember that each Docker host will also maintain its own cache of images, which also needs to be checked.

The Docker distribution project (*https://github.com/docker/distribution/*) is currently working on supporting highly available and scalable registry deployments using techniques such as mirroring.

Continuous Deployment/Delivery

Continuous delivery is the extension of continuous integration to production; engineers should be able to make changes in development, have them run through testing, and then have them be available for deployment at the touch of a button. Continuous deployment takes this a step further and automatically pushes changes that pass testing to deployment.

We saw in Chapter 8 how to set up a continuous integration system using Jenkins. Extending this to continuous deployment can be achieved by pushing images to the production registry and migrating running containers to the new image. Migrating images without downtime requires bringing up new containers and rerouting traffic before stopping the old containers. As discussed in "Testing in Production", there are several possible ways to achieve this in a safe manner, such as blue/green deployments and ramped deployments. Implementing these techniques is often done with in-house tooling, although frameworks such as Kubernetes offer built-in solutions, and I expect to see specialist tools arrive on the market.

Conclusion

We've covered a great deal of information in this chapter-there are a lot of different aspects to consider when deploying containers to production, even with something as simple as identidock.

Although the container space is still very young, there are already several production-grade options for hosting containers. The best option to choose is dependent on the size and complexity of your system and how much effort and money you are willing to expend on deployment and maintenance. Small deployments can be managed by simply running a Docker Engine on a VM in the cloud, but this incurs a large maintenance burden with larger deployments. This can be mitigated by using systems such as Kubernetes and Mesos, which are discussed in Chapter 12, or by using a specialist hosting service such as Giant Swarm, Triton, or ECS.

In this chapter, we looked at some of the issues commonly faced in production, from tasks as seemingly simple as launching containers to thorny issues such as passing secrets, handling data volumes, and continuous deployment. Some of these issues require new approaches in a containerized system, especially when it is comprised of dynamic microservices. New patterns and best practices will be developed to deal with these issues, leading to new tooling and frameworks. Containers can already be used reliably in production, but the future is even brighter.

CHAPTER 10

Logging and Monitoring

Effective monitoring and logging of running containers is essential if you want to keep any nontrivial system up and running and debug issues effectively. In a microservice architecture, logging and monitoring become even more important due to the increased number of machines. Given the ephemeral nature of containers, a given container may no longer exist when debugging an issue, making centralized logs an indispensable tool.

In recent weeks and months, the number of solutions available for both logging and monitoring has exploded. Existing monitoring and logging vendors have begun to offer specialist container solutions and integrations. This chapter will try to give an overview of the various options and techniques available, with a focus on free and open source offerings. We will see how to extend the identidock application with a logging and monitoring solution that could easily be scaled out for larger applications.

The code for this chapter is available at GitHub (*https://github.com/ using-docker/logging*). As with Chapter 9, the examples use images from the Hub, but you can replace the identidock container with your own if you wish.

You can check out the code for the start of the chapter using the v0 tag:

```
$ git clone -b v0 \
  https://github.com/using-docker/logging/
...
```

Later tags represent the progression of the code through the chapter.

Alternatively, you can download the code for any tag from the Releases page on the GitHub project (*https://github.com/using-docker/logging/releases*).

Logging

We'll start by taking a look at how the default logging works in Docker, then we'll look at adding a full logging solution to identidock before moving on to look at some alternatives and considering production issues.

The Default Docker Logging

It's simplest to begin by describing what Docker provides out of the box. If you don't specify any arguments or install any logging software, Docker will log everything sent to STDOUT and STDERR. The logs can then be retrieved with the docker logs command. For example:

```
$ docker run --name logtest debian sh
-c 'echo "stdout"; echo "stderr" >&2'
stderr
stdout
$ docker logs logtest
stderr
stdout
```

We can also get the timestamp by using the -t argument:

```
$ docker logs -t logtest
2015-04-27T10:30:54.002057314Z stderr
2015-04-27T10:30:54.005335068Z stdout
```

And we can also stream the logs from a running container with -f:

```
$ docker run -d --name streamtest debian \
        sh -c 'while true; do echo "tick"; sleep 1; done;'
13aa6ee6406a998350781f994b23ce69ed6c38daa69c2c83263c863337a38ef9
$ docker logs -f streamtest
```

```
tick
tick
tick
tick
tick
tick
...
```

We can also do this from the Docker Remote API,[1] which opens possibilities for programmatically routing and processing logs. If you are using Docker Machine, you should be able to do something like:

```
$ curl -i --cacert ~/.docker/machine/certs/ca.pem \
        --cert ~/.docker/machine/certs/ca.pem \
        --key ~/.docker/machine/certs/key.pem \
        "https://$(docker-machine ip default):2376/containers/\
$(docker ps -lq)/logs?stderr=1&stdout=1"
tick
tick
tick
...
```

If you are using Mac OS, note that curl works slightly differently and that you will need to create a single certificate that contains both the *ca.pem* and *key.pem* details. There is more detail on this on the Open Solitude blog (*http://bit.ly/1IaCxjC*).

There are some shortcomings with the default logging. It can only handle STDOUT and STDERR, which is problematic if your application only logs to file. Also there is no log rotation, which means if you try to use an application such as yes (which just repeatedly writes "yes" to STDOUT) to keep a container running, you will find the container quickly eats all the free space on your disk drive.[2] For example:

```
$ docker run -d debian yes
ba054389b7266da0aa4e42300d46e9ce529e05fc4146fea2dff92cf6027ed0c7
```

There are several other logging methods available that can be started by using the --log-driver argument to docker run. The default logger can be changed by passing the --log-driver argument when starting the Docker daemon. The possible values for the logger are:

json-file
: The default logging we've just looked at.

syslog
: The syslog driver, which we'll look at shortly.

---

1 See the official docs (*http://bit.ly/1QMFApf*) for more information on the Remote API and how to enable it.

2 Yes, I was stupid enough to find this out the hard way.

journald
> The driver for the systemd journal.

gelf
> The Graylog Extended Log Format (GELF) driver.

fluentd
> Forwards log messages to fluentd (*http://www.fluentd.org*).

none
> Turns off logging.

Turning off logging can be useful in situations such as the preceding yes example.

Aggregating Logs

No matter which logging driver you use, it will only provide a partial solution, especially in multihost systems. What we want to do is aggregate all logs—potentially across hosts—into a single location so that we can run analytic and monitoring tools on them.

There are two basic approaches to doing this:

- Run a secondary process inside all our containers that acts as an agent and forwards logs to our aggregation service.
- Collect the logs on the host, or in a separate, standalone container and forward to the aggregation service.

The first technique works, and is sometimes used, but bloats images and unnecessarily increases the number of running processes, so we will only consider the second technique.

There are several ways we can access the container logs from the host:

- We can use the Docker API to programmatically access the logs. This has the advantage of being officially supported, at the cost of some overhead from using the HTTP connection. We'll see an example of using Logspout to do this in the next section.
- If using the syslog driver, we can use syslog functionality to automatically forward the logs, as shown in "Forwarding Logs with rsyslog".
- We can just directly access the log files from the Docker directory. This is described in "Grabbing Logs from File".

If the application you are using insists on logging to file rather than STDOUT or STDERR, have a look at Handling Applications that Log to File for a couple of work-arounds.

Logging with ELK

To add logging to our identidock application, we're going to use what's sometimes known as the ELK stack, which is short for Elasticsearch, Logstash, and Kibana:

Elasticsearch (https://github.com/elastic/elasticsearch)
> A text search engine with near real-time search. It is designed to easily scale across nodes in order to handle large volumes of data and is perfect for searching through masses of log data.

Logstash (https://github.com/elastic/logstash)
> A tool for reading in raw logs, then parsing and filtering them, before sending them onto another service, such as index or store (in our case, Logstash will forward to Elasticsearch). It has support for a wide range of input and output types as well as preexisting parsers for various application logs.

Kibana (https://github.com/elastic/kibana)
> A JavaScript-based graphical interface to Elasticsearch. It can be used to run Elasticsearch queries and visualize the results in various charts. Dashboards can be set up to provide an instant overview of the state of the system.

We'll run this stack locally, based on the *prod.yml* from the last chapter.[3] In an ideal setup, we would move the ELK containers to a separate host to maintain a clear separation of concerns. In Chapter 11, we'll take a look at how this can be done; but for the sake of simplicity, we'll keep everything on one host for this chapter.

The first thing we need to do is figure out how to send our Docker logs to Logstash. For this, we will use Logspout (*https://github.com/gliderlabs/logspout*), a Docker-specific tool that uses the Docker API to stream logs from running containers to a given endpoint (something like rsyslog for Docker). Because we want to use Logstash as our endpoint, we will also install the logspout-logstash adapter (*https://github.com/looplab/logspout-logstash*), which formats the Docker logs in a manner easily read by Logstash. Logspout is designed to be as small and efficient as possible so that it can be run on each Docker host while using the minimum of resources. To achieve this, Logspout is written in Go and built on top of the extremely minimal Alpine Linux image. Because the default container for Logspout doesn't include the logstash adapter, we'll use one I prepared earlier.

---

3 If you want to run this in the cloud, go ahead, but you might find you need to upgrade your server to run all the services.

The overall setup we are aiming for looks something like Figure 10-1, with the container logs on the left being collated by Logspout, then parsed and filtered by Logstash before being deposited in Elasticsearch. Finally, Kibana is used to visualize and investigate the data in the Elasticsearch container.

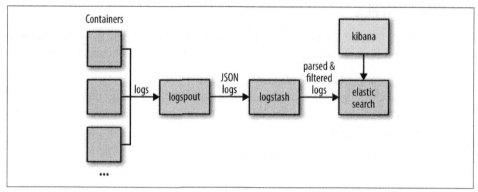

Figure 10-1. Container logging with Logspout and ELK

Start by creating a new file, *prod-with-logging.yml*, which should contain:

```
proxy:
  image: amouat/proxy:1.0
  links:
    - identidock
  ports:
   - "80:80"
  environment:
    - NGINX_HOST=45.55.251.164 ❶
    - NGINX_PROXY=http://identidock:9090
identidock:
  image: amouat/identidock:1.0 ❷
  links:
    - dnmonster
    - redis
  environment:
    ENV: PROD
dnmonster:
  image: amouat/dnmonster:1.0
redis:
  image: redis:3

logspout:
  image: amouat/logspout-logstash:1.0
  volumes:
    - /var/run/docker.sock:/var/run/docker.sock ❸
  ports:
    - "8000:80" ❹
```

❶ Replace the IP address with your host's IP.

❷ I've used my identidock image from the Hub, but feel free to replace with your own version.

❸ Mounts the Docker socket so that Logspout can connect to the Docker API.

❹ Publishes Logspout's HTTP interface for viewing logs. Don't leave this exposed in a production system.

Now, if you bring up the application again, you should be able to connect to Logspout's streaming HTTP interface:

```
$ docker-compose -f prod-with-logging.yml up -d
...
$ curl localhost:8000/logs
```

Open identidock in a browser, and you should start seeing some logs in the terminal:

```
logging_proxy_1|192.168.99.1 - - [24/Sep/2015:11:36:53 +0000] "GET / HTTP/1....
logging_identidock_1|[pid: 6|app: 0|req: 1/1] 172.17.0.14 () {40 vars in 660...
logging_identidock_1|Cache miss
        logging_proxy_1|192.168.99.1 - - [24/Sep/2015:11:36:53 +0000] "GET /mon...
logging_identidock_1|[pid: 6|app: 0|req: 2/2] 172.17.0.14 () {42 vars in 788...
logging_identidock_1|[pid: 6|app: 0|req: 3/3] 172.17.0.14 () {42 vars in 649...
```

Great, that part seems to be working, and you might find this interface useful in the future. Next, we need to send the output somewhere useful—in this case, to a Logstash container. Note that in multihost systems, you will need to run one Logspout container per host, which will route to a centralized Logstash instance. Let's wire up Logstash now. Start by updating our Compose file:

```
...
logspout:
  image: amouat/logspout-logstash:1.0
  volumes:
    - /var/run/docker.sock:/var/run/docker.sock
  ports:
    - "8000:80"
  links:
    - logstash ❶
  command: logstash://logstash:5000 ❷
logstash:
  image: logstash:2.3.4
  volumes:
    - ./logstash.conf:/etc/logstash.conf ❸
  environment:
    LOGSPOUT: ignore ❹
  command: -f /etc/logstash.conf
```

❶ Add a link to the Logstash container.

❷ Use the "logstash" prefix, which tells Logspout to use the `Logstash` module for output.

❸ Map in the configuration file for Logstash.

❹ Logspout will not gather logs from any container that has the environment variable `LOGSPOUT` set. We don't want to gather logs from the Logstash container as it risks starting a cycle where a malformed log entry causes an error in Logstash, which gets logged and sent back to Logstash, which causes a new error that gets logged and sent back, and so on.

The configuration file should be saved as *logstash.conf* with the following contents:

```
input {
  tcp {
    port => 5000
    codec => json ❶
  }
  udp {
    port => 5000
    codec => json ❶
  }
}

output {
  stdout { codec => rubydebug } ❷
}
```

❶ To work with the Logspout output, we need to use the `json` codec.

❷ For testing, we'll output the logs to `STDOUT`.

Now let's run it and see what happens:

```
$ docker-compose -f prod-with-logging.yml up -d
...
$ curl -s localhost > /dev/null
$ docker-compose -f prod-with-logging.yml logs logstash
...

logstash_1   | {
logstash_1   |           "message" => "172.17.0.1 - - [26/Jul/2016:12:53:33 +...
logstash_1   |            "stream" => "stdout",
logstash_1   |            "docker" => {
logstash_1   |               "name" => "/logging_proxy_1",
logstash_1   |                 "id" => "4883fa86ef383b32c66a1ed263309a55f628...
logstash_1   |              "image" => "amouat/proxy:1.0",
logstash_1   |           "hostname" => "4883fa86ef38"
```

```
logstash_1   |     },
logstash_1   |       "@version" => "1",
logstash_1   |     "@timestamp" => "2016-07-26T12:53:33.434Z",
logstash_1   |           "host" => "172.17.0.5"
logstash_1   | }
...
```

You should see a few entries in Ruby format like the preceding code. Note that the output includes fields such as name of the container and its ID, which have been added by Logspout. Logstash has taken the JSON output, ingested it, and spat it out in its Ruby debug format. But there's a lot more we can do with Logstash; we can filter and mutate the logs as needed. For example, you might want to remove personally identifiable or sensitive information before passing it on to another service for further processing or storage. In our case, it would be nice to pull apart the nginx log message into its constituent parts. We can do this by adding a `filter` section to the Logstash configuration file:

```
input {
  tcp {
    port => 5000
    codec => json
  }
  udp {
    port => 5000
    codec => json
  }
}

filter {
  if [docker][image] =~ /^amouat\/proxy.*/ {
    mutate { replace => { type => "nginx" } }
    grok {
      match => { "message" => "%{COMBINEDAPACHELOG}" }
    }
  }
}

output {
  stdout { codec => rubydebug }
}
```

This filter checks the message to see if it comes from an image with the name `amouat/proxy`. If it does, the message is parsed using the existing Logstash filter `COMBINEDAPACHELOG`, which results in a few extra fields being added to the output. If you add the preceding filter and restart the application, you should find log entries like the following:

```
logstash_1 | {
logstash_1 |         "message" => "172.17.0.1 - - [26/Jul/2016:15:26:00...
logstash_1 |          "stream" => "stdout",
logstash_1 |          "docker" => {
```

```
logstash_1    |              "name" => "/logging_proxy_1",
logstash_1    |                "id" => "6a9ea7cf0ef0a40b8abc96e1d4922d4e77...
logstash_1    |             "image" => "amouat/proxy:1.0",
logstash_1    |          "hostname" => "6a9ea7cf0ef0"
logstash_1    |      },
logstash_1    |       "@version" => "1",
logstash_1    |     "@timestamp" => "2016-07-26T15:26:00.997Z",
logstash_1    |           "host" => "172.17.0.5",
logstash_1    |           "type" => "nginx",
logstash_1    |       "clientip" => "172.17.0.1",
logstash_1    |          "ident" => "-",
logstash_1    |           "auth" => "-",
logstash_1    |      "timestamp" => "26/Jul/2016:15:26:00 +0000",
logstash_1    |           "verb" => "GET",
logstash_1    |        "request" => "/",
logstash_1    |    "httpversion" => "1.1",
logstash_1    |       "response" => "200",
logstash_1    |          "bytes" => "265",
logstash_1    |       "referrer" => "\"-\"",
logstash_1    |          "agent" => "\"curl/7.35.0\""
logstash_1    | }
```

Note that the filter has extracted a whole bunch of extra information such as the response code, the request type, and URL. Using a similar technique, you can set up filters for logging of all your various images.

The next step is to connect the Logstash container to an Elasticsearch container. We'll also add in the Kibana container at the same time, as it will provide our interface to Elasticsearch.

Update our Compose file so that it now includes:

```
...
logspout:
  image: amouat/logspout-logstash:1.0
  volumes:
    - /var/run/docker.sock:/var/run/docker.sock
  ports:
    - "8000:80"
  links:
    - logstash
  command: logstash://logstash:5000

logstash:
  image: logstash:2.3.4
  volumes:
    - ./logstash.conf:/etc/logstash.conf
  environment:
    LOGSPOUT: ignore
  links:
    - elasticsearch ❶
  command: -f /etc/logstash.conf
```

```
elasticsearch: ❷
  image: elasticsearch:2.3
  environment:
    LOGSPOUT: ignore

kibana: ❸
  image: kibana:4.5
  environment:
    LOGSPOUT: ignore
    ELASTICSEARCH_URL: http://elasticsearch:9200
  links:
    - elasticsearch
  ports:
    - "5601:5601"
```

❶ Adds a link to the Elasticsearch container.

❷ Creates an Elasticsearch container based on the official image.

❸ Creates a Kibana 4 container. Note that we add a link to the Elasticsearch container and expose port 5601 for the interface.

We also need to update the output section of the *logstash.conf* file to point to our Elasticsearch container:

```
...
output {
  elasticsearch { hosts => ["elasticsearch"] } ❶
  stdout { codec => rubydebug } ❷
}
```

❶ Outputs data in a format readable by Elasticsearch to the remote host called "elasticsearch."

❷ If you want to, you can now remove this line; it's only necessary for debugging and is currently causing logs to be duplicated.

Let's restart the application and take a look:

```
$ docker-compose -f prod-with-logging.yml up -d
Recreating logging_dnmonster_1...
Recreating logging_redis_1...
Recreating logging_elasticsearch_1...
Recreating logging_kibana_1...
Recreating logging_identidock_1...
Recreating logging_proxy_1...
Recreating logging_logstash_1...
Recreating logging_logspout_1...
```

Then open up *localhost* in your browser and play around with the identidock application for a while so that our logging stack has some data to analyze. When you're ready, open *localhost:5601* in your browser to start the Kibana application. You should see something like Figure 10-2.

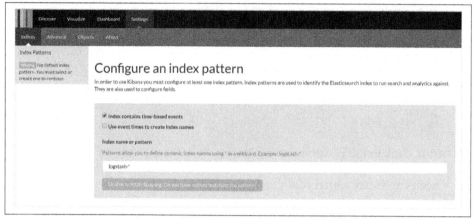

Figure 10-2. Kibana configuration page

Select @timestamp as the time-field name and click "Create." You should then get a page with all the fields Elasticsearch has found, including our nginx and Docker ones.

If you then click on "Discover," you should get a page with a histogram showing log volumes above a list of recent logs, similar to Figure 10-3.

Figure 10-3. Kibana Discover page

You can easily change the time period by clicking the clock icon in the top right. Logs can be filtered by searching for the presence of terms in certain fields. For example, try searching for "Cache miss" on the "message" field to get a histogram of cache misses over time. More advanced charts and visualizations can be generated using the "Visualize" tab, including line charts and pie charts as well data tables and custom metrics.

Kibana 3 Versus 4

If you use a pre-4.0 version of Kibana, you will need to make sure your *browser* can access the *Elasticsearch* container by forwarding a port to the host. This is because Kibana is a JavaScript-based application that runs in the client. From version 4 on, connections are proxied through Kibana, removing this requirement.

This chapter isn't meant as a full introduction to advanced log analysis, so we won't go any further with Kibana. Suffice to say that Kibana and similar solutions offer powerful and highly visual ways to investigate your application and data.

Log Storage and Rotation

Whatever log driver and analysis solution you end up using, you still need to decide how you're going to store your logs and for how long. If you haven't thought about this at all, you likely have containers using the default logging that are slowly eating up all the hard disk until they crash the host.

The Linux logrotate utility can be used to manage the growth of logfiles. Typically, several generations of logfiles are used, with files being moved through the generations at regular intervals. For example, in addition to the current log, you may have father, grandfather, and great-grandfather logs. The grandfather and great-grandfather logs are compressed to save storage. Every day, the current log is moved to the father log, the old father log is compressed and moved to the grandfather log, the grandfather becomes great-grandfather, and the old great-grandfather log is deleted.

You can use the following logrotate configuration to achieve this, which should be saved to a new file under */etc/logrotate.d/* (e.g., */etc/logrotate.d/docker*), or added to */etc/logrotate.conf*:

```
/var/lib/docker/containers/*/*.log {
    daily ❶
    rotate 3 ❷
    compress ❸
    delaycompress ❸
    missingok ❹
```

```
    copytruncate ❺
}
```

❶ Rotate the logs every day.

❷ Keep three generations of log files.

❸ Use compression but delay by one generation.

❹ Stop logrotate from throwing an error if files are missing.

❺ Rather than moving the current logfile, copy it then truncate it (set the size to 0).
This is needed to ensure Docker doesn't get upset when the file disappears. There
is a chance of data loss if the application logs data between the copy and truncate.

By default, you'll probably find that logrotate is executed as a cron job once a day; if
you want to tidy up logs more often than that, you'll need to change this.

For more permanent and robust log storage, forward your logs to a robust database
such as PostgreSQL. You can easily add this as second output from Logstash or an
equivalent tool. Do not rely purely on indexing solutions like Elasticsearch for stor‐
age, as they don't have the same fault-tolerance guarantees of mature databases like
PostgreSQL. Note that you can use Logstash filters to cut out data such as personably
identifiable information if required.

 Handling Applications that Log to File

If you have an application that logs to file rather than STDOUT/
STDERR, you still have a couple of options available. If you are
already using the Docker API to do your logging (e.g., with the
Logspout container), the simplest solution is to run a process (nor‐
mally `tail -F`) that just prints the file to STDOUT. An elegant way
to do this that maintains the single process to a container philoso‐
phy is to use a second container that mounts the log files with
`--volumes-from`.

For example, if we have a container called "tolog" that declares a
volume at */var/log*, we can use the following:

```
$ docker run -d --name tolog-logger \
          --volumes-from tolog \
          debian tail -F
/dev/log/*
```

If you don't want to take this approach, you can also mount the
logs to a known directory on the host and run a collector such as
fluentd (*http://www.fluentd.org/*) on them.

Docker Logging with syslog

Assuming your Docker host has syslog support, you can use the syslog driver, which will send the container logs to syslog on the host. This is perhaps best explained with an example:

```
$ ID=$(docker run -d --log-driver=syslog debian \
       sh -c 'i=0; while true; do i=$((i+1)); echo "docker $i"; sleep 1; done;')
$ docker logs $ID
"logs" command is supported only for "json-file" logging driver (got: syslog) ❶
$ tail /var/log/syslog ❷
Sep 24 10:17:45 reginald docker/181b6d654000[3594]: docker 48
Sep 24 10:17:46 reginald docker/181b6d654000[3594]: docker 49
Sep 24 10:17:47 reginald docker/181b6d654000[3594]: docker 50
Sep 24 10:17:48 reginald docker/181b6d654000[3594]: docker 51
Sep 24 10:17:49 reginald docker/181b6d654000[3594]: docker 52
Sep 24 10:17:50 reginald docker/181b6d654000[3594]: docker 53
Sep 24 10:17:51 reginald docker/181b6d654000[3594]: docker 54
Sep 24 10:17:52 reginald docker/181b6d654000[3594]: docker 55
Sep 24 10:17:53 reginald docker/181b6d654000[3594]: docker 56
Sep 24 10:17:54 reginald docker/181b6d654000[3594]: docker 57
```

❶ At the time of writing, the docker `logs` command only works with the default logging.

❷ On my Ubuntu host, docker logs were being sent to */var/log/syslog*. This may be different on other Linux distributions.

The syslog log file with the container messages probably also contains messages for various other services, as well as other containers. As the log messages have the container ID (in short form), we can easily use the grep tool to find messages pertaining to a given container:

```
$ grep ${ID:0:12} /var/log/syslog ❶
Sep 24 10:16:58 reginald docker/181b6d654000[3594]: docker 1
Sep 24 10:16:59 reginald docker/181b6d654000[3594]: docker 2
Sep 24 10:17:00 reginald docker/181b6d654000[3594]: docker 3
Sep 24 10:17:01 reginald docker/181b6d654000[3594]: docker 4
Sep 24 10:17:02 reginald docker/181b6d654000[3594]: docker 5
Sep 24 10:17:03 reginald docker/181b6d654000[3594]: docker 6
Sep 24 10:17:04 reginald docker/181b6d654000[3594]: docker 7
...
```

❶ The logs use the shortform ID, which means we have to reduce the full ID to 12 characters.

The Docker Events API

In addition to the container logs and Docker daemon logs, there is another set of data you may want to monitor and react to—Docker events. Events are logged for most of the stages in the lifecycle of a Docker container. These events include create, destroy, die, export, kill, pause, attach, restart, start, stop, and unpause. Most of these should be self-explanatory, but note that die occurs when a container exits and destroy occurs when it is deleted (i.e., docker rm is invoked). Figure 10-4 shows the lifecycle as a chart.

The untag and delete events are logged for images. untag occurs when a tag is deleted, which will happen whenever docker rmi is successfully invoked. The delete event occurs when the underlying image is deleted (this event does not always occur on docker rmi because there may be multiple tags for an image). Timestamps are displayed in RFC 3339 format (*https://www.ietf.org/rfc/rfc3339.txt*).

We can retrieve events using the docker events command:

```
$ docker events
2015-09-24T15:23:28.000000000+01:00 44fe57bab...: (from debian) create
2015-09-24T15:23:28.000000000+01:00 44fe57bab...: (from debian) attach
2015-09-24T15:23:28.000000000+01:00 44fe57bab...: (from debian) start
2015-09-24T15:23:28.000000000+01:00 44fe57bab...: (from debian) die
```

As the docker events command returns a stream, you will need to run some Docker commands from another terminal before you see any results. The docker events command also takes arguments for filtering results and controlling the time period for which to return results. Events can be filtered by containers, images, and events. Timestamps used in arguments need to be formatted according to RFC 3339 (e.g., "2006-01-02T15:04:05.000000000Z07:00") or given as seconds since the Unix epoch (e.g., "1378216169").

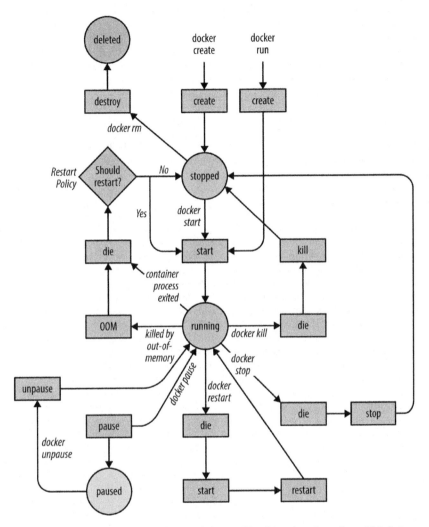

Figure 10-4. The Docker lifecycle (adapted from official Docker docs (http://bit.ly/ 1QMFApf), originally by Mat Good, Glider labs, released under CC-BY-SA 4.0 (http:// bit.ly/cc-by-sa-4) license)

The Docker events API can be very useful when you want want to automatically react to container events. For example, the Logspout utility uses the API to notice when containers are started and begin streaming logs from them. The nginx-proxy from Jason Wilder discussed in "Supercharged Config File Generation" uses the events API to automatically load balance containers when they come up. In addition, you may simply want to log the data in order to perform analysis on the lifecycles of your containers.

We can make things a little better by setting up syslog to put our Docker logs in a separate log file. Docker logs to the "daemon" facility in syslog speak, so you can easily set up syslog to messages for *all* daemons to a given file, but filtering for just the Docker messages is a little harder.[4] If you're using rsyslog version 7 or above (and there's a good chance you are), you can use the following rule, which will place all Docker container messages in */var/log/containers.log*:

```
:syslogtag,startswith,"docker/" /var/log/containers.log
```

Save this rule to an rsyslog configuration file. On Ubuntu at least, you can make a new file */etc/rsyslog.d/30-docker.conf* and save it there. Then restart syslog and the logs will appear in our new file:

```
$ sudo service rsyslog restart
rsyslog stop/waiting
rsyslog start/running, process 15863
$ docker run -d --log-driver=syslog debian \
  sh -c 'i=0; while true; do i=$((i+1)); echo "docker $i"; sleep 1; done;'
$ cat /var/log/containers.log
Sep 24 10:30:46 reginald docker/1a1a57b885f3[3594]: docker 1
Sep 24 10:30:47 reginald docker/1a1a57b885f3[3594]: docker 2
Sep 24 10:30:48 reginald docker/1a1a57b885f3[3594]: docker 3
Sep 24 10:30:49 reginald docker/1a1a57b885f3[3594]: docker 4
Sep 24 10:30:50 reginald docker/1a1a57b885f3[3594]: docker 5
Sep 24 10:30:51 reginald docker/1a1a57b885f3[3594]: docker 6
Sep 24 10:30:52 reginald docker/1a1a57b885f3[3594]: docker 7
```

At the moment, logging will also be going to other files (e.g., */var/log/syslog*). To stop this, add a line immediately after our rule with &stop For example:

```
:syslogtag,startswith,"docker/" /var/log/containers.log
&stop
```

---

4 It shouldn't be, but it seems that parts of syslog have yet to emerge from the '80s....

Syslog and Docker Machine VMs

At the time of writing, syslog isn't running by default in the boot2docker VMs provisioned by Machine. You can start it for testing purposes by logging into the VM and running syslogd. For example:

```
$ docker-machine ssh default
...
docker@default:~$ syslogd
```

You can make this change permanent by calling syslogd from the file */var/lib/boot2docker/bootsync.sh* inside the boot2docker VM, which the VM will execute before starting Docker. For example:

```
$ docker-machine ssh default
...
docker@default:~$ cat /var/lib/boot2docker/bootsync.sh
#!/bin/sh
syslogd
```

Note that the boot2docker VM uses busybox's default syslog implementation, which isn't as flexible as rsyslogd.

You can set syslog as the default logging option for Docker containers by adding --log-driver=syslog to the daemon initialization, normally by editing the configuration file for the docker service (e.g., add to DOCKER_OPTS in the file */etc/default/docker* on Ubuntu).

Forwarding Logs with rsyslog

We can also tell rsyslog to forward our logs onto another server rather than store them locally. This can be used to provide logs to a central service such as Logstash, or another syslog server without the overhead of using something like Logspout.

To replace Logspout with rsyslog in our identidock example, we need to change the Logstash config to expect syslog input, forward a port on the host to Logstash for rsyslog to talk to, and tell rsyslog to send logs over the network rather than to a file.

We can start by reconfiguring Logstash. Update the config file to:

```
input {
  syslog {
    type => syslog
      port => 5544
  }
}

filter {
  if [type] == "syslog" {
    syslog_pri { }
    date {
```

```
      match => [ "syslog_timestamp", "MMM d HH:mm:ss", "MMM dd HH:mm:ss" ]
    }
  }
}

output {
  elasticsearch { hosts => ["elasticsearch"] }
  stdout { codec => rubydebug }
}
```

Now let's configure rsyslog. The configuration is almost the same as above, except rather than specify the file */var/log/containers.log*, we will use the syntax `@@local host:5544`. For example:

```
:syslogtag,startswith,"docker/" @@localhost:5544
&stop
```

This will tell rsyslog to send the logs using TCP to port 5544 on localhost. To use UDP instead, use only a single @.[5]

The final piece of configuration is rewrite our Compose file. Before we do this, it's best to stop any running identidock instances:

```
$ docker-compose -f prod-with-logging.yml stop
...
```

Now we can safely remove Logspout from the Compose file and publish a port on the host for rsyslog to talk to Logstash over:

```
...
logstash:
  image: logstash:2.3.4
  volumes:
    - ./logstash.conf:/etc/logstash.conf
  environment:
    LOGSPOUT: ignore
  links:
    - elasticsearch
  ports:
    - "127.0.0.1:5544:5544"  ❶
  command: -f /etc/logstash.conf

elasticsearch:
  image: elasticsearch:2.3
  environment:
    LOGSPOUT: ignore

kibana:
  image: kibana:4.5
```

---

5 I know, obvious, right?

```
    environment:
      LOGSPOUT: ignore
      ELASTICSEARCH_URL: http://elasticsearch:9200
    links:
      - elasticsearch
    ports:
      - "5601:5601"
```

❶ Publish the port 5544. We only bind to the interface `127.0.0.1` so that the host can connect to the port but other machines on the network cannot.

Finally, restart rsyslog and identidock. Now we can see our logs are sent to Logstash through rsyslog, rather than the slower Logspout method. There's still some work to be done configuring filters to get all the information we had from Logspout into Logstash, but using rsyslog for forwarding logs is a very efficient and robust solution.

Guaranteed Logging

When designing your logging infrastructure, you will—whether you are aware of it or not—trade the need for complete accuracy and reliability for efficiency. If you just need your logs for debugging and monitoring purposes, you can likely just use whatever solution you find simplest. If, however, there are certain log messages that must result in an immediate alert, or your logs must be verifiably complete for compliance with policies, it is essential that you consider the properties and guarantees of the various links in your logging infrastructure.

Some key points to consider:

- What transport protocol is being used to send your logs? UDP is faster but offers less reliability guarantees than TCP (but TCP is still not guaranteed to be reliable).

- What happens in the case of a network outage? Note that many tools, including rsyslog, can be configured to buffer messages until the remote server can be reached.

- How are your messages being stored and backed up? Databases offer greater reliability and fault-tolerance guarantees than filesystems.

An overlapping concern is security of logs; your logs likely contain sensitive information, and it's important to control who has access to them. You will want to make sure that any logs traveling over the public Internet are encrypted and that only the appropriate people can access stored logs.

Grabbing Logs from File

Another efficient way of forwarding logs is to access the raw logs on the filesystem.

If you're using the default logging, Docker currently keeps the container log files at */var/lib/docker/containers/<container id>/<container id>-json.log*.

Taking logs directly from file is efficient but relies on internal Docker implementation details rather than an exposed API. For this reason, it is possible that logging solutions based on this method will break with updates to the Docker engine.

Monitoring and Alerting

In a microservice system, you are likely to have dozens, possibly hundreds or thousands, of running containers. You are going to want as much help as you can get to monitor the state of running containers and the system in general. A good monitoring solution should show at a glance the health of the system and give advance warning if resources are running low (e.g., disk space, CPU, memory). We also want to be alerted should things start going wrong (e.g., if requests start taking several seconds or more to process).

Monitoring with Docker Tools

Docker comes with a basic CLI tool, `docker stats`, that returns a live stream of resource usage. The command takes the name of one or more containers and prints various statistics for them, in much the same way as the Unix application `top`. For example:

```
$ docker stats logging_logspout_1
CONTAINER             CPU %  MEM USAGE/LIMIT    MEM %  NET I/O
logging_logspout_1    0.13%  1.696 MB/2.099 GB  0.08%  4.06 kB/9.479 kB
```

The stats cover CPU and memory usage as well as network utilization. Note that unless you have set memory limits on the container, the limit you see on memory will represent the total amount of memory on the host, rather than the amount of memory available to the container.

Get Stats On All Running Containers

Most of the time, you will want to get stats from all the running containers on the host (in my opinion, this should be the default). You can do this with a bit of shell script fu:

```
$ docker stats \
    $(docker inspect -f {{.Name}} $(docker ps -q))
CONTAINER                 CPU %   MEM USAGE/LIMIT      ...
/logging_dnmonster_1      0.00%   57.51 MB/2.099 GB
/logging_elasticsearch_1  0.60%   337.8 MB/2.099 GB
/logging_identidock_1     0.01%   29.03 MB/2.099 GB
/logging_kibana_1         0.00%   61.61 MB/2.099 GB
/logging_logspout_1       0.14%   1.7 MB/2.099 GB
/logging_logstash_1       0.57%   263.8 MB/2.099 GB
/logging_proxy_1          0.00%   1.438 MB/2.099 GB
/logging_redis_1          0.14%   7.283 MB/2.099 GB
```

The docker ps -q gets the IDs of all running containers, used as input to docker inspect -f {{.Name}}, which turns the IDs to names which are passed to docker stats.

This is useful in as far as it goes, and also hints at the existence of a Docker API that can be used to get such data programmatically. This API does indeed exist and you can call the endpoint at /containers/<id>/stats to get a stream of various statistics on the container, with more detail than the CLI. This API is somewhat inflexible; you can stream updates for all values every second, or only pull all stats once, but there are no options to control frequency or filtering. This means you are likely to find the stats API incurs too much overhead for continuous monitoring, but is still useful for ad hoc queries and investigations.

Most of the various metrics exposed by Docker are also available directly from the Linux kernel, through the CGroups and namespaces features, which can be accessed by various libraries and tools, including Docker's runc library (*https://github.com/opencontainers/runc*). If you have a specific metric you want to monitor, you can write an efficient solution using runc or making kernel calls directly. You will need to use a language that allows you to make low-level kernel calls, such as Go or C. There are also a few gotchas you should be aware of, such as how to avoid forking new processes for updating metrics. The Docker article Runtime Metrics (*https://docs.docker.com/v1.8/articles/runmetrics/*) explains how to do this and goes into depth about the various metrics available from the kernel. Once you've exposed the values you need, you may want to look into tools such as statsd (*https://github.com/etsy/statsd*) for aggregating and calculating metrics, InfluxDB (*http://influxdb.com/*) and OpenTSDB (*http://opentsdb.net*) for storage, and Graphite (*http://graphite.readthe docs.org*) and Grafana (*https://github.com/grafana/grafana*) for displaying the results.

Monitoring and Alerting with Logstash

While Logstash is very much a logging tool, it's worth pointing out that you can already achieve a level of monitoring with Logstash, and that the logs themselves are an important metric to monitor.

For example, you could check nginx status codes and automatically email or message an alert upon receiving a high volume of 500s. Logstash also has output modules for many common monitoring solutions, including Nagios, Ganglia, and Graphite.

In the majority of cases, you will want to use a preexisting tool for gathering and aggregating metrics and producing visualizations. There are many commercial solutions to this, but we will look at the leading open source and container-specific solutions.

cAdvisor

Google's cAdvisor (a contraction of Container Advisor) is the most commonly used Docker monitoring tool. It provides a graphical overview of the resource usage and performance metrics of containers running on the host.

As cAdvisor is available as a container itself, we can get it up and running in a flash. Just launch the cAdvisor container with the following arguments:

```
$ docker run -d \
  --name cadvisor \
  -v /:/rootfs:ro \
  -v /var/run:/var/run:rw \
  -v /sys:/sys:ro \
  -v /var/lib/docker/:/var/lib/docker:ro \
  -p 8080:8080 \
  google/cadvisor:latest
```

If you're on a Red Hat (or CentOS) host, you'll also need to mount the cgroups folder with `--volume=/cgroup:/cgroup`.

Once the container is running, point your browser at *http://localhost:8080*. You should see a page with a bunch of graphs, something like Figure 10-5. You can drill down to specific containers by clicking the "Docker Containers" link and then clicking the name of the container you're interested in.

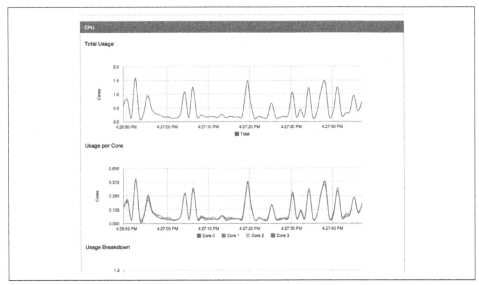

Figure 10-5. cAdvisor graph of CPU usage

cAdvisor aggregates and processes various stats and also makes these available through a REST API for further processing and storage. The data can also be exported to InfluxDB, a database designed for storing and querying time series data, including metrics and analytics. The roadmap for cAdvisor includes features such as hints on how to improve and tune the performance of containers, and usage-prediction information to cluster orchestration and scheduling tools.

Cluster Solutions

cAdvisor is great, but is a per-host solution. If you're running a large system, you will want to get statistics on containers across all hosts as well on the hosts themselves. You will want to get stats on how groups of containers are doing, representing both subsystems as well as slices of functionality across instances. For example, you may want to look at the memory usage of all your nginx containers, or the CPU usage of a set of containers running a data analysis task. Because the required metrics tend to be application and problem specific, a good solution will provide you with a query language that can be used to construct new metrics and visualizations.

Google has developed a cluster monitoring solution built on top of cAdvisor called Heapster, but at the time of writing, it only supports Kubernetes and CoreOS, so we won't consider it here.

Instead we'll take look at Prometheus, an open source cluster-monitoring solution from SoundCloud that can take input from a wide range of sources, including cAdvisor. It is designed to support large microservice architectures and is used by both SoundCloud and Docker, Inc.

Prometheus

Prometheus (*http://prometheus.io*) is unusual in that it operates on a *pull*-based model. Applications are expected to expose metrics themselves, which are then pulled by the Prometheus server rather than sending metrics directly to Prometheus. The Prometheus UI can be used to query and graph data interactively, and the separate *PromDash* can be used to save graphs, charts, and gauges to a dashboard. Prometheus also has an *Alertmanager* component that can aggregate and inhibit alerts and forward to notification services, such as email, and specialist services, such as PagerDuty (*http://www.pagerduty.com*) and Pushover (*https://pushover.net*).

Let's take a look at Prometheus with identidock. We won't add any specialist metrics in, but we could easily do this by using the Python client library to decorate calls in our Python code.

Instead, we'll connect Prometheus to our cAdvisor container. We could also have used the container-exporter project (*http://bit.ly/1HzVqSo*), which also uses Docker's libcontainer library. If you already have the cAdvisor container running, you can see the metrics it exposes to Prometheus at the /metrics endpoint:

```
$ curl localhost:8080/metrics
# HELP container_cpu_system_seconds_total Cumulative system cpu time consume...
# TYPE container_cpu_system_seconds_total counter
container_cpu_system_seconds_total{id="/",name="/"} 97.89
container_cpu_system_seconds_total{id="/docker",name="/docker"} 40.66
container_cpu_system_seconds_total{id="/docker/071c24557187c14fb7a2504612d4c...
container_cpu_system_seconds_total{id="/docker/1a1a57b885f33d2e16e85cee7f138...
...
```

Starting the Prometheus container is straightforward, but does require us to create a configuration file. Save the following file as *prometheus.conf*:

```
global:
  scrape_interval: 1m    ❶
  scrape_timeout: 10s
  evaluation_interval: 1m

scrape_configs:

- job_name: prometheus
  scheme: http    ❷
  target_groups:
  - targets:
    - 'cadvisor:8080'
    - 'localhost:9090'    ❸
```

❶ Tells Prometheus to retrieve statistics every five seconds, arguably a relatively high value. In a production environment, you will need to choose an interval by weighing the cost of scraping against the cost of out-of-date metrics.

❷ Tells Prometheus the URL to scrape cAdvisor on (we'll use a link to set the host-name up).

❸ Also scrape Prometheus' own metrics endpoint on port 9090.

Start the Prometheus container with:

```
$ docker run -d --name prometheus -p 9090:9090 \
              -v $PWD/prometheus.conf:/prometheus.conf \
              --link cadvisor:cadvisor \
              prom/prometheus -config.file=/prometheus.conf
```

You should now be able to open the Prometheus application at *http://localhost:9090*. The home page will give you some information on how Prometheus has been config-ured and the status of endpoints it is scraping. If you go to the "Graph" tab, you can start investigating the data inside Prometheus. Prometheus has its own query lan-guage that includes support for filters, regular expressions, and various operators. As a simple example, try entering the expression:

```
sum(container_cpu_usage_seconds_total {name=~"logging*"}) by (name)
```

This should provide the CPU usage for each of our identidock containers across time. The {name=~"logging*"} expression filters out containers that are not part of our Compose application (e.g., cAdvisor and Prometheus itself). You will need to replace "logging" with the name of your Compose project or folder. The sum function is required as CPU usage is reported per CPU. You should get a result similar to Figure 10-6.

We can take this further and set up a dashboard with the PromDash container. This is reasonably straightforward and left as an exercise for the reader. Figure 10-7 shows a dashboard with the above CPU metric and a graph of memory usage. PromDash also supports displaying graphs from multiple distributed Prometheus instances, which can be useful in displaying graphs per geographical location or across departments.

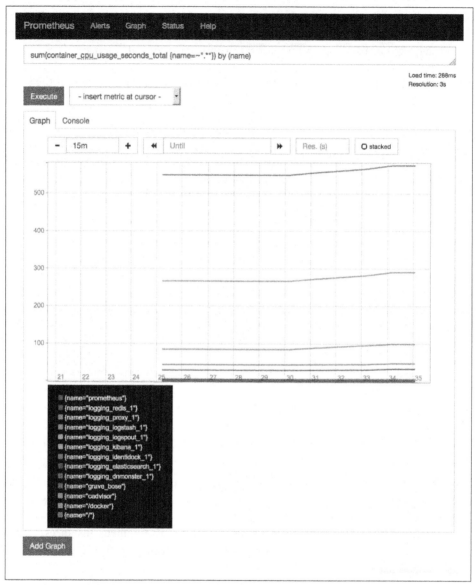

Figure 10-6. Prometheus graph of container CPU usage

This of course is very basic use of Prometheus. A real-world installation would involve scraping far more endpoints over distributed hosts, setting up dashboards and in-depth visualizations with PromDash, and altering with the Alertmanager.

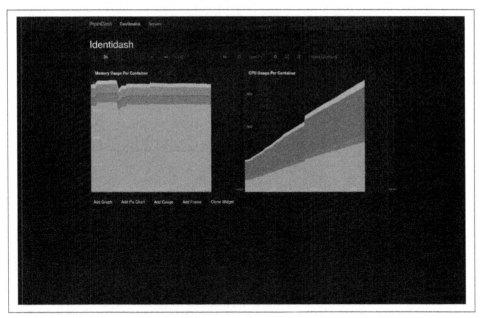

Figure 10-7. PromDash dashboard for identidock

Commercial Monitoring and Logging Solutions

I've intentionally only looked in depth at open source and on-premise solutions in this chapter, but there are many commercial solutions that are well developed and supported. The area is highly contested and fought over. Rather than mention specific solutions in this rapidly evolving space, I'll just say that it is definitely worth looking into, especially if you are seeking a mature or hosted solution.

Conclusion

Effective logging and monitoring is critical to running a microservice-based application. This chapter showed how we could add effective logging and monitoring identidock using the ELK stack alongside cAdvisor and Prometheus. Although this solution is much more heavyweight than our application itself (to the extent that logging and monitoring itself dominates the metrics), we have seen how quick and simple it is to get an effective solution in place.

In the future, we will see much more logging support and options from Docker itself. Commercial offerings are very strong across logging, monitoring, and alerting, so expect to see all vendors coming up with specialist Docker and microservice offerings.

PART III

Tools and Techniques

This part goes into advanced details about the tools and techniques needed to run clusters of Docker containers safely and reliably.

We start by looking at networking and service discovery, a task that quickly becomes essential when dealing with containers on more than one host. To put it another way, how do your containers find one another and how do you connect them?

We then look into software solutions designed to help with orchestration and clustering of containers. These tools help developers address issues such as load balancing, scaling, and failover, and help operations schedule containers and maximize resource usage. Any long-lived application will run into these issues sooner rather than later—knowing the problems and potential solutions ahead of time is a significant advantage.

The final chapter covers how to ensure the security of containers and microservice deployments. Containers pose new challenges for security but also offer new tools and techniques. Despite its position at the end of the book, this is an important topic that everyone involved with containers should familiarize themselves with.

CHAPTER 11

Networking and Service Discovery

The line between service discovery and networking can become surprisingly blurred in a container context. Service discovery is the process of automatically providing clients[1] of a service with connection information (normally IP address and port) for an appropriate[2] instance of that service. This problem is easy in a static, single-host system where there is exactly one instance of everything, but is much more complicated in a distributed system with multiple instances of services that come and go over time. One way to approach discovery is for the client simply to request the service by name (e.g., db or api), and do some magic on the backend to have this resolve to the appropriate location. This "magic" can take the form of simple ambassador containers, a service discovery solution such as Consul, a networking solution such as Weave (which includes service discovery features), or some combination of the previous.

For our purposes, networking can be regarded as the process of connecting containers together. It does not involve plugging in physical Ethernet cables, although it often involves software equivalents such as veth. Container networking starts from the assumption that there is a route available between hosts, whether that route involves traversing the public Internet or just a fast local switch.

So, service discovery allows clients to discover instances, and networking takes care of putting the connections in place. Networking and service discovery solutions tend to overlap in functionality, as service discovery solutions can point across networks, and networking solutions often include service discovery features (such as Weave). A

---

1 I mean "client" in the broadest sense here; primarily, I mean applications and other services running on the backend, but also peers (in the sense of a cluster of cooperating instances) and end-user clients such as browsers.

2 Where "appropriate" is very context dependent, possibly meaning "any," "the fastest," "the one nearest my data," etc.

pure service discovery solution, like Consul, will likely offer richer functionality in terms of health checking, failover, and load balancing. Networking solutions offer different possibilities for connecting and routing containers[3] in addition to features such as traffic encryption and isolating groups of containers.

Quite often, you will need to use both a service discovery solution and a networking one (and you always need some sort of networking). Exactly what is required will depend on your situation, and best practices are still evolving. Networking is likely to change between development, testing, and production environments, but service discovery typically involves decisions at the application level and will remain the same across environments.

This chapter attempts to move through the networking and service discovery space in terms of complexity, so we start off by looking at the simplest cross-host solution (i.e., ambassador containers) before looking at service discovery solutions (including etcd and Consul) and moving on to look at Docker networking details and solutions such as Weave, Flannel, and Project Calico.

Ambassadors

One way to connect containers across hosts is through the use of *ambassadors*. These are proxy containers that stand in for the real container (or service) and forward traffic to the actual service. Ambassadors provide a separation of concerns that make them useful in many scenarios, not just for connecting services across hosts.

The major advantage of ambassador containers is that they allow the production network architecture to differ from the development architecture without requiring changes to code. Developers can use local versions of databases and other resources, safe in the knowledge that ops can rewire the application to use their own clustered services, or remote resources, without touching the code. Ambassadors can also be rewired to use a different backing service on the fly, whereas using links to directly connect to the service would require a restart of the client container.

The disadvantage of ambassador containers is that they require extra configuration, incur overhead, and are a potential point of failure. They can can quickly become overly complex and a management burden when multiple connections are required.

In Figure 11-1, we see a typical development setup where the developer directly links the application to a database container using Docker links, both running on her local

---

3 Using service discovery "alone" will still require the use of some networking, whether it is the default Docker "bridge" network with ports exposed to the host, or "host" networking, both of which require management of ports.

laptop. This is great for making quick changes and being able to throw things away and start over while developing.

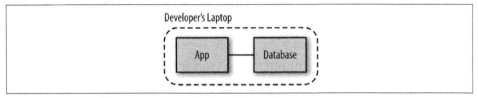

Figure 11-1. Development setup without ambassadors

In Figure 11-2, we see a common production setup where ops have used an ambassador to link the application to their production service, which is running on a separate server. All ops needed to do was to configure the ambassador to pass traffic through to the service and use links to connect the application to the ambassador. The code continues to use the same hostnames and ports as before with the new setup being handled inside the ambassador.

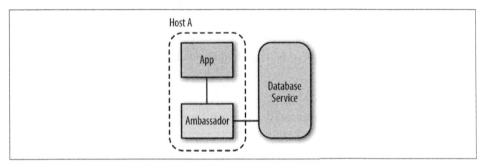

Figure 11-2. Using an ambassador to link to a production service

In Figure 11-3, we see a setup where the application is talking to a container on a remote host, which is itself behind an ambassador. This setup allows the remote host to move traffic to a new container on a new address by just updating the ambassador. Again, no changes were needed to the code to use the new setup.

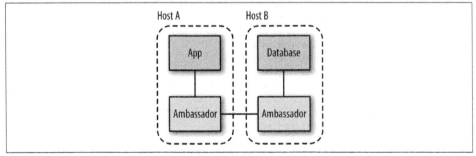

Figure 11-3. Using ambassadors to link to a remote container

The ambassador itself can be a very simple container—all it needs to do is set up a connection between the application and the service. There's no official image for creating ambassadors, so you will need to either roll your own or choose from a user image on the Hub.

The amouat/ambassador Image

This chapter uses an image called `amouat/ambassador`. The image is a simple port of Sven Dowideit's ambassador (*https://hub.docker.com/r/svendowideit/ambassador/*), modified to use the `alpine` base image and run as an automated build on the Docker Hub.

The image uses the socat tool (*http://www.dest-unreach.org/socat/*) to set up a relay between the ambassador and the destination. Environment variables in the same form as those created by Docker links (e.g., `REDIS_PORT_6379_TCP=tcp://172.17.0.1:6379`) define where to connect the relay to. This means a relay to a locally linked container (such as Host B in Figure 11-3) can be set up with very little configuration.

As the image is built on the minimal Alpine Linux distribution, it clocks in at just over 7 MB, so is small enough to be quickly downloaded and adds little overhead to the system.

Let's look at how we can use ambassadors to link up our identidock application with a Redis container running on a separate host, per Figure 11-3. We'll provision two VirtualBox VMs with Docker machine (see "Provisioning Resources with Docker Machine") to do this, but you could also easily run this example using Docker hosts in the cloud. Let's get the hosts ready:

```
$ docker-machine create -d virtualbox redis-host
...
$ docker-machine create -d virtualbox identidock-host
...
```

Now set up a Redis container (called `real-redis`) and an ambassador (called `real-redis-ambassador`) on `redis-host`:

```
$ eval $(docker-machine env redis-host)
$ docker run -d --name real-redis redis:3
Unable to find image 'redis:3' locally
3: Pulling from redis
...
60bb8d255b950b1b34443c04b6a9e5feec5047709e4e44e58a43285123e5c26b
$ docker run -d --name real-redis-ambassador \
          -p 6379:6379 \ ❶
          --link real-redis:real-redis \ ❷
```

```
                        amouat/ambassador
        be613f5d1b49173b6b78b889290fd1d39dbb0fda4fbd74ee0ed26ab95ed7832c
```

❶ We need to publish the port 6379 on the host to allow remote connections

❷ The ambassador uses the environment variables from the linked real-redis
   container to set up a relay that will stream requests that come in on port 6379 to
   to the real-redis container.

Now set up an ambassador on identidock-host:

```
$ eval $(docker-machine env identidock-host)
$ docker run -d --name redis_ambassador --expose 6379 \
        -e REDIS_PORT_6379_TCP=tcp://$(docker-machine ip redis-host):6379 \  ❶
        amouat/ambassador
Unable to find image 'amouat/ambassador:latest' locally
latest: Pulling from amouat/ambassador
31f630c65071: Pull complete
cb9fe39636e8: Pull complete
3931d220729b: Pull complete
154bc6b29ef7: Already exists
Digest: sha256:647c29203b9c9aba8e304fabfd194429a4138cfd3d306d2becc1a10e646fcc23
Status: Downloaded newer image for amouat/ambassador:latest
26d74433d44f5b63c173ea7d1cfebd6428b7227272bd52252f2820cdd513f164
```

❶ We need to manually set up an environment variable to tell the ambassador to
   connect to the remote host. The IP address of the remote host is retrieved by
   using the docker-machine ip command.

Finally, start up identidock and dnmonster, linking identidock to our ambassador:

```
$ docker run -d --name dnmonster amouat/dnmonster:1.0
Unable to find image 'amouat/dnmonster:1.0' locally
1.0: Pulling from amouat/dnmonster
...
c7619143087f6d80b103a0b26e4034bc173c64b5fd0448ab704206b4ccd63fa
$ docker run -d --link dnmonster:dnmonster \
        --link redis_ambassador:redis \
        -p 80:9090 \
        amouat/identidock:1.0
Unable to find image 'amouat/identidock:1.0' locally
1.0: Pulling from amouat/identidock
...
5e53476ee3c0c982754f9e2c42c82681aa567cdfb0b55b48ebc7eea2d586eeac
```

Give it a whirl:

```
$ curl $(docker-machine ip identidock-host)
<html><head>...
```

Sweet! We've just got identidock running across hosts without changing any code,
just through the use of two small ambassador containers. This approach might be a

little fiddly and requires the use of extra containers, but it is also very simple and flexible. It is easy to imagine scenarios involving more sophisticated ambassadors such as:

- Encrypting traffic across an untrusted link
- Automatically connecting containers when they start by monitoring the Docker event stream
- Proxying read requests to a read-only server and write requests to a different server

In all cases, the client doesn't need to know about the extra intelligence in the ambassador.

However, while ambassador containers can be useful, in most cases, it is easier and more scalable to use networking and/or service discovery solutions to find and connect to remote services and containers.

Service Discovery

At the start of the chapter, we defined service discovery as *the process of automatically providing clients of a service with connection information for an appropriate instance of that service.*

For the client application, this means they will need to request, or be given, the address of the service in some way. We'll see solutions that require clients to make explicit calls to an API for the service address as well as DNS-based solutions, which can be easily integrated with existing applications.

This section will cover the major service discovery solutions being used with Docker today. We'll take an in-depth look at etcd, Consul, and SkyDNS before a quick round-up of some other notable solutions. None of these have been written specifically for containers, but all are designed for use in large distributed systems.

etcd

etcd is a distributed key-value store. It is an implementation of the Raft consensus algorithm (*https://raftconsensus.github.io/*) in Go, designed to be both efficient and fault tolerant. *Consensus* is the process of multiple members agreeing on values, a process that quickly becomes complicated in the face of failures and errors. The Raft algorithm ensures values are consistent and that new values can be added whenever a majority of members are available.

Each member in an etcd cluster runs an instance of the etcd binary, which will communicate with the other members. Clients access etcd through a REST interface that runs on all the members.

The recommended minimum size of an etcd cluster is 3 to provide fault tolerance in the case of failure. However, for the following example, we'll use just 2 members to show how etcd works.

Optimal Cluster Size

For both etcd and Consul, a cluster size of 3, 5, or 7 is recommended, striking a balance between failure tolerance and performance.

If there is only a single member, data will be lost in the event of failure. If there are two members and one fails, the remaining member will be unable to reach a quorum (basically a "majority," in plain English) and further writes will fail until the second member returns.

Table 11-1. Cluster size implications

Servers	No. required for majority	Failure tolerance
1	1	0
2	2	0
3	2	1
4	3	1
5	3	2
6	4	2
7	4	3

As can be seen in Table 11-1, adding further members improves failure tolerance. However, more members also mean that writes require agreement and communication between more nodes, slowing down the system. Once the size of the cluster grows beyond 7, the likelihood of enough nodes failing to bring down the system is low enough that adding further nodes isn't worth the performance trade-off. Also note that even numbers are generally best avoided, as they increase the cluster size (and hence decrease performance) but do not improve failure tolerance.

Of course, many distributed systems run with far more than 7 hosts. In these cases, 5 or 7 hosts are used to form the cluster, and the remaining nodes run clients that can query the system but do not take part in consensus replication. These is done via *proxies* in etcd and *client mode* in Consul.

We'll start by creating the new hosts with Docker machine:

```
$ docker-machine create -d virtualbox etcd-1
...
$ docker-machine create -d virtualbox etcd-2
...
```

Now we can launch the etcd containers. Because we know the members of the etcd cluster in advance, we'll just explicitly list them when starting the containers. It's also possible to use a URL- or DNS-based discovery mechanism for clusters where the addresses aren't known in advance. There are a lot of flags that need to be set when starting etcd, so I've used environment variables to hold the VM IP addresses, which makes things a little simpler:

```
$ HOSTA=$(docker-machine ip etcd-1)
$ HOSTB=$(docker-machine ip etcd-2)
$ eval $(docker-machine env etcd-1)
$ docker run -d -p 2379:2379 -p 2380:2380 -p 4001:4001 \
  --name etcd quay.io/coreos/etcd \ ❶
  -name etcd-1 -initial-advertise-peer-urls http://${HOSTA}:2380 \ ❷
  -listen-peer-urls http://0.0.0.0:2380 \
  -listen-client-urls http://0.0.0.0:2379,http://0.0.0.0:4001 \
  -advertise-client-urls http://${HOSTA}:2379 \
  -initial-cluster-token etcd-cluster-1 \
  -initial-cluster \
     etcd-1=http://${HOSTA}:2380,etcd-2=http://${HOSTB}:2380 \ ❸
  -initial-cluster-state new
...
d4c12bbb16042b11252c5512ab595403fefcb2f46abb6441b0981103eb596eed
```

❶ Gets the official etcd image from the Quay.io registry.

❷ Sets up various URLs for accessing etcd. We need to make sure etcd listens on IP 0.0.0.0 for remote and local connections, but tells other clients and peers to connect via the IP address of the host. In a real setup, the etcd nodes should communicate on an internal network not exposed to the outside world (i.e., not obtained through docker-machine ip).

❸ We explicitly list all the nodes in the cluster, including the node being launched. This can be replaced with other discovery methods.

The setup is almost the same on the second VM, except we need to advertise the IP of etcd-2 to external clients:

```
$ eval $(docker-machine env etcd-2)
$ docker run -d -p 2379:2379 -p 2380:2380 -p 4001:4001 \
  --name etcd quay.io/coreos/etcd \
  -name etcd-2 -initial-advertise-peer-urls http://${HOSTB}:2380 \
  -listen-peer-urls http://0.0.0.0:2380 \
  -listen-client-urls http://0.0.0.0:2379,http://0.0.0.0:4001 \
  -advertise-client-urls http://${HOSTB}:2379 \
  -initial-cluster-token etcd-cluster-1 \
  -initial-cluster \
     etcd-1=http://${HOSTA}:2380,etcd-2=http://${HOSTB}:2380 \
  -initial-cluster-state new
```

```
...
2aa2d8fee10aec4284b9b85a579d96ae92ba0f1e210fb36da2249f31e556a65e
```

Our etcd cluster is now up and running. We can ask etcd for a list of members with a simple `curl` query against the HTTP API:

```
$ curl -s http://$HOSTA:2379/v2/members | jq '.'
{
  "members": [
    {
      "clientURLs": [
        "http://192.168.99.100:2379"
      ],
      "peerURLs": [
        "http://192.168.99.100:2380"
      ],
      "name": "etcd-1",
      "id": "30650851266557bc"
    },
    {
      "clientURLs": [
        "http://192.168.99.101:2379"
      ],
      "peerURLs": [
        "http://192.168.99.101:2380"
      ],
      "name": "etcd-2",
      "id": "9636be876f777946"
    }
  ]
}
```

I've used the jq tool here to pretty print the output. Members can be dynamically added and deleted from the cluster by sending POST and DELETE HTTP requests to the same endpoint.

The next step is to add some data and make sure it can be read from both hosts. Data is stored in directories in etcd and returned as JSON. The following example stores the value `service_address` in the directory *service_name* by using an HTTP PUT request:

```
$ curl -s http://$HOSTA:2379/v2/keys/service_name \
        -XPUT -d value="service_address" | jq '.'
{
  "node": {
    "createdIndex": 17,
    "modifiedIndex": 17,
    "value": "service_address",
    "key": "/service_name"
  },
  "action": "set"
}
```

To get it back, we just need to do a GET on the directory:

```
$ curl -s http://$HOSTB:2379/v2/keys/service_name | jq '.'
{
  "node": {
    "createdIndex": 17,
    "modifiedIndex": 17,
    "value": "service_address",
    "key": "/service_name"
  },
  "action": "get"
}
```

By default, etcd returns some metadata on the key as well as its value. Note that we set the data on etcd-1 and read it from etcd-2. Because they are part of the same cluster, it doesn't matter which host you use for operations; they will both give the same answer.

There is also a command-line client called etcdctl that can be used to talk to the etcd cluster. Rather than install it, we can just use a container:

```
$ docker run binocarlos/etcdctl -C ${HOSTB}:2379 get service_name
service_address
```

You can get a better feel for how etcd works by looking at the logs for the etcd containers, which will show how the members cooperate to elect leaders among other details. A full description and specification of the underlying Raft algorithm can be found at *https://raftconsensus.github.io/*.

We can now see how we could write an application that uses etcd for service discovery directly. In the case of identidock, we would make a simple HTTP request in the Python code to find the address of the Redis and dnmonster services. The dnmonster and Redis containers could also be changed to register their addresses with etcd when they start, completely automating the system.

Rather than modify the identidock code, we will see in the following section on SkyDNS how we can build a discovery solution on top of etcd that doesn't require any changes to the code.

SkyDNS

The SkyDNS utility (*https://github.com/skynetservices/skydns*) provides DNS-based service discovery on top of etcd. Most notably, it is used by Google Container Engine to provide service discovery in its Kubernetes offering (see "Kubernetes").

We can use SkyDNS to complete the etcd solution and get identidock running across two hosts with no changes to the code. If you followed along with the last example, you will have two servers running an etcd cluster: etcd-1, whose IP address is $HOSTA, and etcd-2, whose IP address is $HOSTB. By the time we've finished, we will have the system shown in Figure 11-4, with the identidock container using SkyDNS to find the dnmonster and Redis containers.

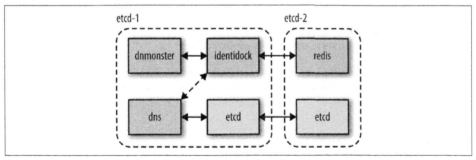

Figure 11-4. Cross-host identidock with SkyDNS and etcd

The first thing to do is to add some SkyDNS configuration settings to etcd so that it knows what to do when it comes up:

```
$ curl -XPUT http://${HOSTA}:2379/v2/keys/skydns/config \
      -d value='{"dns_addr":"0.0.0.0:53", "domain":"identidock.local."}' | jq .
{
  "action": "set",
  "node": {
    "key": "/skydns/config",
    "value": "{\"dns_addr\":\"0.0.0.0:53\", \"domain\":\"identidock.local.\"}",
    "modifiedIndex": 6,
    "createdIndex": 6
  }
}
```

This will tell SkyDNS to listen to all interfaces on port 53 and that it is an authority for the domain *identidock.local*.

It makes sense for us to use a container for SkyDNS, but it can also be run as a host process. We'll use the `skynetservices/skydns` image[4] created by the SkyDNS developers. Let's spin it up on `etcd-1` now:

```
$ eval $(docker-machine env etcd-1)
$ docker run -d -e ETCD_MACHINES="http://${HOSTA}:2379,http://${HOSTB}:2379" \
      --name dns skynetservices/skydns:2.5.2a
...
f95a871247163dfa69cf0a974be6703fe1dbf6d07daad3d2fa49e6678fa17bd9
```

---

4 At the time of writing, the SkyDNS image isn't an automated build, which makes it something of a black box. You may prefer to build your own SkyDNS container so that you can be certain of what is in it. There is a Dockerfile available on the SkyDNS GitHub project (*https://github.com/skynetservices/skydns*) for this purpose.

We had to give it some extra config to tell it where to find its etcd backend, but we now have a working DNS server. Except we haven't told it about any services yet. We'll start by bringing up our Redis server on etcd-2 and adding that to SkyDNS:

```
$ eval $(docker-machine env etcd-2)
$ docker run -d -p 6379:6379 --name redis redis:3
...
d9c72d30c6cbf1e48d3a69bc6b0464d16232e45f32ec00dcebf5a7c6969b6aad
$ curl -XPUT http://${HOSTA}:2379/v2/keys/skydns/local/identidock/redis \
        -d value='{"host":"'$HOSTB'","port":6379}' | jq .
{
  "action": "set",
  "node": {
    "key": "/skydns/local/identidock/redis",
    "value": "{\"host\":\"192.168.99.101\",\"port\":6379}",
    "modifiedIndex": 7,
    "createdIndex": 7
  }
}
```

We used a path ending */local/identidock/redis* for the curl request, which maps to the domain *redis.identidock.local*. The JSON data specifies the IP address and port we want the name to resolve to. We have used the IP address of the host rather than the Redis container, as the container IP is local to etcd-2.

At this point, we can try things out to see how they work. We'll start a new container and use the --dns flag to point it to our DNS container for lookups:

```
$ eval $(docker-machine env etcd-1)
$ docker run --dns $(docker inspect -f {{.NetworkSettings.IPAddress}} dns) \
        -it redis:3 bash
...
root@3baff51314d6:/data# ping redis.identidock.local
PING redis.identidock.local (192.168.99.101): 48 data bytes
56 bytes from 192.168.99.101: icmp_seq=0 ttl=64 time=0.102 ms
56 bytes from 192.168.99.101: icmp_seq=1 ttl=64 time=0.090 ms
56 bytes from 192.168.99.101: icmp_seq=2 ttl=64 time=0.096 ms
^C--- redis.identidock.local ping statistics ---
3 packets transmitted, 3 packets received, 0% packet loss
round-trip min/avg/max/stddev = 0.090/0.096/0.102/0.000 ms
root@3baff51314d6:/data# redis-cli -h redis.identidock.local ping
PONG
```

Pretty good! The only issue is that *redis.identidock.local* is a bit of a mouthful. It would be much better if we could just say *redis*, but that's a no go:

```
root@3baff51314d6:/data# ping redis
ping: unknown host
```

If we start a new container and add *identidock.local* as a search domain, the OS will automatically try to resolve *redis.identidock.local* if *redis* doesn't resolve:

```
root@3baff51314d6:/data# exit
$ docker run --dns $(docker inspect -f {{.NetworkSettings.IPAddress}} dns) \
            --dns-search identidock.local \
            -it redis:3 redis-cli -h redis ping
PONG
```

Excellent, that's pretty much what we need, but we don't want to have to specify the --dns and --dns-search flags every time we run a container. Instead, we could give them as options to the Docker daemon, but this has a bit of a chicken-and-egg problem when the DNS server is a container itself,[5] so we're going to go with another option. We'll add the relevant values to the host's *etc/resolv.conf* file,[6] which controls where the OS will look for domain names and is automatically propagated to containers:

```
$ docker-machine ssh etcd-1
. . .
docker@etcd-1:~$ echo -e "domain identidock.local \nnameserver " \
  $(docker inspect -f {{.NetworkSettings.IPAddress}} dns) > /etc/resolv.conf
docker@etcd-1:~$ cat /etc/resolv.conf
domain identidock.local
nameserver 172.17.0.3
docker@etcd-1:~$ exit
```

Make it work:

```
$ docker run redis:3 redis-cli -h redis ping
PONG
```

Now we can start dnmonster and add it to the DNS:

```
$ docker run -d --name dnmonster amouat/dnmonster:1.0
$ DNM_IP=$(docker inspect -f {{.NetworkSettings.IPAddress}} dnmonster)
$ curl -XPUT http://$HOSTA:2379/v2/keys/skydns/local/identidock/dnmonster \
      -d value='{"host": "'$DNM_IP'","port":8080}'
. . .
```

We've used the internal container IP for dnmonster here, so it will only be accessible from etcd-1. If we had multiple SkyDNS servers operating on several hosts, we would want to mark this record as being *host local* so that it doesn't confuse the other servers. This can be done by defining a host local domain when starting SkyDNS.

Finally, start up identidock and make sure it works, without a link in sight:

---

5 If you want to do this, you can expose port 53 on the DNS container to the host and use the address of the Docker bridge for the DNS server.

6 The VirtualBox VM will actually re-create this file on reboot, undoing our changes; the instructions here are intended as an example only. Production hosts may also have different methods for changing *resolv.conf*, such as the resolvconf utility.

```
$ docker run -d -p 80:9090 amouat/identidock:1.0
$ curl $HOSTA
<html><head><title>...
```

So now we have a service discovery interface that doesn't require any changes to our implementation and is running on top of the distributed and fault-tolerant etcd store.

Digging into SkyDNS

If you want to see how SkyDNS works, you can use the dig utility that is included in the SkyDNS image. For example:

```
$ docker exec -it dns sh
/ # dig @localhost SRV redis.identidock.local
dig @localhost SRV redis.identidock.local

; <<>> DiG 9.10.1-P2 <<>> @localhost SRV redis.identidock.local
; (2 servers found)
;; global options: +cmd
;; Got answer:
;; ->>HEADER<<- opcode: QUERY, status: NOERROR, id: 51805
;; flags: qr aa rd ra; QUERY: 1, ANSWER: 1, AUTHORITY: 0, ADDITIONAL: 1

;; QUESTION SECTION:
;redis.identidock.local.        IN   SRV

;; ANSWER SECTION:
redis.identidock.local. 3600  IN   SRV  10 100 6379 redis.identidock.local.

;; ADDITIONAL SECTION:
redis.identidock.local. 3600  IN   A    192.168.99.101

;; Query time: 4 msec
;; SERVER: ::1#53(::1)
;; WHEN: Sat Jul 25 17:18:39 UTC 2015
;; MSG SIZE  rcvd: 98
```

Here the DNS server has returned the SRV record for redis.identidock.local. The information includes the IP address and port number, as well as the priority, weight, and TTL.

SkyDNS uses SRV or service records as well as the traditional A records (which perform IPv4 resolution). Among other fields, SRV records include the port for the service, its time-to-live (TTL), priority, and weight. Setting a TTL allows records to be automatically expunged if a client or agent does not regularly update the value, which can be used to implement failover and more graceful error handling than simply timing out.

Other features include grouping multiple hosts into address pools, which can be used as a form of load balancing, and support for publishing metrics and stats to services such as Prometheus and Graphite.

Consul

Consul (*https://consul.io*) is HashiCorp's answer to the service discovery problem. In addition to being a distributed, highly available key-value store, it also boasts advanced health-checking features and a DNS server by default.

CAP Theorem

When looking into key-value stores and service discovery, you will quickly run into the CAP theorem (*https://en.wikipedia.org/wiki/CAP_theorem*), which roughly states that a distributed system cannot simultaneously be *consistent*, *available*, and *partition tolerant*.[7]

An AP system will favor availability over consistency, so reads and writes should nearly always be possible (and are typically fast), but may not always be up to date (in some cases, old data may be returned). A CP system will favor consistency, so writes may fail in some cases, but whenever data is returned, it will be correct and up to date.

In practice, the water seems to be a bit more muddy, in particular with regard to Consul. Both etcd and Consul are based on the Raft algorithm, which provides a CP solution. However, Consul has three different modes ("default," "consistent," and "stale") that provide different levels of consistency versus availability trade-off.

Every host runs an instance of the Consul agent, in either server or client mode. The agent can check the status of various services as well as general stats like memory usage, keeping complexity out of the client application. A subset of hosts (normally 3, 5, or 7; see "Optimal Cluster Size") will run the agent in server mode, which is responsible for writing and storing data and collaborating with the other server agents. Agents in client mode will forward requests to server agents.

Getting started is just as easy, especially if we use Docker containers. In this case, we'll use a container from GliderLabs (*http://gliderlabs.com/*). Again, we'll start by creating two new VMs for this purpose:

---

7 See "Brewer's Conjecture and the Feasibility of Consistent, Available, Partition-Tolerant Web Services" (*https://www.comp.nus.edu.sg/~gilbert/pubs/BrewersConjecture-SigAct.pdf*) for precise definitions of these terms.

```
$ docker-machine create -d virtualbox consul-1
...
$ docker-machine create -d virtualbox consul-2
...
```

Now start up the Consul containers. Again, we'll save the IPs of the VMs to variables to save some work:

```
$ HOSTA=$(docker-machine ip consul-1)
$ HOSTB=$(docker-machine ip consul-2)
$ eval $(docker-machine env consul-1)
$ docker run -d --name consul -h consul-1 \
        -p 8300:8300 -p 8301:8301 -p 8301:8301/udp \
        -p 8302:8302/udp -p 8400:8400 -p 8500:8500 \
        -p 172.17.42.1:53:8600/udp \
        gliderlabs/consul agent -data-dir /data -server \   ❶
            -client 0.0.0.0 \   ❷
            -advertise $HOSTA -bootstrap-expect 2   ❸
...
ff226b3114541298d19a37b0751ca495d11fabdb652c3f19798f49db9cfea0dc
```

❶ Starts the Consul agent in server mode and saves data to the */data* directory.

❷ Specifies the address to listen for client API requests. This defaults to 127.0.0.1, which is only addressable inside the container.

❸ The -advertise flag specifies the address other hosts should contact the server on (in this case, the IP address of the host). We also set the -bootstrap-expect flag to tell Consul to wait for a second server to join the cluster.

Here we are using the public IPs returned from Docker machine to link the hosts. In production, you will want to use a private address that cannot be reached from the Internet at large.

Bring up the second container, this time using the -join command to link the first server:

```
$ eval $(docker-machine env consul-2)
$ docker run -d --name consul -h consul-2 \
        -p 8300:8300 -p 8301:8301 -p 8301:8301/udp \
        -p 8302:8302/udp -p 8400:8400 -p 8500:8500 \
        -p 172.17.42.1:53:8600/udp \
        gliderlabs/consul agent -data-dir /data -server \
            -client 0.0.0.0 \
            -advertise $HOSTB -join $HOSTA
...
```

We can check that they've both been added to the cluster with the Consul CLI:

```
$ docker exec consul consul members
Node      Address            Status  Type   Build  Protocol  DC
```

```
consul-1  192.168.99.100:8301  alive   server  0.5.2  2         dc1
consul-2  192.168.99.101:8301  alive   server  0.5.2  2         dc1
```

We can see how the key-value store works by setting and getting some data:

```
$ curl -XPUT http://$HOSTA:8500/v1/kv/foo -d bar
true
$ curl http://$HOSTA:8500/v1/kv/foo | jq .
[
  {
    "Value": "YmFy",
    "Flags": 0,
    "Key": "foo",
    "LockIndex": 0,
    "ModifyIndex": 39,
    "CreateIndex": 16
  }
]
```

Hmm, we get something back, but what's this `"Value":"YmFy"`? It turns out that Consul base64 encodes data on the fly. We can get the original back by using the jq and base64 tools:[8]

```
$ curl -s http://$HOSTA:8500/v1/kv/foo | jq -r '.[].Value' | base64 -d
bar
```

A bit more work, but we're there.

There's a separate API for adding services to Consul, which ties into Consul's service discovery and health-checking functionality. Generally, the key-value store is just used for storing configuration details and small amounts of metadata.

Let's see how we can use Consul services to get identidock working across the hosts. We'll aim for the same structure as before, with Redis running on consul-2 and identidock and dnmonster running on consul-1. Start by bringing up Redis:

```
$ eval $(docker-machine env consul-2)
$ docker run -d -p 6379:6379 --name redis redis:3
...
2f79ea13628c446003ebe2ec4f20c550574c626b752b6ffa3b70770ad3e1ee6c
```

And now tell Consul about our Redis service via the *service/register* endpoint:

```
$ curl -XPUT http://$HOSTA:8500/v1/agent/service/register \
    -d '{"name": "redis", "address":"'$HOSTB'","port": 6379}'
$ docker run amouat/network-utils dig @172.17.42.1 +short redis.service.consul
...
192.168.99.101
```

---

8 We're using the GNU Linux version of base64 here. If you're running the MacOS version, use the argument -D instead of -d.

Next, we need to configure consul-1 to use Consul for DNS resolution. We'll take a different approach to the previous etcd example and configure the Docker daemon rather than the host */etc/resolv.conf* file. To do this, we need to edit the file */var/lib/boot2docker/profile* so it includes the --dns and --dns-search flags:

```
$ docker-machine ssh consul-1
...
docker@consul-1:~$ sudo vi /var/lib/boot2docker/profile
...
docker@consul-1:~$ cat /var/lib/boot2docker/profile

EXTRA_ARGS='
--label provider=virtualbox
--dns 172.17.42.1
--dns-search service.consul ❶
'
CACERT=/var/lib/boot2docker/ca.pem
DOCKER_HOST='-H tcp://0.0.0.0:2376'
DOCKER_STORAGE=aufs
DOCKER_TLS=auto
SERVERKEY=/var/lib/boot2docker/server-key.pem
SERVERCERT=/var/lib/boot2docker/server.pem
```

❶ This argument allows us to use short names like "redis" rather than the full name "redis.service.consul."

You'll then need to restart the Daemon and bring Consul back up. I found it easiest to restart the VM:

```
docker@consul-1:~$ exit
$ eval $(docker-machine env consul-1)
$ docker start consul
consul
```

A quick test:

```
$ docker run redis:3 redis-cli -h redis ping
PONG
```

Start up dnmonster on consul-1 and add the service:

```
$ docker run -d --name dnmonster amouat/dnmonster:1.0
...
41c8a78989803737f65460d75f8bed1a3683ee5a25c958382a1ca87f27034338
$ DNM_IP=$(docker inspect -f {{.NetworkSettings.IPAddress}} dnmonster)
$ curl -XPUT http://$HOSTA:8500/v1/agent/service/register \
    -d '{"name": "dnmonster", "address":"'$DNM_IP'","port": 8080}'
```

Finally, get identidock running:

```
$ docker run -d -p 80:9090 amouat/identidock:1.0
...
22cfd97bfba83dc31732886a4f0aec51e637b8c7834c9763e943e80225f990ec
```

```
$ curl $HOSTA
<html><head><title>...
```

And again, we have identidock working without links.

One of the most interesting features of Consul is the support for *health checking* to ensure the various parts of the system are alive and functioning. We can write tests for the host node itself (e.g., to check disk space or memory), or for particular services. The following code defines a simple HTTP test for the dnmonster service:

```
$ curl -XPUT http://$HOSTA:8500/v1/agent/service/register \
      -d '{"name": "dnmonster", "address":"'$DNM_IP'","port": 8080,
         "check": {"http": "http://'$DNM_IP':8080/monster/foo",
                  "interval": "10s"}
         }'
```

The check will ensure the container responds to an HTTP request on the given URL with a 2xx status code. Note that this check has to be run on consul-1 for the test to pass. We can can examine the status of the test by hitting the */health/checks/dnmonster/* endpoint:

```
$ curl -s $HOSTA:8500/v1/health/checks/dnmonster | jq '.[].Status'
"passing"
```

Tests can also be written using scripts, which will pass if the script returns 0, allowing for arbitrarily complex checks. By combining health checks with Consul's support for *watches* (which are used to monitor data for updates), it is relatively simple to implement failover solutions and/or automatically notify administrators of problems.

Other notable features include support for multiple datacenters and encryption of network traffic.

Registration

In the preceding examples, we have manually performed the final step of service discovery—*registration*; we had to write a curl request to register the Redis and dnmonster services with both SkyDNS and Consul. We could instead add logic to Redis or dnmonster container to do this automatically on start,[9] but it's also possible write a service that automatically registers containers when they start by monitoring Docker events.

This is the purpose of Registrator (*https://github.com/gliderlabs/registrator*) from GliderLabs. Registrator works alongside Consul, etcd, or SkyDNS to provide automatic registration of containers. It works by monitoring the Docker event stream for con-

---

9 If we don't want to, or can't, modify the service inside the container, this can be done with a wrapper script or "side-kick" process.

tainer creation and adds relevant entries to the underlying framework based on the container metadata.

DNS-Based Service Discovery Pros and Cons

Many of the solutions here provide a DNS interface for service discovery. In some cases, this is the primary, or only interface; in other cases, it is a convenience in addition to other APIs.

There are important reasons for favoring DNS for service discovery:

- DNS includes out-of-the-box support for legacy applications. This can be worked around when using other service discovery mechanisms by adding ambassador containers, but this requires extra effort from both development and operations.
- Developers don't need to do anything special or learn a new API. Applications using DNS will work without modification on a wide range of platforms.
- DNS is a well-known and trusted protocol with multiple implementations and wide support.

There are also several downsides to DNS-based discovery, which means you may want to consider other mechanisms in certain scenarios. We will discount the criticism that DNS is slow—in a service discovery scenario, we are talking about fast, local lookups as opposed to slow, remote ones. The remaining issues are:

- Normal DNS lookups do not return port information, so this either has to be assumed or looked up through another channel (DNS SRV records do return port information, but applications and frameworks almost invariably only use the hostname).
- Applications (and operating systems) may also cache DNS responses, leading to delays updating clients when a service moves.
- Most DNS services only provide limited support for health checking and load balancing. Typically load balancing is limited to round-robin or random selection, which will only satisfy a subset of users. Health checking can be built on top of TTL, but more sophisticated and in-depth checks typically require additional services.
- Clients are free to implement logic that selects between services based on attributes such as the versions of APIs available and capacity.

Other Solutions

There are several other choices for service discovery you may want to consider:

ZooKeeper (https://zookeeper.apache.org/)
A centralized, reliable, and readily available store, used for coordinating services in both Mesos and Hadoop. ZooKeeper is written in Java and is accessed via a Java API, although bindings are available for several languages. Clients are required to maintain active connections to ZooKeeper servers and perform keep-alives, which requires significant coding work (but note that libraries like Curator (*https://curator.apache.org*) exist to help with this).

The major advantage of ZooKeeper is that it is mature, stable, and battle-tested. If you already have infrastructure using ZooKeeper, it may well be a good choice. If not, the extra work of integrating and building on top of ZooKeeper is likely not worth it, especially if you're not using Java.

SmartStack (http://nerds.airbnb.com/smartstack-service-discovery-cloud/)
Airbnb's solution for service discovery. It is made up of two components: Nerve (*https://github.com/airbnb/nerve*), for health checking and registration, and Synapse (*https://github.com/airbnb/synapse*), for discovery.

Synapse runs on each host that consumes services and assigns each service to a port, which is proxied to the actual service. Synapse uses HAProxy (*http://www.haproxy.org/*) to do routing and will automatically update and restart HAProxy when changes occur. It can be configured to get the list of services to proxy from a store (such as ZooKeeper or etcd) or by watching the Docker event stream for container creation events (similar to Registrator).

Each service will have a corresponding Nerve process or container, which will check the health of the service and automatically register it with the store used by Synapse (e.g., ZooKeeper or etcd).

Eureka (https://github.com/Netflix/eureka/wiki)
Netflix's solution for load balancing and failover in AWS. Designed as a "middle-tier" solution to deal with the ephemerality of AWS nodes. If you are intending to run a large service on AWS infrastructure, this is definitely worth investigating.

WeaveDNS (http://docs.weave.works/weave/latest_release/weavedns.html)
WeaveDNS is the service discovery component of the Weave networking solution. Containers register their host or container name with WeaveDNS when they start, providing a fully automated solution. WeaveDNS runs as part of the Weave router on each host and communicates with other Weave routers in the network so that all container names can be resolved. WeaveDNS also provides a simple form of load balancing. See "Weave" for more information.

docker-discover (http://jasonwilder.com/blog/2014/07/15/docker-service-discovery/)
Essentially a Docker native implementation of SmartStack, using etcd as a back-end. Like SmartStack, it is made up of two components: docker-register (*https://github.com/jwilder/docker-register*), the Nerve equivalent for health checking and

registration, and docker-discover (*https://github.com/jwilder/docker-discover*), the Synapse equivalent for discovery. As with SmartStack, docker-discover uses HAProxy to handle routing. A very interesting project, but the lack of updates and supporting organization mean development and support is likely to be patchy.

Finally, it is important to note that the new networking features coming to Docker ("New Docker Networking") also provide a limited form of service discovery via the service object. This form of service discovery relies on working with either the Docker Overlay networking driver or another compatible plugin, such as Calico.

Networking Options

As we've seen, both ambassador containers and service discovery solutions can be used to connect service across hosts, where the underlying network allows. However, this requires exposing ports through the host, which requires manual management and doesn't scale well. A better solution is to provide IP connectivity between containers, which is the focus of the solutions described in this chapter.

However, before we start looking into full cross-host networking solutions, it's worth understanding how the default Docker networking works and what options are available. There are four basic modes available: *bridge*, *host*, *container*, and *none*.

Bridge

The default bridge network is great in development, providing a painless way to get containers talking to each other. In production, it's not so great; all the plumbing required behind the scenes has considerable overhead.

Figure 11-5 shows what the Docker bridge network looks like. There is a Docker bridge, normally called docker0 and running on 172.17.42.1, which is used to connect containers. When a container is started, Docker will instantiate a veth pair—essentially the software equivalent of an Ethernet cable—connecting eth0 in the container to the bridge. External connectivity is provided by IP forwarding and iptables rules that set up IP masquerading—a form of network address translation (NAT).

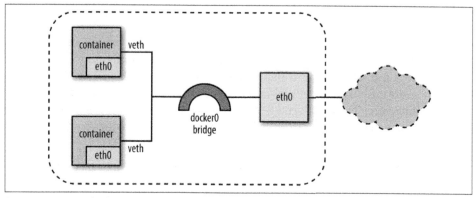

Figure 11-5. Default Docker bridge networking

By default, all containers can talk to each other, regardless of whether or not they are linked or if they export or publish ports (for an example of this, see "Limit Container Networking"). You can stop this by setting intercontainer communication off by passing the `--icc=false` flag when starting the Docker daemon, which will set an iptables rule. By setting `--icc=false` and `--iptables=true`, you can allow only *linked* containers to communicate, which is again done by adding iptables rules.

All of this works, and is very useful in development, but efficiency concerns mean that it may not be appropriate for production.

Host

A container running with `--net=host` shares the networking namespace of the host, fully exposing it to the public network. This means the container has to share the IP address of the host, but also cuts out all of the plumbing of the bridge network, meaning it is as fast as normal host networking.

As the IP address is shared, containers that need to talk to each other will have to co-ordinate over ports on the host, which will require some thought and probably changes to applications.

There are also security implications, as you may unintentionally expose ports to the outside world, which can be managed by a firewall layer.

The significantly improved efficiency means you may want to consider a hybrid networking model where externally facing and network-heavy containers such as proxies and caches use host networking, but the rest of your containers sit on the internal bridge network. Note that you can't use links to connect containers on the bridge network to containers on the host network, but containers on the bridge network can talk to containers on the host by using the IP address of the `docker0` bridge.

Container

Uses the networking namespace from another container. This can be very useful in certain situations (e.g., where you bring up a container preconfigured with the networking stack and tell all other containers to use that stack). This allows the creation and easy reuse of efficient network stacks specialized to a given scenario or datacenter architecture. The disadvantage is that all containers sharing a network stack will need to use the same IP address, which can make intercontainer communication difficult.

This can work well in certain situations and is notably used by Kubernetes (discussed in "Kubernetes").

None

Just as it sounds—turns off networking completely for a container. This can be useful for containers that don't need any network, such as a compiler container that writes its output to a volume.

The none networking mode can also be useful when you need to set up your own networking from scratch. If this is the case, you may find tools such as pipework (*https://github.com/jpetazzo/pipework*) to be very useful for working with networking inside cgroups and namespaces.

New Docker Networking

At the time of writing, the Docker networking stack and interface is going through a major overhaul. This will most likely be completed by the time this book goes to print and represents a large change in the way Docker networks are created and used (although the code in this book should continue to work unchanged). This section looks at these changes based on the work released in the experimental Docker channel. As this isn't finalized, there are likely to be minor differences between what is presented here and what ends up in the stable Docker release.

The immediate change is that Docker gets two new top-level "objects": *network* and *service*. This allows "networks"[10] to be created and managed separately from containers. When containers are launched, they can be assigned to a given network and will only be able to directly connect to other containers on the same network. Containers can publish *services* that allow them to be contacted via name, replacing the need for links (which can still be used, but will be less useful).

---

10 Arguably, using the term "network" is misleading. In many respects, a Docker network is really a namespace for containers that allows them to be grouped and segregated, plus communication channels.

This is best explained by a few examples.

The `network ls` subcommand will list the current networks and their IDs:

```
$ docker network ls
NETWORK ID          NAME                TYPE
d57af6043446        none                null
8fcc0afef384        host                host
30fa18d442b5        bridge              bridge
```

We can create a service with the `--publish-service` flag when starting a container. The following creates the db service on the bridge network:

```
$ docker run -d --name redis1 --publish-service db.bridge redis
9567dd9eb4fbd9f588a846819ec1ea9b71dc7b6cbd73ac7e90dc0d75a00b6f65
```

We can see the existing services with the `service ls` subcommand:

```
$ docker service ls
SERVICE ID          NAME                NETWORK             CONTAINER
f87430d2f240        db                  bridge              9567dd9eb4fb
```

Now we can create a new container on the same network and talk to the `redis1` container without the need for links by using the "db" service:

```
$ docker run -it redis redis-cli -h db ping
PONG
```

Containers belonging to different networks will be unable to communicate by default.

If we do use links, we can see it really just sets up services underneath the hood:

```
$ docker run -d --name redis2 redis
7fd526b2c7a6ad8a3faf4be9c1c23375dc5ae4cd17ff863a293c67df816a2b09
$ docker run --link redis2:redis2 redis redis-cli -h redis2 ping
PONG
$ docker service ls
SERVICE ID          NAME                NETWORK             CONTAINER
59b749c7fe0b        redis2              bridge              7fd526b2c7a6
f87430d2f240        db                  bridge              9567dd9eb4fb
```

Getting more interesting, we can reassign the containers that provide services using the `service attach` and `service detach` subcommands:

```
$ docker run redis redis-cli -h db set foo bar      ❶
OK
$ docker run redis redis-cli -h redis2 set foo baz  ❷
OK
$ docker run redis redis-cli -h db get foo
bar
$ docker service detach redis1 db
$ docker service attach redis2 db
$ docker run redis redis-cli -h db get foo          ❸
baz
```

❶ Adds some data to `redis1`, currently exposed by the `db` service.

❷ Adds some data to `redis2`.

❸ Now `redis2` is exposed by the `db` service.

So we can see the new model offers a lot more flexibility and oversight when wiring up containers and maintaining systems, while still supporting the previous networking paradigm.

Network Types and Plugins

You probably noticed that networks have different *types*.[11] There is a type for each of the "classic" networking options—host, none, and bridge, which we covered earlier—but there is also the *overlay* type and the ability to add new types in the form of *networking plugins*. The default network can be set on the Docker daemon. If a default network is not set, the bridge network is used.

Plugins

Docker plugins, including network drivers,[12] can be added to Docker by installing them under the */usr/share/docker/plugins* directory. This is commonly achieved by running a container that mounts this directory.

Plugins can be written in any language, as long as they can interface with Docker's JSON-RPC API (*http://www.jsonrpc.org/*).

We'll see an example of using the Project Calico network plugin in "Project Calico". I expect to see a wide range of plugins to appear, tailored to different scenarios and using different underlying technologies, including IPVLAN (*https://github.com/torvalds/linux/blob/master/Documentation/networking/ipvlan.txt*) and Open vSwitch (*http://openvswitch.org/*)).

Networking Solutions

The following section takes a look at the various solutions that can be put in place for cross-host networking clusters of containers. We'll look at *Overlay*, the Docker "batteries included" solution that will ship with the new networking stack; *Weave*, a

---

11 Also referred to as network *drivers*.

12 New *volume* drivers can also be loaded via a plugin such as Flocker (*https://github.com/ClusterHQ/flocker-docker-plugin*). At the time of writing, there is work on creating a top-level volume object, but this is still some time away from fruition.

---

feature-rich solution designed for ease of use; *Flannel*, the CoreOS solution; and *Project Calico*, Metaswitch's layer 3–based solution.

> Docker networking is a very nascent and fluid sector. On top of this, it is a very rich space, with the potential to support many different solutions tailored to various scenarios. While the tools presented here are the state of the art at the time of writing, the sector is changing rapidly—by the time this book is in print, there will be changes to the way these solutions work, and new solutions will be available. You should do your own research before settling on any solution outlined here.

Overlay

Overlay is the "batteries included" Docker implementation for cross-host networking. It uses VXLAN tunnels to connect hosts with their own IP space and NAT for external connectivity. The serf library (*https://serfdom.io/*) is used for communication between peers.

Linking containers into the network is handled in much the same way as the standard bridge network; a Linux bridge is set up for the Overlay network, and a veth pair is used to connect to the container.

> ### Experimental Warning!
>
> The VMs used in this example are running the experimental build of Docker, which means *there will differences from your version*. By the time you read this book, the stable release of Docker will support networking plugins, which you should use instead.
>
> This example uses the following versions of Docker and Consul:
>
> ```
> docker@overlay-1:~$ docker --version
> Docker version 1.8.0-dev, build 5fdc102, experimental
> docker@overlay-1:~$ docker run gliderlabs/consul version
> Consul v0.5.2
> Consul Protocol: 2 (Understands back to: 1)
> ```

As an example, I have provisioned two hosts overlay-1 and overlay-2 with the experimental branch of Docker and Consul as a key-value store. We'll set up identidock in the same manner as before, with Redis running on overlay-2 and both the dnmonster and identidock containers running on overlay-1.

By the time this book is released, you should be able to do something very similar with the stable branch. I've directly ssh'd into the VMs here to make sure the same version of the Docker client and daemon is used.

Start by sshing into overlay-2:

```
$ docker-machine ssh overlay-2
...
```

First, we'll create a new network called "ovn" using the overlay driver:

```
docker@overlay-2:~$ docker network create -d overlay ovn
5d2709e8fd689cb4dee6acf7a1346fb563924909b4568831892dcc67e9359de6
docker@overlay-2:~$ docker network ls
NETWORK ID          NAME                TYPE
f7ae80f9aa44        none                null
1d4c071e42b1        host                host
27c18499f9e5        bridge              bridge
5d2709e8fd68        ovn                 overlay
```

We can get more details on the network from the network info subcommand:

```
docker@overlay-2:~$ docker network info ovn
Network Id: 5d2709e8fd689cb4dee6acf7a1346fb563924909b4568831892dcc67e9359de6
Name: ovn
Type: overlay
```

Now it's time to start up Redis, using the --publish-service redis.ovn argument to expose the container as a service on the "ovn" network with the name "redis":

```
docker@overlay-2:~$ docker run -d --name redis-ov2 \
                        --publish-service redis.ovn redis:3
...
29a02f672a359c5a9174713418df50c72e348b2814e88d537bd2ab877150a4a5
```

If we now exit overlay-2 and ssh to overlay-1, we can see that it has access to the same network:

```
docker@overlay-2:~$ exit
$ docker-machine ssh overlay-1
docker@overlay-1:~$ docker network ls
NETWORK ID          NAME                TYPE
7f9a4f144131        none                null
528f9267a171        host                host
dfec33441302        bridge              bridge
5d2709e8fd68        ovn                 overlay
```

Start the dnmonster and identidock containers in the same way, using --publish-service to connect to the ovn network:

```
docker@overlay-1:~$ docker run -d --name dnmonster-ov1 \
                        --publish-service dnmonster.ovn amouat/dnmonster:1.0
...
37e7406613f3cbef0ca83320cf3d99aa4078a9b24b092f1270352ff0e1bf8f92
docker@overlay-1:~$ docker run -d --name identidock-ov1 \
                        --publish-service identidock.ovn amouat/identidock:1.0
...
41f328a59ff3644718b8ce4f171b3a246c188cf80a6d0aa96b397500be33da5e
```

And finally check that it all works:

```
docker@overlay-1:~$ docker exec identidock-ov1 curl -s localhost:9090
<html><head><title>Hello...
```

Very simply and very quickly we got identidock running across two hosts. As implementation details and usage is likely to change, we won't go deep into details of how the Overlay driver works.

Weave

Weave (*http://weave.works/*) is a developer-friendly networking solution designed to work across a wide range of environments with minimal work. Weave is perhaps the most complete solution available, as it includes WeaveDNS for service discovery and load balancing, has built-in *IP address management* (IPAM), and support for encrypting communications.

Let's see how easy it is to get identidock running with Weave across two hosts. We'll stick with the architecture we used in the ambassador and service discovery examples where Redis runs on one host (`weave-redis` in this case) and the identidock and dnmonster containers on the other host (`weave-identidock`). Again, we'll use Docker machine to provide us with VMs. I used Weave version 1.1.0 for this example; you can expect to see minor differences when running newer versions.

We'll start by building `weave-redis`:

```
$ docker-machine create -d virtualbox weave-redis
...
```

Now `ssh` in and install Weave:

```
$ docker-machine ssh weave-redis
...
docker@weave-redis:~$ sudo curl -sL git.io/weave -o /usr/local/bin/weave
docker@weave-redis:~$ sudo chmod a+x /usr/local/bin/weave
docker@weave-redis:~$ weave launch
Setting docker0 MAC (mitigate https://github.com/docker/docker/issues/14908)
Unable to find image 'weaveworks/weaveexec:v1.1.0' locally
v1.1.0: Pulling from weaveworks/weaveexec
...
Digest: sha256:8b5e1b692b7c2cb9bff6f9ce87360eee88540fe32d0154b27584bc45acbbef0a
Status: Downloaded newer image for weaveworks/weaveexec:v1.1.0
Unable to find image 'weaveworks/weave:v1.1.0' locally
v1.1.0: Pulling from weaveworks/weave
Digest: sha256:c34b8ee7b72631e4b7ddca3e1157b67dd866cae40418c279f427589dc944fac0
Status: Downloaded newer image for weaveworks/weave:v1.1.0
```

The preceding commands have downloaded Weave, then pulled and started the containers providing the Weave infrastructure. We'll go into more details about what each of these containers does later.

The next step is to point our Docker client at the Weave proxy rather than the Docker daemon. This gives Weave a chance to set up various networking hooks whenever a container is started:

```
docker@weave-redis:~$ eval $(weave env)
```

And now we can launch our Redis container, and it will be automatically connected to the Weave network:

```
docker@weave-redis:~$ docker run --name redis -d redis:3
Unable to find image 'redis:3' locally
3: Pulling from redis
...
3c97d635be5107f5a79cafe3cfaf1960fa3d14eec3ed5fa80e2045249601583f
docker@weave-redis:~$ exit
```

Now for the identidock and dnmonster host. This time we'll just run ssh commands from docker-machine rather than logging in, as it makes configuration a little easier. Start by creating the weave-identidock VM and installing Weave:

```
$ docker-machine create -d virtualbox weave-identidock
...
$ docker-machine ssh weave-identidock \
    "sudo curl -sL https://git.io/weave -o /usr/local/bin/weave && \
    sudo chmod a+x /usr/local/bin/weave"
```

This time when we run weave launch, we need to pass the IP of the weave-redis host:

```
$ docker-machine ssh weave-identidock \
        "weave launch $(docker-machine ip weave-redis)"
Unable to find image 'weaveworks/weaveexec:v1.1.0' locally
v1.1.0: Pulling from weaveworks/weaveexec
...
Digest: sha256:8b5e1b692b7c2cb9bff6f9ce87360eee88540fe32d0154b27584bc45acbbef0a
Status: Downloaded newer image for weaveworks/weaveexec:v1.1.0
Unable to find image 'weaveworks/weave:v1.1.0' locally
v1.1.0: Pulling from weaveworks/weave
Digest: sha256:c34b8ee7b72631e4b7ddca3e1157b67dd866cae40418c279f427589dc944fac0
Status: Downloaded newer image for weaveworks/weave:v1.1.0
```

Now it's time to check the networking. We'll ssh into weave-identidock and see if we can access the Redis container running on weave-redis. Again, note that we need to set up the Weave proxy:

```
$ docker-machine ssh weave-identidock
...
docker@weave-identidock:~$ eval $(weave env)
```

```
docker@weave-identidock:~$ docker run redis:3 redis-cli -h redis ping
...
PONG
```

Success! To finish the example, let's start up the dnmonster and identidock containers
and make sure the application works:

```
docker@weave-identidock:~$ docker run --name dnmonster -d amouat/dnmonster:1.0
...
1bc9cdd5c3dd532d4f6a56529be8e2a068a9402c1e07df69ec33971f5c4b89b9
docker@weave-identidock:~$ docker run --name identidock -d -p 80:9090 \
    amouat/identidock:1.0
...
9b5e9c89a7807bcad2cff49dc0692d0e8d064494288df5405a6573d886c0208d
docker@weave-identidock:~$ exit
$ curl $(docker-machine ip weave-identidock)
<html><head>...
$ curl -s $(docker-machine ip weave-identidock)/monster/gordon | head -c 4
◆PNG
```

Great, we've got cross-host networking working with DNS resolution of container
names and not a link in sight.

To understand how this works, it's worth looking at the containers Weave has started
to manage its infrastructure:

```
$ docker ps
CONTAINER ID ... PORTS                                      NAMES
0b7693194bb9                                                weaveproxy
b6e515f4d02b    172.17.42.1:53->53/udp, 0.0.0.0:6783->6783/t... weave
```

These containers and the identidock containers are shown in Figure 11-6.

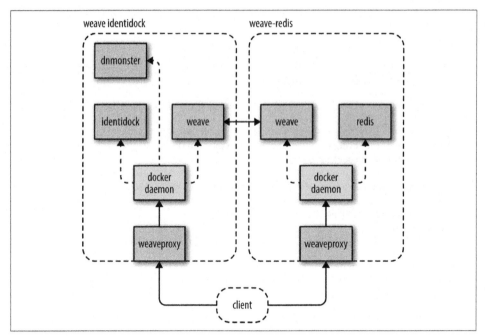

Figure 11-6. Identidock running on Weave

Both hosts are running the same Weave images, which were started by the `weave launch` commands earlier. These containers take care of the various parts of the weave infrastructure:

weave

This container holds the Weave router, which is responsible for handling networking routes and talking to the other hosts on the weave network. Weave routers talk to each other via TCP to establish communication and share information on the network topology. Network traffic is sent via UDP connections set up separately. Weave routers learn the network topology over time, allowing them to route efficiently and deal with changing networks without full connectivity. The router also handles DNS, which allows developers to refer to containers by name across hosts.

weaveproxy

This container is responsible for the magic that allows us to run normal `docker run` commands but have them attached to the Weave network. The container intercepts `docker run` requests to the Docker daemon to allow Weave a chance to set up networking and modify the run request so the container uses the Weave networking stack. Once this is done, the modified request is forwarded onto the Docker daemon. This interception technique is enabled by the `eval $(weave` `proxy-env`) line that sets the `DOCKER_HOST` environment variable to point to the weave proxy rather than the actual Docker daemon.

Weave creates a weave bridge, which you can see by running `ifconfig`. Each container including the weave router is connected to the bridge via a veth pair.

Weave includes the ability to put containers on separate subnets so that applications can be segregated from each other and support for encryption so that Weave networks can span untrusted links.

For full information on the Weave architecture and features, see the official documentation (*http://docs.weave.works/weave/latest_release/index.html*).

The focus of Weave is on building a great developer experience, where containers can be networked and discovered across hosts with a minimum of fuss.

Running Weave as a Plugin

Weave can also be run using the Docker plugin framework, which effectively replaces the proxy container.

At the time of writing, there are several limitations to this method that make the instructions here preferable, mainly relating to ongoing work in the networking plugin API to provide Weave and other networking plugins with all the information and hooks that are needed. For example, there is currently an issue with Weave losing configuration information if the cluster is restarted.

These issues may well have been resolved by the time you read this.

Flannel

Flannel (*https://github.com/coreos/flannel*) is the cross-host networking solution from CoreOS. It's primarily used with CoreOS-based clusters, but there's no reason why it can't be used with other stacks.

Flannel will assign a subnet to each host, which is then used to assign IPs to containers. Flannel works well with Kubernetes (see "Kubernetes"), where it can be used to assign a unique and routable IP to each pod. Flannel runs a daemon on each host that retrieves its configuration from etcd (see "etcd"); for this reason, the cluster must have already been configured to use etcd. A variety of backends are available including:

udp
    The default backend that forms an overlay network where layer 2 networking information is encapsulated in UDP packets sent over the existing network.

vxlan

Uses VXLAN to encapsulate network packets. As this is done inside the kernel, this is potentially much faster than UDP, which has to go through user space.

aws-vpc

For setting up networks on Amazon EC2.

host-gw

Sets up IP routes to subnets using remote IP addresses. Requires that hosts have direct layer 2 connectivity with each other.

gce

For setting up networks on Google Compute engine.

We'll use Docker Machine again to get started with Flannel, but this time, things are a bit more complicated—the Flannel daemon needs to configure the flannel0 network bridge before the Docker engine starts up, which makes it tricky to run Flannel as a container. We could do some funky bootstrapping involving running Flannel with a secondary Docker daemon, but it's easier to just run flannel as a process on the host. In addition, Flannel has a dependency on etcd, which we will also run as a native process.

Admittedly, Docker machine–provisioned VMs aren't really a good fit for this use case due to the extra configuration we have to do, which includes undoing various bits of machine config. However, it is an enlightening exercise that should help you get started with Flannel on your own network infrastructure.

Flannel and etcd Version

These examples use version 2.0.13 of etcd and 0.5.1 of Flannel. As Flannel is in heavy development, you can expect to find some differences if you use a newer version.

In this example, we will set up two hosts, flannel-1 and flannel-2, and check that the containers on each hosts can connect. We'll start by provisioning two VirtualBox VMs to act as our hosts:

```
$ docker-machine create -d virtualbox flannel-1
...
$ docker-machine create -d virtualbox flannel-2
...
$ docker-machine ip flannel-1 flannel-2
192.168.99.102
192.168.99.103
```

Note the IP addresses of each machine. You'll need these to set up etcd, which we'll now install on flannel-1. But first we need to stop the Docker daemon and delete the docker0 bridge:

```
$ docker-machine ssh flannel-1
...
docker@flannel-1:~$ sudo /usr/local/etc/init.d/docker stop
docker@flannel-1:~$ sudo ip link delete docker0
```

Now download and extract etcd:

```
docker@flannel-1:~$ curl -sL https://github.com/coreos/etcd/releases/download/\
v2.0.13/etcd-v2.0.13-linux-amd64.tar.gz -o etcd.tar.gz
docker@flannel-1:~$ tar xzvf etcd.tar.gz
```

Time to launch etcd. Using a couple of environment variables makes this easier to read:

```
docker@flannel-1:~$ HOSTA=192.168.99.102
docker@flannel-1:~$ HOSTB=192.168.99.103
docker@flannel-1:~$ nohup etcd-v2.0.13-linux-amd64/etcd \
  -name etcd-1 -initial-advertise-peer-urls http://$HOSTA:2380 \
  -listen-peer-urls http://$HOSTA:2380 \
  -listen-client-urls http://$HOSTA:2379,http://127.0.0.1:2379 \
  -advertise-client-urls http://$HOSTA:2379 \
  -initial-cluster-token etcd-cluster-1 \
  -initial-cluster \
etcd-1=http://$HOSTA:2380,etcd-2=http://$HOSTB:2380 \
  -initial-cluster-state new &
```

The nohup utility is used so that etcd remains running after we log out of the host. It will log output to the file *nohup.out*.

So now we have etcd set up on flannel-1. We'll come back and finish installing Flannel after we've got things running on flannel-2:

```
docker@flannel-1:~$ exit
$ docker-machine ssh flannel-2
docker@flannel-2:~$ sudo /usr/local/etc/init.d/docker stop
docker@flannel-2:~$ sudo ip link delete docker0
docker@flannel-2:~$ curl -sL https://github.com/coreos/etcd/releases/\
download/v2.0.13/etcd-v2.0.13-linux-amd64.tar.gz -o etcd.tar.gz
docker@flannel-2:~$ tar xzvf etcd.tar.gz
```

Starting etcd is the same as before, except the IPs are reversed:

```
docker@flannel-2:~$ HOSTA=192.168.99.102
docker@flannel-2:~$ HOSTB=192.168.99.103
docker@flannel-2:~$ nohup etcd-v2.0.13-linux-amd64/etcd \
  -name etcd-2 -initial-advertise-peer-urls http://$HOSTB:2380 \
  -listen-peer-urls http://$HOSTB:2380 \
  -listen-client-urls http://$HOSTB:2379,http://127.0.0.1:2379 \
  -advertise-client-urls http://$HOSTB:2379 \
  -initial-cluster-token etcd-cluster-1 \
```

```
    -initial-cluster \
etcd-1=http://$HOSTA:2380,etcd-2=http://$HOSTB:2380 \
    -initial-cluster-state new &
```

Now it's time to download Flannel:

```
docker@flannel-2:~$ curl -sL https://github.com/coreos/flannel/releases/\
download/v0.5.1/flannel-0.5.1-linux-amd64.tar.gz -o flannel.tar.gz
docker@flannel-2:~$ tar xzvf flannel.tar.gz
```

Next, we need to set some configuration in etcd to tell Flannel which IP range it can use:

```
docker@flannel-2:~$ ./etcd-v2.0.13-linux-amd64/etcdctl
                set /coreos.com/network/config '{ "Network": "10.1.0.0/16" }'
```

And now we can start up the Flannel daemon. Note that we need to tell Flannel to use the interface eth1, which allows communication with the other VM:

```
docker@flannel-2:~$ nohup sudo ./flannel-0.5.1/flanneld -iface=eth1 &
```

Flannel is now running, and if you run ifconfig, you should see the Flannel bridge:

```
docker@flannel-2:~$ ifconfig flannel0
flannel0  Link encap:UNSPEC  HWaddr 00-00-00-00-00-00-00-00-00-00-00-00-00-00-...
          inet addr:10.1.37.0  P-t-P:10.1.37.0  Mask:255.255.0.0
          UP POINTOPOINT RUNNING NOARP MULTICAST  MTU:1472  Metric:1
          RX packets:4 errors:0 dropped:0 overruns:0 frame:0
          TX packets:4 errors:0 dropped:0 overruns:0 carrier:0
          collisions:0 txqueuelen:500
          RX bytes:216 (216.0 B)  TX bytes:221 (221.0 B)
```

Note that it has been given an address within the range specified in the Flannel configuration.

The next thing to do is to configure Docker to use Flannel. If we're using a different VM image or bare metal, we could use the *mk-docker-opts.sh* script distributed with Flannel to automatically configure the Docker engine. However, our VirtualBox image doesn't include bash, so we'll just do it by hand instead. First, take a look at the file */run/flannel/subnet.env* Flannel has created for us:

```
docker@flannel-2:~$ cat /run/flannel/subnet.env
FLANNEL_SUBNET=10.1.79.1/24
FLANNEL_MTU=1472
FLANNEL_IPMASQ=false
```

We need to set the Docker daemon flag --bip to the value of the FLANNEL_SUBNET and --mtu to the value of FLANNEL_MTU, which will tell Docker to use an IP and MTU[13] compatible with Flannel. Docker daemon flags are configured in the

---

13 *MTU* is the *maximum transmission unit*, which controls how big data packets can get in the network.

file */var/lib/boot2docker/profile*. After updating the file (which can be done with sudo vi in the VM), it should look something like:

```
docker@flannel-2:~$ cat /var/lib/boot2docker/profile

EXTRA_ARGS='
--label provider=virtualbox
--bip 10.1.79.1/24
--mtu 1472
'
CACERT=/var/lib/boot2docker/ca.pem
DOCKER_HOST='-H tcp://0.0.0.0:2376'
DOCKER_STORAGE=aufs
DOCKER_TLS=auto
SERVERKEY=/var/lib/boot2docker/server-key.pem
SERVERCERT=/var/lib/boot2docker/server.pem
```

We can now restart the Docker engine:

```
docker@flannel-2:~$ sudo /etc/init.d/docker start
hostname: flannel-2: Unknown host
Need TLS certs for flannel-2,,10.0.2.15,192.168.99.103
docker@flannel-2:~$ exit
```

Finally, we need to repeat these steps on flannel-1:

```
$ docker-machine ssh flannel-1
...
docker@flannel-1:~$ curl -sL https://github.com/coreos/flannel/releases/\
download/v0.5.1/flannel-0.5.1-linux-amd64.tar.gz -o flannel.tar.gz
v0.5.1/flannel-0.5.1-linux-amd64.tar.gz -o flannel.tar.gz
docker@flannel-1:~$ tar xzvf flannel.tar.gz
...
docker@flannel-1:~$ nohup sudo ./flannel-0.5.1/flanneld -iface=eth1 &
docker@flannel-1:~$ cat /run/flannel/subnet.env
FLANNEL_SUBNET=10.1.83.1/24 ❶
FLANNEL_MTU=1472
FLANNEL_IPMASQ=false
docker@flannel-1:~$ sudo vi /var/lib/boot2docker/profile
...
docker@flannel-1:~$ sudo /etc/init.d/docker start
hostname: flannel-1: Unknown host
Need TLS certs for flannel-1,,10.0.2.15,192.168.99.102
docker@flannel-1:~$ exit
```

❶ Note that this value should be different than flannel-2 so that both hosts allocate container IPs from different ranges.

Now everything should be working, so let's make sure our containers can communicate. On flannel-1, we'll start up the Netcat utility to listen for connections on a given port:

```
$ eval $(docker-machine env flannel-1)
$ docker run --name nc-test -d amouat/network-utils nc -l 5001
...
```

 Network Tools Container

In order to test various networky things when stuff goes wrong, it's handy to have an image with some network tools installed. I've set up an image called amouat/network-utils that can be used for this purpose. Inside you'll find stuff like curl, Netcat, traceroute, and dnsutils, as well as jq for pretty printing JSON output from REST APIs.

Example usage:

```
$ docker run -it amouat/network-utils
root@7e80c9731ea0:/# curl -s https://api.github.com\
/repos/amouat/network-utils-container\
    | jq '. .description'
"Docker container with some network utilities"
```

Now find the IP address Flannel has assigned to the container:

```
$ IP=$(docker inspect -f {{.NetworkSettings.IPAddress}} nc-test)
$ echo $IP
10.1.83.2
```

Note that this is within the range we requested earlier. Now let's start up Netcat on flannel-2 and test connecting to the nc-test container:

```
$ eval $(docker-machine env flannel-2)
$ docker run -e IP=$IP \
    amouat/network-utils sh -c 'echo -n "hello" | nc -v $IP 5001'
Unable to find image 'amouat/network-utils:latest' locally
...
Status: Downloaded newer image for amouat/network-utils:latest
Connection to 10.1.83.2 5001 port [tcp/*] succeeded!
```

And if we look in the logs for the nc-test container, we can see the message we sent:

```
$ eval $(docker-machine env flannel-1)
$ docker logs nc-test
hello
```

And there you go: two containers talking across hosts using their own IPs. It may have felt like a lot of work to get there, but remember this is something that will hopefully be automated for new hosts joining the cluster, and users of CoreOS stacks can expect it to work out of the box.

But we still can't get identidock running though. Although we have cross-host networking, we don't have service discovery, which requires one of the previously discussed solutions, such as SkyDNS or rewriting identidock to use etcd.

Project Calico

Project Calico (henceforth, simply Calico) takes a slightly different approach to networking. This is most easily described in terms of the OSI model (*https://en.wikipe dia.org/wiki/OSI_model*), which divides networking into seven conceptual layers. Most other networking solutions, such as Weave and Flannel (when using the UDP backend), build an overlay network by encapsulating layer 2 traffic into a higher layer.[14] Calico instead uses standard IP routing and networking tools to provide a layer 3 solution.[15]

The major advantages of a pure layer 3 solution are in simplicity and efficiency. Calico's primary operating mode requires no encapsulation and is designed for datacenters where the organization has control over the physical network fabric. Routing within a Calico network is established using the Border Gateway Protocol or BGP—a venerable protocol that underpins much of the wider Internet—to connect routers within, and at the edges of, the datacenter network. This approach allows Calico to work on top of a wide variety of layer 2 and layer 3 physical topologies. There is no requirement to use NAT for external connectivity in Calico; containers can be connected directly to public IPs where security policy and IP availability allows.

The disadvantage of Calico is that its primary mode doesn't work in public clouds, where users don't have control over the network fabric. Calico can still be used in public clouds, but normally requires the use of IP-in-IP tunneling to provide connectivity.

Also notable is Calico's security model, which allows fine-grained control over which containers can talk to each other.

---

14 Layer 2 is the "Data Link Layer" in the OSI model, which is where MAC addresses come in.

15 Layer 3 is the "Network Layer" in the OSI model, which is where IPv4 and IPv6 come in.

Experimental Warning!

The VMs I'm using in this example are using the experimental build of Docker, which means *there will be differences in your version*. By the time you read this book, the stable release of Docker will support networking plugins, which you should use instead.

For the sake of completeness, I ran the following example using Digital Ocean VMs provisioned with the following commands:

```
$ docker-machine create -d digitalocean \
      --digitalocean-access-token=<token> \
      --digitalocean-private-networking \
      --engine-install-url \
       "https://experimental.docker.com" calico-1
...
$ docker-machine create -d digitalocean \
      --digitalocean-access-token=<token> \
      --digitalocean-private-networking \
      --engine-install-url \
       "https://experimental.docker.com" calico-2
...
$ docker-machine ssh calico-1
root@calico-1:~# docker -v
Docker version 1.8.0-dev, build 3ee15ac, experimental
```

I also manually installed Consul on one of the boxes that was required for the Docker daemons to share network configuration details.

Various things *will* have changed by the time you read this, and you can expect to need to make minor changes to the example. Don't try to use the same versions of Calico and Docker as me—instead, install the latest supported and stable versions of both.

The following assumes we have two Docker Machine provisioned VMs set up, called calico-1 and calico-2, which can communicate with each other on the addresses <calico-1 ipv4> and <calico-2 ipv4> (these addresses may be internal and not accessible from the Internet). In this case, I am using the Digital Ocean cloud, but other clouds should be very similar.

The first thing we need to do is to set up etcd on each host, which is used by Calico to share information about the network between hosts:

```
$ HOSTA=<calico-1 ipv4>
$ HOSTB=<calico-2 ipv4>
$ eval $(docker-machine env calico-1)
$ docker run -d -p 2379:2379 -p 2380:2380 -p 4001:4001 \
  --name etcd quay.io/coreos/etcd \
  -name etcd-1 -initial-advertise-peer-urls http://${HOSTA}:2380 \
  -listen-peer-urls http://0.0.0.0:2380 \
  -listen-client-urls http://0.0.0.0:2379,http://0.0.0.0:4001 \
```

```
  -advertise-client-urls http://${HOSTA}:2379 \
  -initial-cluster-token etcd-cluster-1 \
  -initial-cluster \
etcd-1=http://${HOSTA}:2380,etcd-2=http://${HOSTB}:2380 \
  -initial-cluster-state new
...
b9a6b79e42a1d24837090de4805bea86571b75a9375b3cf2100115e49845e6f3
$ eval $(docker-machine env calico-2)
$ docker run -d -p 2379:2379 -p 2380:2380 -p 4001:4001 \
  --name etcd quay.io/coreos/etcd \
  -name etcd-2 -initial-advertise-peer-urls http://${HOSTB}:2380 \
  -listen-peer-urls http://0.0.0.0:2380 \
  -listen-client-urls http://0.0.0.0:2379,http://0.0.0.0:4001 \
  -advertise-client-urls http://${HOSTB}:2379 \
  -initial-cluster-token etcd-cluster-1 \
  -initial-cluster \
etcd-1=http://${HOSTA}:2380,etcd-2=http://${HOSTB}:2380 \
  -initial-cluster-state new
...
2aa2d8fee10aec4284b9b85a579d96ae92ba0f1e210fb36da2249f31e556a65e
```

Now that we have etcd running, let's install Calico. This will be somewhat out-of-date by the time you read this, but the rough steps should still be similar. Start by downloading Calico:

```
$ docker-machine ssh calico-1
...
root@calico-1:~# curl -sSL -o calicoctl \
  https://github.com/Metaswitch/calico-docker/releases/download/v0.5.2/calicoctl
root@calico-1:~# chmod +x calicoctl
```

Load the xt_set kernel module, which is needed for some IP tables features used by Calico:

```
root@calico-1:~# modprobe xt_set
```

We need to tell Calico what address range it can assign IPs from. This is done using the pool add subcommand:

```
root@calico-1:~# sudo ./calicoctl pool add 192.168.0.0/16 --ipip --nat-outgoing
```

The --ipip flag tells calico to set up an IP-in-IP tunnel between hosts, which is only needed if the hosts don't have direct layer 2 connectivity. This command only needs to be run on one host.

Next, we start up the Calico services, including the Docker network plugin, which runs as a container:

```
root@calico-1:~# sudo ./calicoctl node --ip=<calico-1 ipv4>
WARNING: ipv6 forwarding is not enabled.
Pulling Docker image calico/node:v0.5.1
Calico node is running with id: d72f2eb6f10ea24a76d606e3ee75bf...
```

Now set up the other host in the same way:

```
$ docker-machine ssh calico-2
...
root@calico-2:~# curl -sSL -o calicoctl \
  https://github.com/Metaswitch/calico-docker\
/releases/download/v0.5.2/calicoctl
root@calico-2:~# chmod +x calicoctl
root@calico-2:~# modprobe xt_set
root@calico-2:~# sudo ./calicoctl node --ip=<calico-2 ipv4>
WARNING: ipv6 forwarding is not enabled.
Pulling Docker image calico/node:v0.5.1
Calico node is running with id: b880fac45feb7ebf3393ad4ce63011a2...
root@calico-2:~#
```

And now we can get identidock running once more. Start by launching Redis on calico-2 using the --publish-service redis.anet.calico argument, which will create a new Calico network called "anet" and the "redis" service:

```
root@calico-2:~# docker run --name redis -d \
       --publish-service redis.anet.calico redis:3
....
6f0db3fe01508c0d2fc85365db8d3dcdf93edcdaae1bcb146d34ab1a3f87b22f
```

If we now log in to calico-1, we can connect to the same network and reach the Redis container:

```
root@calico-2:~# exit
$ docker-machine ssh calico-1
root@calico-1:~# docker run --name redis-client \
       --publish-service redis-client.anet.calico \
       redis:3 redis-cli -h redis ping
...
PONG
```

Now let's start up the dnmonster and identidock containers on the same network:

```
root@calico-1:~# docker run --name dnmonster \
       --publish-service dnmonster.anet.calico -d amouat/dnmonster:1.0
...
fba8f7885a2e1700bc0e263cc10b7d812e926ca7447e98d9477a08b253cafe0
root@calico-1:~# docker run --name identidock \
       --publish-service identidock.anet.calico -d amouat/identidock:1.0
...
589f6b6b17266e59876dfc34e15850b29f555250a05909a95ed5ea73c4ee7115
```

Time to make sure things are working:

```
root@calico-1:~# docker exec identidock curl -s localhost:9090
<html><head><title>Hello...
```

Great, we now have identidock up and running with Calico. We've accessed identidock from the container, as we need the client to be on the Calico network. Of course, it is possible to expose the application to other networks, such as the public Internet, but it requires a little more work and is likely to change, so we won't cover it here.

Behind the scenes, there's a few pieces in place that make this work:

etcd
Stores and distributes information on hosts and containers.

BIRD
The BIRD Internet Routing Daemon (or BIRD)[16] uses BGP to route IP traffic between hosts and containers.

Felix
The Calico agent that runs on each compute host to configure local network policy, using data in etcd.

The Calico plugin
Responsible for setting up network connections when a Docker container is created and recording it in etcd.

The current focus of Calico is providing efficient, and comparatively simple, networking for VMs and containers in situations where the organization controls the networking fabric, such as private clouds used by large companies. At the same time, the Calico plugin looks set to provide a comparatively efficient and simple solution for networking containers running on the same public cloud.

Conclusion

Service discovery is often an essential feature in modern distributed and dynamic systems. Containers and services are constantly in flux, being stopped, started, and moved in response to demand or failures. Under such circumstances, solutions that require manual work to reroute connections simply won't work.

Most of the service discovery solutions we've seen support DNS-based lookups, where clients can simply address services by name and the system takes care of routing to the appropriate instance. This is excellent in terms of simplicity at the client end and for supporting existing applications and tools, but DNS can become a hindrance in highly dynamic systems. DNS responses are often cached, resulting in delays and errors when a service moves host. Load balancing is typically round-robin at best, which is rarely ideal. In addition, clients may want to include their own logic for selecting between potential services, which becomes much simpler with richer APIs.

---

16 As far as I can tell, the *B* doesn't stand for anything except BIRD itself, in a recursive and annoying fashion.

Which service discovery tool you need to use is very use-case specific. Most projects already use a relevant tool due to software requirements or existing platform tooling (e.g., Mesos uses ZooKeeper, and GKE uses etcd). In such cases, it makes sense to use what is already there rather than bringing another tool into the mix. Choosing between etcd (or etcd plus SkyDNS) and Consul is much more difficult. Both are relatively new projects (etcd is slightly older), but are based on sound underlying algorithms. Consul includes DNS support and some advanced features by default, which will often swing the balance. etcd is arguably less "opinionated" than Consul and has a more advanced key-value store, which may make it a better choice in scenarios requiring a lot of customization. The DNS support of Consul and SkyDNS may not be relevant if you use APIs to discover services or are already including a networking solution that provides name resolution.

Choosing a networking solution is an even more difficult task, mainly due to the immaturity of the space. We will eventually see more solutions become available (especially in the form of networking plugins) and clearer differentiation between them. So far, I haven't undertaken any performance or scalability testing of the solutions, as I expect the numbers will change wildly in the future as vendors work on optimizations and tailor themselves to particular use cases. That being said, from the current crop of solutions, I would say the following:

- Docker's Overlay network is likely to become the most-used solution during development, simply because it is the "batteries included" option. Depending on how stable and efficient it becomes, it may also be appropriate for small deployments running on the cloud.

- Weave is focusing heavily on ease of use and the developer experience, making it another good choice for development. Weave also includes features such as encryption and firewall traversal that will make it very attractive in situations such as cross-cloud deployments.

- Flannel is used in CoreOS stacks and offers specialist backends for various scenarios. At the time of writing, Flannel may be too much work to use in development (this should change as plugins are developed) but offers an efficient and simple solution in several production scenarios.

- Project Calico's primary target is large organizations or datacenters that control their own network fabric. In such cases, Project Calico's layer 3 approach can offer a simple and efficient solution. That being said, the Project Calico network plugin looks to be both easy to use and comparatively fast, potentially making it attractive in development and single-cloud deployments.

- In some circumstances, rolling-your-own may be appropriate. For instance, ops engineers often know exactly how they want to wire things up for efficiency. In this case, you can create your own networking plugin or use tools like pipework to insert specialist plumbing. You also may be able to use the container or host networking modes, which will remove the overhead of the Docker bridge and NAT rules but means containers have to share IP addresses.

The correct choice here is very much dependent on your particular needs and the platform you are running on top of. You may find that certain solutions operate considerably faster or slower than others or enable use cases not available in other solutions. Nothing will beat actually trying out the different solutions in tests that replicate the conditions your application will run under.

CHAPTER 12

Orchestration, Clustering, and Management

Most software systems evolve over time. New features are added and old ones pruned. Fluctuating user demand means an efficient system must be able to quickly scale resources up and down. Demands for near-zero downtime require automatic failover to preprovisioned backup systems, normally in a separate datacenter or region.

On top of this, organizations often have multiple such systems to run, or need to run occasional tasks such as data mining that are separate from the main system, but require significant resources or talk to the existing system.

When using multiple resources, it is important to make sure they are efficiently used (i.e., that they're not sitting idle), but can still cope with spikes in demand. Balancing cost effectiveness against the ability to quickly scale is a difficult task that can be approached in a variety of ways.

All of this means that running a nontrivial system is full of administrative tasks and challenges, the complexity of which should not be underestimated. It quickly becomes impossible to look after machines on an individual level; rather than patching and updating machines one by one, they must be treated identically. When a machine develops a problem, it should be destroyed and replaced, rather than nursed back to health.[1]

Various software tools and solutions exist to help with these challenges and cover each of the following areas to a greater or lesser degree:

---

[1] The distinction between these approaches is often known as "pets versus cattle."

Clustering
> Grouping "hosts"—either VMs or bare metal—and networking them together. A cluster should feel like a single resource rather than a group of disparate machines.

Orchestration
> Making all the pieces work together. Starting containers on appropriate hosts and connecting them. An orchestration system may also include support for scaling, automatic failover, and node rebalancing.

Management
> Providing oversight into the system and supporting various administrative tasks.

We will start by looking at the primary orchestration and clustering tools in the Docker ecosystem: Swarm, Fleet, Kubernetes, and Mesos. Swarm is the Docker native clustering solution, which also tackles orchestration to a large degree, particularly when used with Docker Compose. Fleet is a low-level clustering and scheduling system used by CoreOS. Kubernetes is a higher-level and somewhat opinionated orchestration solution that builds in failover and scaling features by default, and can run on top of other clustering solutions. Mesos is a low-level clustering solution that works with higher-level "frameworks" to provide a robust and complete solution to clustering and orchestration.

> The code for this chapter is available at this book's GitHub (*https://github.com/using-docker/orchestration*).
>
> You can check out the code for this chapter using:
>
> ```
> $ git clone -b \
>   https://github.com/using-docker/orchestration/
>   ...
> ```
>
> Alternatively, you can download the code directly from the GitHub project.

Clustering and Orchestration Tools

This section investigates the primary clustering and orchestration tools available for Docker—Swarm, Fleet, Kubernetes, and Mesos. For each tool, we will look at its unique features and see how they can be used to run our identidock example.

Swarm

Swarm (*https://docs.docker.com/swarm/*) is the native clustering tool for Docker. Swarm uses the standard Docker API—that is containers can be launched using normal docker run commands and Swarm will take care of selecting an appropriate host to run the container on. This also means that other tools that use the Docker API—

---

such as Compose and bespoke scripts—can use Swarm without any changes and take advantage of running on a cluster rather than a single host.

The basic architecture of Swarm is fairly straightforward: each host runs a Swarm *agent* and one host runs a Swarm *manager* (on small test clusters this host may also run an agent). The manager is responsible for the orchestration and scheduling of containers on the hosts. Swarm can be run in a high-availability mode where etcd, Consul, or ZooKeeper is used to handle failover to a backup manager. There are several different methods for how hosts are found and added to a cluster, which is known as *discovery* in Swarm. By default, *token*-based discovery is used, where the addresses of hosts are kept in a list stored on the Docker Hub.

As a quick way to get started with Swarm[2], let's set up a small cluster of VMs. We'll use Docker Machine to create the VMs and the default Swarm token-based discovery method for linking them together. Start by creating the token for our cluster using `swarm create`:

```
$ SWARM_TOKEN=$(docker run swarm create)
$ echo $SWARM_TOKEN
26a4af8d51e1cf2ea64dd625ba51a4ff
```

We can now create the manager (or master) host:

```
$ docker-machine create -d virtualbox \
        --engine-label dc=a \
        --swarm --swarm-master \
        --swarm-discovery token://$SWARM_TOKEN \
        swarm-master
Running pre-create checks...
(swarm-master) Creating VirtualBox VM...
...
Configuring swarm...
Checking connection to Docker...
Docker is up and running!
To see how to connect your Docker Client to the Docker Engine running on the...
```

Machine has created a new VirtualBox VM called `swarm-master` and attached it to the Swarm cluster with the token we generated previously. We've also attached the label dc=a to the Docker engine on the host, for reasons that will become clear later. Next, we'll create two further VMs, `swarm-1` and `swarm-2`, to make up our cluster:

```
$ docker-machine create -d virtualbox \
    --engine-label dc=a \
    --swarm \
    --swarm-discovery token://$SWARM_TOKEN \
    swarm-1
...
```

---

2 These examples were tested with Swarm version 1.2.2.

```
$ docker-machine create -d virtualbox \
    --engine-label dc=b \
    --swarm \
    --swarm-discovery token://$SWARM_TOKEN \
    swarm-2
...
```

Note that we have labeled swarm-1 as dc=a and swarm-2 as dc=b.

We can manually verify that these nodes have been added to the cluster by looking at the Hub API:

```
$ curl https://discovery-stage.hub.docker.com/v1/clusters/$SWARM_TOKEN
["192.168.99.102:2376","192.168.99.101:2376","192.168.99.100:2376"]
```

The IPs shown are the addresses of the VMs we created. These IPs have to be address-able by the Swarm manager, but will not normally be publicly addressable. We can get the same information (regardless of the discovery method) by issuing the swarm list command. You could download the Swarm binary to do this, but it's easiest just to use the Swarm image, as we did when creating the token:

```
$ docker run swarm list token://$SWARM_TOKEN
192.168.99.102:2376
192.168.99.101:2376
192.168.99.100:2376
```

We can see a diagram of the simple cluster we've created in Figure 12-1. The labels dc=a and dc=b are intended to indicate datacenter A and datacenter B, respectively. While 2 VMs running on a laptop have about as much in common with a datacenter as a midge does with a jumbo jet, it serves our example well and you could easily add powerful cloud resources to your cluster with very similar commands.

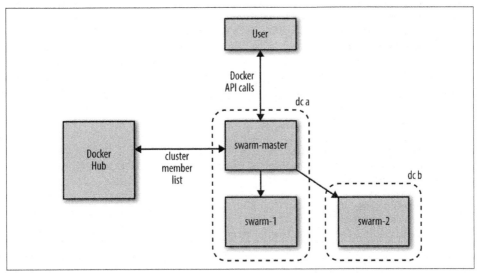

Figure 12-1. Swarm cluster example

Swarm Discovery

The default token-based discovery is very useful for getting started quickly, but has a significant disadvantage—it requires all hosts to be able to access the Hub, which becomes a single point of failure.

There are several other discovery mechanisms available, including simply providing the Docker manager with a list of IP addresses and using a distributed store such as etcd, Consul, or ZooKeeper.

For full information on the discovery methods available, see the documentation (*https://docs.docker.com/swarm/discovery/*).

Let's connect our Docker client to the Swarm master and see what `docker info` tells us:

```
$ eval $(docker-machine env --swarm swarm-master)
$ docker info
Containers: 4
 Running: 4
 Paused: 0
 Stopped: 0
Images: 3
Server Version: swarm/1.2.2
Role: primary
Strategy: spread
Filters: health, port, containerslots, dependency, affinity, constraint
Nodes: 3
```

```
swarm-1: 192.168.99.101:2376
  └ ID: 2KBB:7N6P:YJ5Y:UC5L:CEUK:VQTW:3XEV:6AFD:XFNO:AAE2:JS5X:XG7I
  └ Status: Healthy
  └ Containers: 1
  └ Reserved CPUs: 0 / 1
  └ Reserved Memory: 0 B / 1.021 GiB
  └ Labels: dc=a, executiondriver=, kernelversion=4.4.8-boot2docker, operat...
  └ Error: (none)
  └ UpdatedAt: 2016-05-25T14:29:59Z
  └ ServerVersion: 1.11.1
swarm-2: 192.168.99.102:2376
  └ ID: KMFG:KX6S:KE2S:GF6G:EIBG:WC6G:GGDO:7PAM:46MN:VZF3:BIRS:2EOT
  └ Status: Healthy
  └ Containers: 1
  └ Reserved CPUs: 0 / 1
  └ Reserved Memory: 0 B / 1.021 GiB
  └ Labels: dc=b, executiondriver=, kernelversion=4.4.8-boot2docker, operat...
  └ Error: (none)
  └ UpdatedAt: 2016-05-25T14:30:12Z
  └ ServerVersion: 1.11.1
swarm-master: 192.168.99.100:2376
  └ ID: LQGZ:42VT:CUS3:CWY5:DSPM:QLV5:IUN6:GMIY:E3TM:IUDD:LA3B:SXNF
  └ Status: Healthy
  └ Containers: 2
  └ Reserved CPUs: 0 / 1
  └ Reserved Memory: 0 B / 1.021 GiB
  └ Labels: dc=a, executiondriver=, kernelversion=4.4.8-boot2docker, operat...
  └ Error: (none)
  └ UpdatedAt: 2016-05-25T14:29:53Z
  └ ServerVersion: 1.11.1
Plugins:
 Volume:
 Network:
Kernel Version: 4.4.8-boot2docker
Operating System: linux
Architecture: amd64
CPUs: 3
Total Memory: 3.064 GiB
Name: 71ac6178cba8
Docker Root Dir:
Debug mode (client): false
Debug mode (server): false
WARNING: No kernel memory limit support
```

This gives us some detailed information on the cluster, and we can see the three hosts ("nodes" in Swarm parlance) we have created. Each node is running a Swarm agent container that connects it to the cluster, and the `swarm-master` node is also running a Swarm master container for managing the cluster. Running an agent on the same node as the master wouldn't be advisable in a production setting, but it's fine for our demonstration.

Now it's time to test out our cluster!

```
$ docker run -d debian sleep 10 ❶
ebce5d18121002f35b2666da4dd2dce189ece9573c8ebeba531d85f51fbad8e8
$ docker ps
CONTAINER ID  IMAGE   COMMAND     ... NAMES
ebce5d181210  debian  "sleep 10"  ... swarm-1/furious_bell
```

❶ This command will take a short amount of time to complete while the debian image is downloaded. When talking to a Swarm cluster, you won't get updates on download progress.

We can see that our container has been created and automatically scheduled on the swarm-1 host. This may seem slightly underwhelming, but it's pretty neat; behind the scenes, Swarm has intercepted our request, analyzed our cluster, and forwarded our request to the most appropriate host.

Filters

Filters control which nodes are available to run containers on. There are several different types of filter that are applied by default. We can see an example of a default filter in action by starting a few Nginx containers:

```
$ docker run -d -p 80:80 nginx
af0b0dd4e55891210d937ef4831cd90f11274e99671e243b63e20bcd02d1f871
$ docker run -d -p 80:80 nginx
7d1d2323dc85193d5badcb561c4c4269003d62a4638e6276f40eb87490ace617
$ docker run -d -p 80:80 nginx
320f676f72600201ccae2cc2d81904446efafad82440bc0115bfa853e443660e
$ docker ps
CONTAINER ID  IMAGE ... PORTS                                   NAMES
320f676f7260  nginx     192.168.99.101:80->80/tcp, 443/tcp      swarm-1/drunk_e...
7d1d2323dc85  nginx     192.168.99.100:80->80/tcp, 443/tcp      swarm-master/el...
af0b0dd4e558  nginx     192.168.99.102:80->80/tcp, 443/tcp      swarm-2/loving_...
```

Note that Swarm has placed each Nginx container on a different host. What happens if we try to start a fourth container?

```
$ docker run -d -p 80:80 nginx
docker: Error response from daemon: Unable to find a node that satisfies the...
[port 80 (Bridge mode)].
See 'docker run --help'.
```

The *port* filter runs by default and schedules containers which request a specific port on the host to nodes with that port free. By the time we start the fourth container, there are no available hosts with port 80 free, so Swarm denies the request.

The *constraint* filter can be used to select subsets of nodes matching the given key/ value pairs. To see this in action, we can use the labels we applied to the hosts earlier:

```
$ docker run -d -e constraint:dc==b postgres
40741066f905427848db7ec32f91192aacd9e88397d4c20b54add7c8edbc1a11
$ docker run -d -e constraint:dc==b postgres
2393d41ef041a47e65027c4b08208c32c9f7b0e12698477075ab97d87e2cf36d
 docker ps
CONTAINER ID          IMAGE      ... NAMES
2393d41ef041           postgres       swarm-2/jolly_bhabha
40741066f905           postgres       swarm-2/serene_swirles
...
```

Both of the containers have been scheduled on swarm-2, which is the only host with the label dc=b. To prove the point, we can also use constraint:dc==a or constraint:dc!=b:

```
$ docker run -d -e constraint:dc==a postgres
62efba99ef9e9f62999bbae8424bd27da3d57735335ebf553daec533256b01ef
$ docker ps
CONTAINER ID          IMAGE      ... NAMES
62efba99ef9e           postgres       swarm-master/dreamy_noyce
704261c8f3f1           postgres       swarm-2/berserk_yalow
e4d1b2991158           postgres       swarm-2/nostalgic_ptolemy
...
```

We can see that this container was scheduled on swarm-master, which has the label dc=a.

The constraint filter can also be used to filter on various host metadata such as the hostname, storage driver, and operating system.

You can see how constraints could be used to schedule containers to start on hosts in given regions (e.g., constraint:region!=europe) or with special hardware (e.g., constraint:disk==ssd or constraint:gpu==true).

The remaining filters are:

health
> This will only schedule containers on "healthy" hosts.

dependency
> This will coschedule dependent containers (e.g., containers that share a volume or are linked will be placed onto the same host).

affinity
> Allows users to define "attractions" between containers and other containers or images. For example, you can specify a container to be scheduled next to an existing container (e.g. -e affinity:container==loving_sammet) or only to run on hosts that already have the given image (e.g. -e affin ity:image==nginx).

Constraint and Affinity Expression Syntax

Affinity and constraint filter expressions can use the operators == (node must match value) and != (node must not match value).

They can also use regular expressions and globbing patterns. For example:

```
$ docker run -d -e constraint:region==europe* postgres ❶
$ docker run -d -e constraint:node==/swarm-[12]/ postgres ❷
```

❶ Will run on hosts who have region label beginning with europe.

❷ Will run on hosts named swarm-1 or swarm-2 (but not swarm-master).

In addition, "soft" constraints or affinities can be given by placing a ~ before the value. In such cases, the scheduler will attempt to meet the rule, but if it can't it will still run the container on a resource not matching the rule rather than fail completely. For example:

```
$ docker run -d -e constraint:dc==~a postgres
```

This will first attempt to run the container on a host labeled dc=a, but will still run on other hosts if no matching hosts exists with capacity.

Strategies

Assuming there is more than one available host after filter constraints have been applied, how does Swarm choose the host for a container? The answer is it depends on the chosen *strategy*. The following strategies are available:

spread
: Places the container on the host with the *least* number of containers (regardless of state).

binpack
: Places the container on the *most* loaded host that still has capacity.

random
: Places the container on a *random* host.

The spread strategy will result in containers being equally distributed over hosts. The major advantage of this approach is that it limits the number of containers affected when a host goes down. The binpack strategy will fill hosts as much as possible, thereby optimizing machine usage. The random strategy is primarily intended for debugging.

Delete Your VMs

In this chapter, we create a lot of VMs using Docker Machine. These VMs use a lot of resources, so it's important to stop and remove them when you're finished with an example. This can be easily done with Machine commands:

```
$ docker-machine stop swarm-master
$ docker-machine rm swarm-master
Successfully removed swarm-master
```

The major advantage of Swarm is that it only uses straight Docker API calls, which means it requires almost no effort by developers to start using. This should also mean Swarm workloads are straightforward to port between clusters, whereas using Mesos or Kubernetes may result in a more difficult to port architecture.

Fleet

Fleet (*https://coreos.com/fleet/*) is the cluster management tool from CoreOS. It bills itself as a "low-level cluster engine"—that is, it is expected to form a "foundation layer" for higher-level solutions such as Kubernetes.

The most distinguishing feature of Fleet is that it builds on top of systemd (*https://wiki.freedesktop.org/www/Software/systemd/*). While systemd provides system and service initialization for a single machine, Fleet extends this to a cluster of machines. Fleet reads systemd unit files, which are then scheduled on a machine or machines in the cluster.

The technical architecture of Fleet is shown in Figure 12-2. Each machine runs an *engine* and an *agent*. Only one engine is active in the cluster at any time, but all agents are constantly running (for the sake of the diagram, the active engine is shown separately to the machines, but it will be running on one of them). Systemd unit files (henceforth *units*) are submitted to the engine, which will schedule the job on the "least-loaded" machine. The unit file will normally simply run a container. The agent takes care of starting the unit and reporting state. Etcd is used to enable communication between machines and store the status of the cluster and units.

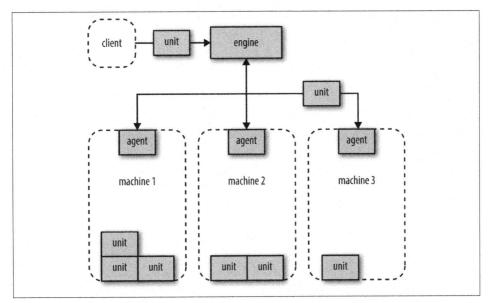

Figure 12-2. Fleet architecture

The architecture is designed to be fault tolerant; if a machine dies, any units scheduled on that machine will be restarted on new hosts. Fleet currently suffers from some scalability limitations that mean it is not recommended for large clusters (more than 100 nodes or 1000 containers).

Fleet supports various scheduling hints and constraints. At the most basic level, units can be scheduled as *global*—that is, an instance will run on all machines, or as a single unit that will run on a single machine. Global scheduling is very useful for utility containers for tasks such as logging and monitoring. Various *affinity* type constraints are supported. So a container that runs a health check can be scheduled to always run next to the application server, for example. Metadata can also be attached to hosts and used for scheduling, so you could ask your containers to run on machines belonging to a given region or with certain hardware, for example.

As Fleet is based on systemd, it also supports the concept of *socket activation* (i.e., a container can be spun up in response to a connection on a given port). The primary advantage of this is that processes can be created just in time, rather than sitting around idle waiting for something to happen. There are potentially other benefits related to management of sockets, such as not losing messages between container restarts.

Let's see how we can get identidock running on a Fleet cluster. For this example, I've created a GitHub project that contains a Vagrant template that will launch three VMs:

```
$ git clone https://github.com/amouat/fleet-vagrant
...
$ cd fleet-vagrant
$ vagrant up
...
$ vagrant ssh core-01 -- -A
CoreOS alpha (758.1.0)
```

We've now brought up a cluster of three VMs running CoreOS, which already have Flannel (see "Flannel") and Fleet installed. We can use the Fleet command-line tool fleetctl to get a list of machines in the cluster:

```
core@core-01 ~ $ fleetctl list-machines
MACHINE        IP              METADATA
0684eb86... 172.17.8.102       -
1b11c461... 172.17.8.103       -
38cd7dd2... 172.17.8.101       -
```

First, we want to install SkyDNS (see "SkyDNS") for DNS-based service discovery. It makes sense to install common services such as this on all nodes in the cluster, so we'll define it to be a *global* unit. The service file is called *skydns.service* and has the following contents (it should already be in your VM):

```
[Unit]
Description=SkyDNS

[Service]
TimeoutStartSec=0
ExecStartPre=-/usr/bin/docker kill dns
ExecStartPre=-/usr/bin/docker rm dns
ExecStartPre=/usr/bin/docker pull skynetservices/skydns:2.5.2b
ExecStart=/usr/bin/env bash -c "IP=$(/usr/bin/ip -o -4 addr list docker0 \
   | awk '{print $4}' | cut -d/ -f1) \
   && docker run --name dns -e ETCD_MACHINES=http://$IP:2379 \
      skynetservices/skydns:2.5.2b"
ExecStop=/usr/bin/docker stop dns

[X-Fleet]
Global=true
```

Apart from the [X-Fleet] section, the rest is just a standard systemd unit file. In ExecStart, we first do some shell hackery to get the IP address of the docker0 bridge for accessing the host's etcd instance. The container is launched without the -d argument, which allows systemd to monitor the application and take care of logging. The [X-Fleet] section tells Fleet we want to run this unit on all machines, rather than the default of a running single instance.

Before we start our DNS servers, we need to add some configuration to etcd:

```
core@core-01 ~ $ etcdctl set /skydns/config \
  '{"dns_addr":"0.0.0.0:53", "domain":"identidock.local."}'
{"dns_addr":"0.0.0.0:53", "domain":"identidock.local."}
```

This tells SkyDNS that it is responsible for the `identidock.local` domain.

Now we can start up the service. Units are launched with the `fleetctl start` command:

```
core@core-01 ~ $ fleetctl start skydns.service
Triggered global unit skydns.service start
```

And we can get the status of all units with the `list-units` command. Once everything is launched and running, you should get output like:

```
core@core-01 ~ $ fleetctl list-units
UNIT                MACHINE                      ACTIVE  SUB
skydns.service  0684eb86.../172.17.8.102     active  running
skydns.service  1b11c461.../172.17.8.103     active  running
skydns.service  38cd7dd2.../172.17.8.101     active  running
```

This shows that a SkyDNS container is running on each of the machines in our cluster.

Now that we have DNS running, let's start up our Redis container and register it with DNS. The config for the Redis unit can be found in the file *redis.service*, which looks like this:

```
[Unit]
Description=Redis
After=docker.service
Requires=docker.service
After=flanneld.service

[Service]
TimeoutStartSec=0
ExecStartPre=-/usr/bin/docker kill redis
ExecStartPre=-/usr/bin/docker rm redis
ExecStartPre=/usr/bin/docker pull redis:3
ExecStart=/usr/bin/docker run --name redis redis:3
ExecStartPost=/usr/bin/env bash -c 'sleep 2 \
  && IP=$(docker inspect -f {{.NetworkSettings.IPAddress}} redis) \
  && etcdctl set /skydns/local/identidock/redis \
      "{\\\"host\\\":\\\"$IP\\\",\\\"port\\\":6379}"'
ExecStop=/usr/bin/docker stop redis
```

This time we haven't included an [`X-Fleet`] section, so only a single instance of Redis will be launched. In the [`ExecStartPost`] section, we've included some code to automatically register Redis with SkyDNS after starting the container. The short `sleep` is required for Docker to set up the network configuration before we grab the IP address. This sort of code is generally best placed in a supporting script, but I've left it in the main unit file for simplicity.

Start up the Redis service and the dnmonster service (the dnmonster unit file follows the same format as the Redis one):

```
core@core-01 ~ $ fleetctl start redis.service
Unit redis.service inactive
Unit redis.service launched on 0684eb86.../172.17.8.102
core@core-01 ~ $ fleetctl start dnmonster.service
Unit dnmonster.service inactive
Unit dnmonster.service launched on 1b11c461.../172.17.8.103
```

You should see the dnmonster and Redis units are scheduled on separate machines, in order to spread the load:

```
core@core-01 ~ $ fleetctl list-units
UNIT                   MACHINE                    ACTIVE   SUB
dnmonster.service      1b11c461.../172.17.8.103   active   running
redis.service          0684eb86.../172.17.8.102   active   running
skydns.service         0684eb86.../172.17.8.102   active   running
skydns.service         1b11c461.../172.17.8.103   active   running
skydns.service         38cd7dd2.../172.17.8.101   active   running
```

It will take some time before the machines have downloaded and started the appropriate containers.

Now let's start the identidock container. The unit file *identidock.service* looks like this:

```
[Unit]
Description=identidock

[Service]
TimeoutStartSec=0
ExecStartPre=-/usr/bin/docker kill identidock
ExecStartPre=-/usr/bin/docker rm identidock
ExecStartPre=/usr/bin/docker pull amouat/identidock:1.0
ExecStart=/usr/bin/env bash -c "docker run --name identidock --link dns \
  --dns $(docker inspect -f {{.NetworkSettings.IPAddress}} dns) \
  --dns-search identidock.local amouat/identidock:1.0"
ExecStop=/usr/bin/docker stop identidock
```

This time I've used Docker's --dns and --dns-search flags to tell the container to resolve DNS queries through the SkyDNS container on its machine. To make things a bit easier, we can also ask Fleet to schedule the container on the machine we're currently logged in to. To do this, first find the ID of the machine using fleetctl list-machines -l:

```
core@core-01 ~ $ fleetctl list-machines -l
MACHINE                              IP              METADATA
0684eb86f0d04353948dfaf7ecda2bfb     172.17.8.102    -
1b11c4610d9c4bb2a3b47dc8018b2d4f     172.17.8.103    -
38cd7dd279c54d09a4b385c8ba3f8cd7     172.17.8.101    -
```

Then add the following to the bottom of the *identidock.service* file:

```
[X-Fleet]
MachineID=<id>
```

Replacing <id> with the ID of the machine you're running on. In my case, this would be:

```
[X-Fleet]
MachineID=38cd7dd279c54d09a4b385c8ba3f8cd7
```

Now we can start the identidock unit and it should be scheduled on the current machine:

```
core@core-01 ~ $ fleetctl start identidock.service
Unit identidock.service inactive
Unit identidock.service launched on 38cd7dd2.../172.17.8.101
```

Once the service has started, we can see if things are working:

```
core@core-01 ~ $ docker exec -it identidock bash
uwsgi@5e578c4df292:/app$ ping redis
PING redis.identidock.local (192.168.67.3): 56 data bytes
64 bytes from 192.168.67.3: icmp_seq=0 ttl=60 time=46.676 ms
64 bytes from 192.168.67.3: icmp_seq=1 ttl=60 time=1.225 ms
^C--- redis.identidock.local ping statistics ---
2 packets transmitted, 2 packets received, 0% packet loss
round-trip min/avg/max/stddev = 1.225/23.951/46.676/22.726 ms
uwsgi@5e578c4df292:/app$ curl localhost:9090
<html><head><title>Hello...
```

We can also test what happens if a machine goes down:

```
core@core-01 ~ $ fleetctl list-units
UNIT                  MACHINE                     ACTIVE  SUB
dnmonster.service     1b11c461.../172.17.8.103    active  running
identidock.service    38cd7dd2.../172.17.8.101    active  running
redis.service         0684eb86.../172.17.8.102    active  running
skydns.service        0684eb86.../172.17.8.102    active  running
skydns.service        1b11c461.../172.17.8.103    active  running
skydns.service        38cd7dd2.../172.17.8.101    active  running
```

Redis is running on 172.17.8.102, which is the core-02 machine. We can use Vagrant to stop the machine:

```
core@core-01 ~ $ exit
$ vagrant halt core-02
==> core-02: Attempting graceful shutdown of VM...
```

Now log back in and check the status:

```
core@core-01 ~ $ fleetctl list-units
UNIT                  MACHINE                     ACTIVE      SUB
dnmonster.service     1b11c461.../172.17.8.103    active      running
identidock.service    38cd7dd2.../172.17.8.101    active      running
redis.service         1b11c461.../172.17.8.103    activating  start-pre
skydns.service        1b11c461.../172.17.8.103    active      running
skydns.service        38cd7dd2.../172.17.8.101    active      running
```

The Redis service has automatically been rescheduled onto a running machine. It will take some time until the host has downloaded the container, but once it has, it will register the new address with SkyDNS and identidock will continue to function. This pause could be largely avoided by preloading the required images onto each host.

As we can see, Fleet has a lot of useful functionality, but is more geared toward long-lived services rather than transient containers for batch tasks and similar. The scheduling strategies are also very basic—"least loaded" works in many cases, but other scenarios will call for more subtle or complex strategies. Finally, there are scaling issues with Fleet which currently limits its use cases to smaller clusters.

Kubernetes

Kubernetes (*http://kubernetes.io/*) is a container-orchestration tool built by engineers at Google, based on their experiences using containers in production over the last decade. Kubernetes is somewhat opinionated and enforces several concepts around how containers are organized and networked. The primary concepts you need to understand are:

Pods

Pods are groups of containers that are deployed and scheduled together. Pods form the atomic unit of scheduling in Kubernetes, as opposed to single containers in other systems. A pod will typically include between one and five containers that work together to provide a service. In addition to these user containers, Kubernetes will run other containers to provide logging and monitoring services. Pods are treated as ephemeral in Kubernetes; you should expect them to be created and destroyed continually as the system evolves.

Flat networking space

Networking works significantly differently in Kubernetes than it does when using the default Docker bridge network. In the default Docker networking, containers live on a private subnet and can't communicate directly with containers on other hosts without forwarding ports on the host or using proxies. In Kubernetes, containers within a pod share an IP address, but the address space is "flat" across all pods—that is, all pods can talk to each other without any network address translation (NAT). This makes multihost clusters much more easy to manage, at the cost of not supporting links and making single host (or, more accurately, single *pod*) networking a little more tricky. As containers in the same pod share an IP, they can communicate by using ports on the localhost address (which means you need to coordinate port usage within a pod).

Labels

Labels are key-value pairs attached to objects in Kubernetes, primarily pods, used to describe identifying characteristics of the object (e.g., version: dev and tier:

frontend). Labels are not normally unique; they are expected to identify groups of containers. *Label selectors* can then be used to identify objects or groups of objects (e.g., all the pods in the frontend tier with environment set to production). By using labels, it is easy to do grouping tasks such as assigning pods to load-balanced groups or moving pods between groups.

Services

Services are stable endpoints that can be addressed by name. Services can be connected to pods by using label selectors. For example, a "cache" service may connect to several "redis" pods identified by the label selector `"type"`: `"redis"`. The service will automatically round-robin requests between the pods. In this way, services can be used to connect parts of a system to each other. Using services provides a layer of abstraction that means applications do not need to know internal details of the service they are calling. For example, application code running inside a pod only needs to know the name and port of the database service to call; it does not care how many pods make up the database, or which pod it talked to last time. Kubernetes will set up a DNS server for the cluster that watches for new services and allows them to be addressed by name in application code and configuration files.

It is also possible to set up services that do not point to pods but to other preexisting services such as external APIs or databases.

Replication controllers

Replication controllers are the normal way to instantiate pods in Kubernetes (typically, you don't use the Docker CLI in Kubernetes). They control and monitor the number of running pods (called replicas) for a service. For example, a replication controller may be responsible for keeping five Redis pods running. Should one fail, it will immediately launch a new one. If the number of replicas is reduced, it will stop any excess pods. Although using replication controllers to instantiate all pods adds an extra layer of configuration, it also significantly improves fault tolerance and reliability.

Figure 12-3 shows part of a Kubernetes cluster, where we have two pods created by a replication controller and exposed by a service. The service round-robins requests between the pods that are selected based on the value of the `tier` label. Within a pod, there is only a single IP address that is shared between all containers. Containers within a pod can communicate by using ports on the `localhost` address. The service has been assigned a separate IP address, which is publicly accessible.

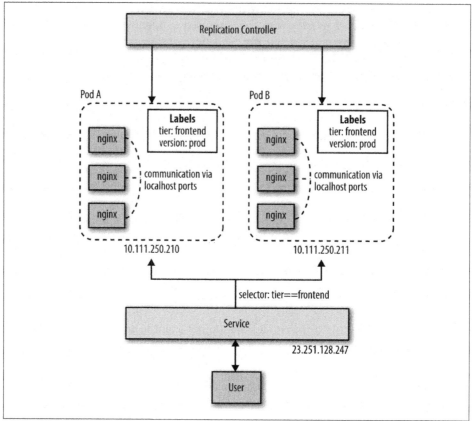

Figure 12-3. Example Kubernetes cluster

To get identidock running on Kubernetes, we'll use separate pods for the dnmonster, identidock, and redis containers. This may sound like overkill, but these services could all potentially scale independently (one identidock service could use a loadbalanced group of two dnmonster services and three redis servers), which means we don't have to rewrite our application to address services using ports on localhost. We don't need to add logging or monitoring containers, as Kubernetes will do this for us. Kubernetes also provides a load-balanced frontend proxy, so we don't need an Nginx proxy container either.

Getting Kubernetes

The Kubernetes GitHub pages contain getting started guides for many different platforms. If you would like to play around with Kubernetes on a local resource, you can run Kubernetes from a set of Docker containers (*https://github.com/GoogleCloudPlat form/kubernetes/blob/master/docs/getting-started-guides/docker.md*) or a Vagrant VM (*https://github.com/GoogleCloudPlatform/kubernetes/blob/master/docs/getting-started-guides/vagrant.md*) available from the Kubernetes GitHub pages. Otherwise, a safe bet for a hosted version of Kubernetes is to use Google Container Engine (GKE) (*https://cloud.google.com/container-engine/*), which is Google's own commercial offering.

If you install Kubernetes yourself, you will need to configure the DNS addon to resolve service names. If you are running on GKE, this will already be configured and running.

These instructions were written using Google Container Engine (GKE) to run Kubernetes, but they should be very similar to other Kubernetes installations.[3] See "Getting Kubernetes" for more information on obtaining or installing Kubernetes. The rest of this section assumes you are at a point where you can successfully run `kubectl` commands and that your Kubernetes installation includes a DNS server.

Let's start by defining the replication controller to start our Redis instance. Create a file called *redis-controller.json* with the following contents:

```
{ "kind":"ReplicationController",
  "apiVersion":"v1",
  "metadata":{ "name":"redis-controller" },
  "spec":{
     "replicas":1,
     "selector":{ "name":"redis-pod" },
     "template":{
        "metadata":{
           "labels":{ "name":"redis-pod" }
        },
        "spec":{
           "containers":[ {
                 "name":"redis",
                 "image":"redis:3",
                 "ports":[ {
                       "containerPort":6379,
                       "protocol":"TCP"
           } ] } ] } } } }
```

Here we are asking Kubernetes to create a replication-controlled pod consisting of a single container running the `redis:3` image, exposing the port 6379. We provide the pod with a label that has the key "name" and value "redis-pod." The replication controller is an object in its own right, with the name "redis-controller."

Let's start this pod using the `kubectl` tool:

---

3 The examples here are for v1 of the API. Later versions of the API can be expected to have slightly different syntax.

```
$ kubectl create -f redis-controller.json
replicationcontroller "redis-controller" created
```

If you then run kubectl get pods, you will get a list of all running and pending pods with their status. For the time being we will only have single running pod. However, we can also get information on some of the infrastructure services that Kubernetes is running for us:

```
$ kubectl get componentstatuses
NAME                  STATUS    MESSAGE              ERROR
scheduler             Healthy   ok
controller-manager    Healthy   ok
etcd-0                Healthy   {"health": "true"}
etcd-1                Healthy   {"health": "true"}
```

Similarly, you can run kubectl get rc to get a list of replication controllers and kubectl get services to get a list of services.

The next step is to define a *service* that will allow other containers to connect to our redis pod without needing to know its IP address. Create a file *redis-service.json* with the following contents:

```
{ "kind":"Service",
  "apiVersion":"v1",
  "metadata":{ "name":"redis" },
  "spec":{
    "ports": [ {
        "port":6379,
        "targetPort":6379,
        "protocol":"TCP"
      } ],
    "selector":{ "name":"redis-pod" }
} }
```

This defines a service that will connect callers to our redis pod. The service is given the name "redis," which will be picked up by the DNS cluster addon (installed in GKE by default) and made resolvable. Importantly, this means our identidock code will work without needing to edit the hostnames. Services can be started in the same way as controllers:

```
$ kubectl create -f redis-service.json
service "redis" created
```

The redis pod is identified by the selector "name":"redis-pod". If we had multiple redis nodes with the label "name":"redis-pod", this selector would match all of them. When there is more than one selected pod, the service will choose a random pod to process the request (it's also possible to set an *affinity* for selecting the pod; e.g., "ClientIP" will consistently assign clients to pods based on the client's IP address). By changing the label on pods, they can be dynamically moved in and out of selector groups, which can be used to accomplish tasks such as temporarily taking a pod out of production for debugging or maintenance.

Next, we can create our dnmonster controller and service in a very similar manner. Create a file *dnmonster-controller.json* with the following contents:

```
{ "kind":"ReplicationController",
  "apiVersion":"v1",
  "metadata":{ "name":"dnmonster-controller" },
  "spec":{
    "replicas":1,
    "selector":{ "name":"dnmonster-pod" },
    "template":{
      "metadata":{
        "labels":{ "name":"dnmonster-pod" } },
      "spec":{
        "containers":[ {
          "name":"dnmonster",
          "image":"amouat/dnmonster:1.0",
          "ports":[ {
            "containerPort":8080,
            "protocol":"TCP"
        } ] } ] } } } }
```

And the dnmonster service as *dnmonster-service.json*:

```
{ "kind":"Service",
  "apiVersion":"v1",
  "metadata":{ "name":"dnmonster" },
  "spec":{
    "ports": [ {
      "port":8080,
      "targetPort":8080,
      "protocol":"TCP"
    } ],
    "selector":{ "name":"dnmonster-pod" }
} }
```

Start them up:

```
$ kubectl create -f dnmonster-controller.json
replicationcontroller "dnmonster-controller" created
$ kubectl create -f dnmonster-service.json
service "dnmonster" created
```

This follows exactly the same pattern as the redis controller and service; we have a dnmonster service that can be accessed using the hostname dnmonster and that forwards to the single dnmonster instance created by the replication controller.

Now we can create our identidock pod and begin to wire it all together. Create a file *identidock-controller.json* with the following contents:

```
{ "kind":"ReplicationController",
  "apiVersion":"v1",
  "metadata":{ "name":"identidock-controller" },
  "spec":{
    "replicas":1,
    "selector":{ "name":"identidock-pod" },
    "template":{
      "metadata":{
        "labels":{ "name":"identidock-pod" } },
      "spec":{
        "containers":[ {
            "name":"identidock",
            "image":"amouat/identidock:1.0",
            "ports":[ {
                "containerPort":9090,
                "protocol":"TCP"
      } ] } ] } } } }
```

Bring it up:

```
$ kubectl create -f identidock-controller.json
replicationcontroller "identidock-controller" created
```

Identidock should now be up and running, but we still need to create the identidock service to make it accessible to the outside world. Create a file *identidock-service.json* with the following contents:

```
{ "kind":"Service",
  "apiVersion":"v1",
  "metadata":{ "name":"identidock" },
  "spec":{
    "type": "LoadBalancer",
    "ports": [ {
        "port":80,
        "targetPort":9090,
        "protocol":"TCP"
      } ],
    "selector":{ "name":"identidock-pod" }
  } }
```

This service is a little bit different. We've set the `"type"` to be `"LoadBalancer"`, which will create an externally accessible load balancer that will listen for connections on port 80 and forward them to our identidock service on port 9090.

Start up the identidock service as expected:

```
$ kubectl create -f identidock-service.json
service "identidock" created
```

If you're running on GKE, you may also need to open port 80 on the firewall, which can be done by creating a rule with the gcloud tool:

```
$ gcloud compute firewall-rules create --allow=tcp:80 identidock-80
```

Now, assuming there is no firewall in the way, you should be able to connect using the external IP address listed for the identidock service (note that it may take some time for Kubernetes to allocate the external IP):

```
$ kubectl get services identidock
NAME         CLUSTER-IP       EXTERNAL-IP      PORT(S)   AGE
identidock   10.147.254.181   192.158.28.231   80/TCP    3m
$ curl 192.158.28.231
<html><head><title>Hello...
```

Volumes in Kubernetes

Volumes are also different in Kubernetes. The major difference is that they are declared at the pod level, rather than the container level, and can be shared between containers within the pod. Kubernetes offers several types of volumes, for various use cases, including:

emptyDir
> This will initialize an empty directory on the pod that the containers can write to. When the pod dies, so does the directory. This is very useful for temporary data that is only needed for the lifetime of the pod, or data that is regularly backed up to another, more persistent store.

gcePersistentDisk
> For users on GKE, this can be used to store data within the Google Cloud. The data will persist beyond the lifetime of the pod.

awsElasticBlockStore
> For users on AWS, this can be used to stored data on Amazon's Elastic Block Store (EBS). The data will persist beyond the lifetime of the pod.

nfs
> For accessing files on a Network File System (NFS) share. Again, data will persist beyond the lifetime of the pod.

secret
> For storing sensitive information such as passwords and API tokens used by pods. Secret volumes must be populated via the Kubernetes API and are stored in tmpfs, which exists entirely in RAM and is never written to disk.

Using Kubernetes took a bit more configuration work but has resulted in a system that supports failover and load balancing out of the box. Rather than having containers hard linked to each other, using services gives us a layer of abstraction that allows us to easily scale and swap the underlying pods and containers. The disadvantage is that Kubernetes has added a considerable amount of extra weight to our simple identidock application; the extra logging and monitoring infrastructure requires significantly more resources and hence increases running costs.

For some applications, the system design and choices enforced by Kubernetes may not be appropriate. For the majority of applications, especially microservices and those with little or well-contained state, it provides an easy-to-use, resilient, and scalable solution for surprisingly little work.

Mesos and Marathon

Apache Mesos (*https://mesos.apache.org*) is an open source cluster manager. It's designed to scale to very large clusters involving hundreds or thousands of hosts. Mesos supports diverse workloads from multiple tenants; one user's Docker containers may be running next to another user's Hadoop tasks.

Apache Mesos was started as a project at the University of California, Berkeley, before becoming the underlying infrastructure used to power Twitter and an important tool at many major companies such as eBay and Airbnb. A lot of continuing development in Mesos and supporting tools (such as Marathon) is undertaken by Mesosphere, a company cofounded by Ben Hindman, one of the original developers of Mesos.

The architecture of Mesos is designed around high availability and resilience. The major components in a Mesos cluster are:

Mesos agent nodes::[4] Responsible for actually running tasks. All agents submit a list of their available resources to the master. There will typically be tens to thousands of agent nodes.

Mesos master
> The master is responsible for sending tasks to the agents. It maintains a list of available resources that are then offered to frameworks. The master decides how many resources to offer based on an allocation strategy. There will typically be two or four standby masters ready to take over in case of a failure.

ZooKeeper
> Used in elections and for looking up address of current master. Typically three or five ZooKeeper instances will be running to ensure availability and to handle failures.

Frameworks
> Frameworks coordinate with the master to schedule tasks onto agent nodes. Frameworks are composed of two parts: the *executor* process that runs on the agents and takes care of running the tasks, and the *scheduler* that registers with

---

4 Previously known as slave nodes.

the master and selects the resources to use based on offers from the master. There may be multiple frameworks running on a Mesos cluster for different kinds of tasks. Users wishing to submit jobs interact with frameworks rather than directly with Mesos.

In Figure 12-4, we see a Mesos cluster that uses the Marathon framework as the scheduler. The Marathon scheduler uses ZooKeeper to locate the current Mesos master it will submit tasks to. Both the Marathon scheduler and the Mesos master have standbys ready to start work should the current master become unavailable.

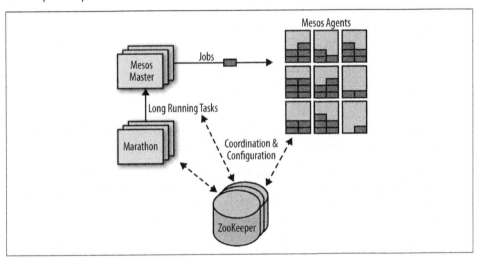

Figure 12-4. Mesos cluster

Typically, ZooKeeper will run on the same hosts as the Mesos master and its standbys. In a small cluster, these hosts may also run agents, but larger clusters require communication with the master, making this less feasible. Marathon may run on the same hosts as well, or may instead run on separate hosts that live on the network boundary and form the access point for clients, thus keeping clients separated from the Mesos cluster itself.

Mesosphere's Marathon (*https://mesosphere.github.io/marathon/*) is designed to start, monitor, and scale long-running[5] applications. Marathon is designed to be flexible about the applications it launches, and can even be used to start other complementary frameworks such as Chronos ("cron" for the datacenter). It makes a good choice of framework for running Docker containers, which are directly supported in Marathon. Like the other orchestration frameworks we've looked at, Marathon supports various affinity and constraint rules. Clients interact with Marathon through a REST

---

5 Presumably this is why they called it Marathon. *Ba-dum-tsh*, indeed.

API. Other features include support for health checks and an event stream that can be used to integrate with load balancers or for analyzing metrics.

To get an idea how Mesos and Marathon work, we'll set up a three-node cluster using Docker Machine that mimics the setup in Figure 12-4. However, we'll only run a single instance of ZooKeeper, the Marathon scheduler, and the Mesos master. All nodes will run a Mesos agent. A production architecture is considerably different and should include multiple instances of the central services for high availability.

Start by creating the hosts, mesos-1, mesos-2, and mesos-3:

```
$ docker-machine create -d virtualbox mesos-1
Creating VirtualBox VM...
...
$ docker-machine create -d virtualbox mesos-2
...
$ docker-machine create -d virtualbox mesos-3
...
```

We also need to do a bit of configuration to allow the mesos hostnames to resolve. This shouldn't be necessary, but I ran into problems without it:

```
$ docker-machine ssh mesos-1 'sudo sed -i "\$a127.0.0.1 mesos-1" /etc/hosts'
$ docker-machine ssh mesos-2 'sudo sed -i "\$a127.0.0.1 mesos-2" /etc/hosts'
$ docker-machine ssh mesos-3 'sudo sed -i "\$a127.0.0.1 mesos-3" /etc/hosts'
```

We'll start by configuring mesos-1, which will run the Mesos master, ZooKeeper, the Marathon framework as well as an agent.

The first thing we want to start is ZooKeeper, which the other containers will use to register and find services. We're using an image I created here, as at the time of writing, there wasn't an official one. I've used --net=host for this container, mainly for efficiency reasons and for consistency with the master and agent containers, which require host networking so they can open new ports for services:

```
$ eval $(docker-machine env mesos-1)
$ docker run --name zook -d --net=host amouat/zookeeper
...
Status: Downloaded newer image for amouat/zookeeper:latest
dfc27992467c9563db05af63ecb6f0ec371c03728f9316d870bd4b991db7b642
```

Save the IP addresses of our nodes into variables to make the following configuration a bit easier:

```
$ MESOS1=$(docker-machine ip mesos-1)
$ MESOS2=$(docker-machine ip mesos-2)
$ MESOS3=$(docker-machine ip mesos-3)
```

Now we can bring up the master:

```
$ docker run --name master -d --net=host \
         -e MESOS_ZK=zk://$MESOS1:2181/mesos \ ❶
```

```
            -e MESOS_IP=$MESOS1 \ ❷
            -e MESOS_HOSTNAME=$MESOS1 \
            -e MESOS_QUORUM=1 \ ❸
            mesosphere/mesos-master:0.28.1 ❹
    ...
    Status: Downloaded newer image for mesosphere/mesos-master:0.23.0-1.0.ubuntu1404
    9de83f40c3e1c5908381563fb28a14c2e23bb6faed569b4d388ddfb46f7d7403
```

❶ Tells the master where to find ZooKeeper and register itself.

❷ Sets the IP to use for the masters.

❸ We're only going to have a single master node for the purposes of the demo.

❹ We're using a mesos image from Mesosphere. This image isn't an automated build, and it's hard to tell exactly what is in it, so I don't recommend using it in production.

And we'll run an agent on the same host:

```
$ docker run --name agent -d --net=host \
            -e MESOS_MASTER=zk://$MESOS1:2181/mesos \
            -e MESOS_CONTAINERIZERS=docker \ ❶
            -e MESOS_IP=$MESOS1 \
            -e MESOS_HOSTNAME=$MESOS1 \
            -e MESOS_EXECUTOR_REGISTRATION_TIMEOUT=10mins \ ❷
            -e MESOS_RESOURCES="ports(*):[80-32000]" \ ❸
            -e MESOS_HOSTNAME=$MESOS1 \
            -v /var/run/docker.sock:/run/docker.sock \ ❹
            -v /usr/local/bin/docker:/usr/bin/docker \
            -v /sys:/sys:ro \ ❺
            mesosphere/mesos-slave:0.28.1
    ...
    Status: Downloaded newer image for mesosphere/mesos-slave:0.23.0-1.0.ubuntu1404
    38aaec1d08a41e5a6deeb62b7b097254b5aa2b758547e03c37cf2dfc686353bd
```

❶ Mesos has the concept of *containerizers*, which provide isolation between tasks and are run on the agent. Adding the docker argument here allows us to execute Docker containers as tasks on the agent.

❷ We need to extend the "registration timeout" to allow the agent time to download images before aborting.

❸ By default, agents will only offer a subset of high-numbered ports to frameworks. As identidock uses some low-numbered ports, we need to explicitly add them to the offered resources. For conciseness, I've neglected to remove the ports used by Mesos from this list, but this can cause a conflict if a framework requests a port already in use.

❹ In order for the agent to be able to start new containers, we mount the Docker sock and binary.

❺ Mounting */sys* is needed for the agent to report accurate details on the resources available on the host.

Now we can start the Marathon framework:

```
$ docker run -d --name marathon -p 9000:8080 \ ❶
            mesosphere/marathon:v1.1.1 --master zk://$MESOS1:2181/mesos \
            --zk zk://$MESOS1:2181/marathon \
            --task_launch_timeout 600000 ❷
...
Status: Downloaded newer image for mesosphere/marathon:v1.1.1
697d78749c2cfd6daf6757958f8460963627c422710f366fc86d6fcdce0da311
```

❶ We need to move Marathon from its default port of 8080 to avoid potentially conflicting with the dnmonster container.

❷ Sets a timeout of 600,000 ms to match the agent executor registration timeout of 10 minutes. This setting addresses a temporary issue and will be removed in a future version.

Next, bring up an agent on the other hosts:

```
$ eval $(docker-machine env mesos-2)
$ docker run --name agent -d --net=host \
            -e MESOS_MASTER=zk://$MESOS1:2181/mesos \
            -e MESOS_CONTAINERIZERS=docker \
            -e MESOS_IP=$MESOS2 \
            -e MESOS_HOSTNAME=$MESOS2 \
            -e MESOS_EXECUTOR_REGISTRATION_TIMEOUT=10mins \
            -e MESOS_RESOURCES="ports(*):[80-32000]" \
            -v /var/run/docker.sock:/run/docker.sock \
            -v /usr/local/bin/docker:/usr/bin/docker \
            -v /sys:/sys:ro \
            mesosphere/mesos-slave:0.28.1
...
Status: Downloaded newer image for mesosphere/mesos-slave:0.28.1
ac1216e7eedbb39475404f45a5655c7dc166d118db99072ed3d460322ad1a1c2
$ eval $(docker-machine env mesos-3)
$ docker run --name agent -d --net=host \
            -e MESOS_MASTER=zk://$MESOS1:2181/mesos \
            -e MESOS_CONTAINERIZERS=docker \
            -e MESOS_IP=$MESOS3 \
            -e MESOS_HOSTNAME=$MESOS3 \
            -e MESOS_EXECUTOR_REGISTRATION_TIMEOUT=10mins \
            -e MESOS_RESOURCES="ports(*):[80-32000]" \
            -v /var/run/docker.sock:/run/docker.sock \
            -v /usr/local/bin/docker:/usr/bin/docker \
            -v /sys:/sys:ro \
```

```
mesosphere/mesos-slave:0.28.1
...
Status: Downloaded newer image for mesosphere/mesos-slave:0.28.1
b5eecb7f56903969d1b7947144617050f193f20bb2a59f2b8e4ec30ef4ec3059
```

Now, if you open *http://$MESOS1:5050* in a browser (replacing *$MESOS1* with the IP address of `mesos-1`), you should see the web interface for Mesos. Similarly the Marathon interface should be available on port 9000.

We now have the infrastructure in place for running containers on Mesos agents via Marathon. But before we can get identidock running, we need to add a service discovery mechanism. In this case, we'll use mesos-dns (*https://github.com/mesosphere/mesos-dns*) and launch it on `mesos-1`.

Marathon jobs are defined in a JSON file that contains details of the job to launch and its resource requirements.

We can use the following JSON file to start `mesos-dns` on `mesos-1`:

```
{
  "id": "mesos-dns",
  "container": {
    "docker": {
      "image": "bergerx/mesos-dns", ❶
      "network": "HOST", ❷
      "parameters": [
          { "key": "env",
            "value": "MESOS_DNS_ZK=zk://192.168.99.100:2181/mesos" },❸
          { "key": "env", "value": "MESOS_DNS_MASTERS=192.168.99.100:5050" },
          { "key": "env", "value": "MESOS_DNS_RESOLVERS=8.8.8.8" },
          { "key": "env", "value": "MESOS_DNS_IPSOURCES=mesos,host"} ❹
      ]
    }
  },
  "cpus": 0.1, ❺
  "mem": 120.0,
  "instances": 1, ❻
  "constraints": [["hostname", "CLUSTER", "192.168.99.100"]] ❼
}
```

❶ We're using a user-provided build of mesos-dns here, as it automatically reads configuration from environment variables, which at the time of writing wasn't supported by the *mesosphere/mesos-dns* image.

❷ Again, it makes sense to use host networking for efficiency, although we could use the bridge network and publish port 53.

❸ We need to set environment variables to configure mesos-dns. This is done by using the `parameter` option, which adds flags to the docker `run` command used to start the image. Replace the IP address 192.168.99.100 with the IP of mesos-1 in your cluster.

❹ This variable tells mesos-dns to advertise the IP addresses of the container *hosts*, not the containers themselves (which are private to each host).

❺ All tasks need to define what resources they need to run. In this case, we're asking for "0.1" CPU resources and 120 megabytes of memory.

❻ For this test, we only need a single instance of mesos-dns.

❼ We'll pin mesos-dns to the mesos-1 host by specifying a hostname constraint with the IP of mesos-1.

Exactly how resources are allocated to a container is dependent on the *isolator* used by Mesos, which is configurable. Normally, CPU will be a relative weighting—that is, when there is contention for CPU, a container with a weighting 0.2 will receive twice as much CPU as one with a weighting of 0.1. The agent will also deduct the CPU value from the resources it offers to Mesos (so if an agent has "8" CPU and runs a task with "1" CPU, it will offer "7" CPU for further tasks).

Save the file as *dns.json* and send to Marathon using the REST API and the following command:

```
$ curl -sX POST http://$MESOS1:9000/v2/apps -d @dns.json \
    -H "Content-type: application/json" | jq .
{
  "tasks": [],
  "deployments": [
    {
      "id": "7613a993-340d-442e-9ed0-4a932f3fb2e3"
...
```

We could also use the marathonctl command-line tool or the web interface to submit jobs.

If you now look at the Marathon web interface, you should see that it is in the process of deploying the mesos-dns application. Once mesos-dns is up and running, we need to tell each of our hosts to use it. The easiest solution is to update *resolv.conf* in each of the hosts, which will be automatically propagated to any containers when they are started.

You can do this by running a sed script on each of the hosts:

```
$ docker-machine ssh mesos-1 \
    "sudo sed -i \"1s/^/domain marathon.mesos\nnameserver $MESOS1\n/\" \
    /etc/resolv.conf"
$ docker-machine ssh mesos-2 \
    "sudo sed -i \"1s/^/domain marathon.mesos\nnameserver $MESOS1\n/\" \
```

```
    /etc/resolv.conf"
$ docker-machine ssh mesos-3 \
    "sudo sed -i \"1s/^/domain marathon.mesos\nnameserver $MESOS1\n/\" \
    /etc/resolv.conf"
```

This should result in a *resolv.conf* on each host that looks like the following:

```
domain marathon.mesos
nameserver 192.168.99.100
...
```

If your *resolv.conf* includes a search line, you will also need to extend it to include *marathon.mesos* or name resolution will fail.

Now create a launcher for each of our containers. We'll put these on the bridge network, but they'll all need to expose a port so that they can be accessed via the host.

As usual, we'll start with Redis. Save the following as *redis.json*:

```
{
    "id": "redis",
    "container": {
      "docker": {
        "image": "redis:3",
        "network": "BRIDGE",
        "portMappings": [
          {"containerPort": 6379, "hostPort": 6379}
        ]

      }
    },
    "cpus": 0.3,
    "mem": 300.0,
    "instances": 1
}
```

And submit:

```
$ curl -X POST http://$MESOS1:9000/v2/apps -d @redis.json \
    -H "Content-type: application/json"
...
```

Similarly for dnmonster, save the following as *dnmonster.json*:

```
{
    "id": "dnmonster",
    "container": {
      "docker": {
        "image": "amouat/dnmonster:1.0",
        "network": "BRIDGE",
        "portMappings": [
          {"containerPort": 8080, "hostPort": 8080}
        ]

      }
```

```
        },
        "cpus": 0.3,
        "mem": 200.0,
        "instances": 1
}
```

And submit:

```
$ curl -X POST http://$MESOS1:9000/v2/apps -d @dnmonster.json \
    -H "Content-type: application/json"
...
```

Finally, save the following as *identidock.json*:

```
{
    "id": "identidock",
    "container": {
      "docker": {
        "image": "amouat/identidock:1.0",
        "network": "BRIDGE",
        "portMappings": [
          {"containerPort": 9090, "hostPort": 80}
        ]

      }
    },
    "cpus": 0.3,
    "mem": 200.0,
    "instances": 1
}
```

And submit:

```
$ curl -X POST http://$MESOS1:9000/v2/apps -d @identidock.json \
    -H "Content-type: application/json"
...
```

Once the agents have downloaded and started the images, you should be able to
access identidock via the IP address of whichever host was assigned the identidock
task. You can find this out from either the web interface or the REST API. For example:

```
$ curl -s http://$MESOS1:9000/v2/apps/identidock | jq '.app.tasks[0].host'
"192.168.99.101"
$ curl 192.168.99.101
<html><head><title>Hello...
```

Marathon will ensure any apps that die are restarted, assuming there are enough
resources available. It's educational to try stopping and restarting the mesos-2 and
mesos-3 machines and see how tasks are migrated and restarted as resources go offline and new ones become available.

More complex health checks can easily be added to apps, normally by implementing a HTTP endpoint Marathon can poll at regular intervals. For example, we can update *identidock.json* to contain the following:

```
{
    "id": "identidock",
    "container": {
      "docker": {
        "image": "amouat/identidock:1.0",
        "network": "BRIDGE",
        "portMappings": [
          {"containerPort": 9090, "hostPort": 80}
        ]

      }
    },
    "cpus": 0.3,
    "mem": 200.0,
    "instances": 1,
    "healthChecks": [
        {
            "protocol": "HTTP",
            "path": "/",
            "gracePeriodSeconds": 3,
            "intervalSeconds": 10,
            "timeoutSeconds": 10,
            "maxConsecutiveFailures": 3
        }]
}
```

This will attempt to fetch the home page for identidock every 10 seconds. If the fetch fails for whatever reason (e.g., the return code isn't between 200 and 399 or a response is received within the timeout), Marathon will test the endpoint twice more before killing the task.

To deploy the health check, just stop the old identidock deployment and start the updated one:

```
$ curl -X DELETE http://$MESOS1:9000/v2/apps/identidock
{"version":"2015-09-02T13:53:23.281Z","deploymentId":"1db18cce-4b39-49c0-8f2f...
$ curl -X POST http://$MESOS1:9000/v2/apps -d @identidock.json \
      -H "Content-type: application/json"
...
```

Now you should be able to find "Health Check Results" if you click through the Marathon web interface.

We've already seen constraints in action in Marathon when we scheduled the mesos-dns container on a host with a given IP address. We can also specify constraints that choose hosts with (or without) given attributes, including being able to spread containers across hosts for fault tolerance.

One problem with the current setup is that the address of the identidock service is dependent on the IP of the host it is scheduled on. Clearly, it's important to have a way of reliably routing to the identidock service from a static endpoint. One way to do this would be to use mesos-dns to discover the current endpoint, but Marathon also provides a servicerouter tool (*https://github.com/mesosphere/marathon/blob/master/bin/servicerouter.py*) that generates an HAProxy (*http://www.haproxy.org/*) config for routing to Marathon apps. Another solution is to roll your own proxy or load-balancing service that listens to Marathon's event bus for application creation and destruction events and forwards requests accordingly.

A second issue is the usage of fixed ports, like 6379 for Redis and 8080 for dnmonster. We've already had to remap the Marathon interface to port 9000 to avoid a conflict with dnmonster. We could fix this by rewriting the application to use dynamic ports assigned by Marathon, but a better solution would be use to a SDN. There are guides available online for installing Weave alongside Mesos, and Mesosphere is working on natively integrating Project Calico (see "Project Calico") with Mesos.

Marathon also features *application groups* that can be used to gather applications together to ensure they are deployed in the correct order to satisfy dependencies (e.g., starting a database before the application server) both on startup and when scaling or performing rolling updates.

A unique feature of Mesos, when compared to the other orchestration solutions, is its support for mixed workloads. Multiple frameworks can be running on the same cluster, allowing Hadoop or Storm data-processing tasks to run alongside Docker containers driving a microservice application. This is one of the features that makes Mesos particularly useful at driving high utilization; it's possible to schedule high-CPU but low-bandwidth tasks on the same host as tasks with the opposite characteristics to maximize resource usage. Efficient usage of a cluster is dependent on accurately requesting resources rather than over-provisioning when submitting tasks to Marathon or other frameworks. In the identidock example, the memory figures were intentionally inflated in order to ensure that not all the tasks would be allocated to the same agent, although in reality, a single host could easily cope. In order to address this, Mesos supports *over-subscription*, which allows "revocable" tasks to be started on an agent that is not offering enough resources, but according to monitoring, still has capacity. These revocable tasks will be stopped if resource usage spikes and hence are normally low-priority tasks, such as running background analytics. For more information on over-subscription in Mesos, see the Mesos site (*http://mesos.apache.org/documentation/latest/oversubscription/*) and GitHub (*https://github.com/mesosphere/serenity*).

Running Swarm or Kubernetes on Mesos

As Mesos itself provides a low-level clustering and scheduling infrastructure, it's possible to run higher-level interfaces such as Kubernetes and Swarm on top of Mesos. At first this might sound foolish—there is a large degree of duplication in the functionality provided. However, running on top of Mesos means you can take advantage of the existing Mesos functionality for fault tolerance, high availability, and resource utilization. You can also take advantage of easy portability to any datacenter or cloud that supports Mesos, while still keeping the features and ease of use of Kubernetes or Swarm. There are significant advantages for operations as well; they can concentrate on providing the underlying Mesos infrastructure while supporting diverse workloads and high utilization.

For more information, see Kubernetes-Mesos (*http://bit.ly/1XLRuBx*).

Conclusion

There are clearly a lot of choices for orchestrating, clustering, and managing containers. That being said, the choices are generally well differentiated. In terms of orchestration, we can say the following:

- Swarm has the advantage (and disadvantage) of using the standard Docker interface. While this makes it very simple to use Swarm and to integrate it into existing workflows, it may also make it more difficult to support the more complex scheduling that may be defined in custom interfaces.

- Fleet is a low-level and fairly simple orchestration layer that can be used as a base for running higher-level orchestration tools, such as Kubernetes or custom systems.

- Kubernetes is an opinionated orchestration tool that comes with service discovery and replication baked in. It may require some redesigning of existing applications, but used correctly, will result in a fault-tolerant and scalable system.

- Mesos is a low-level, battle-hardened scheduler that supports several frameworks for container orchestration, including Marathon, Kubernetes, and Swarm.

At the time of writing, Kubernetes and Mesos are more developed and stable than Swarm. In terms of scale, only Mesos has been proven to support large-scale systems of hundreds or thousands of nodes. However, when looking at small clusters of, say, less than a dozen nodes, Mesos may be an overly complex solution.

CHAPTER 13

Security and Limiting Containers

To use Docker safely, you need to be aware of the potential security issues and the major tools and techniques for securing container-based systems. In this chapter, we will consider security from the viewpoint of running Docker in production, but most of the advice is equally applicable to development. Even with security, it is important to keep the development and production environments similar in order to avoid the issues around moving code between environments that Docker was intended to solve.

Reading online posts and news items and Jonathan Rudenberg's article on image insecurity (*https://titanous.com/posts/docker-insecurity*), but note that the issues in Jonathan's article have been largely addressed by the development of digests and the Notary project.] about Docker can give you the impression that Docker is inherently insecure and not ready for production use.footnote:[The better articles on Docker security include the series by Dan Walsh of Red Hat on Opensource.com (*https://open source.com/business/14/7/docker-security-selinux*) While you certainly need to be aware of issues related to using containers safely, if used properly, containers can provide a more secure and efficient system than using VMs or bare metal alone.

This chapter begins by exploring some of the issues surrounding the security of container-based systems that you should be thinking about when using containers.

Disclaimer!

The guidance in this chapter is based on my opinion. I am not a
security researcher, nor am I responsible for any major public-
facing system. That being said, I am confident that any system that
follows the guidance in this chapter will be in a better security situation than the majority of systems out there. The advice in this
chapter does not form a complete solution and should only be used
to inform the development of your own security procedures and
policy.

Things to Worry About

So what sorts of security issues should you be thinking about in a container-based
environment? The following list is nonexhaustive but should give you food for
thought:

Kernel exploits

Unlike in a VM, the kernel is shared among all containers and the host, magnify-
ing the importance of any vulnerabilities present in the kernel. Should a container cause a kernel panic, it will take down the whole host. In VMs, the
situation is much better: an attacker would have to route an attack through both
the VM kernel and the hypervisor before being able to touch the host kernel.

Denial-of-service (DoS) attacks

All containers share kernel resources. If one container can monopolize access to
certain resources—including memory and more esoteric resources such as user
IDs (UIDs)—it can starve out other containers on the host, resulting in a denial
of service, where legitimate users are unable to access part or all of the system.

Container breakouts

An attacker who gains access to a container should not be able to gain access to
other containers or the host. Because users are not namespaced, any process that
breaks out of the container will have the same privileges on the host as it did in
the container; if you were root in the container, you will be root on the host.[1]
This also means that you need to worry about potential *privilege escalation*
attacks—where a user gains elevated privileges such as those of the root user,
often through a bug in application code that needs to run with extra privileges.
Given that container technology is still in its infancy, you should organize your

---

[1] There is currently ongoing work to automatically map the root user in a container to a nonprivileged user on
the host. This would dramatically reduce the capabilities of an attacker in the event of a breakout, but would
create problems with the ownership of volumes.

security around the assumption that container breakouts are unlikely, but possible.

Poisoned images

How do you know that the images you are using are safe, haven't been tampered with, and come from where they claim to come from? If an attacker can trick you into running her image, both the host and your data are at risk. Similarly, you want to be sure the images you are running are up to date and do not contain versions of software with known vulnerabilities.

Compromising secrets

When a container accesses a database or service, it will likely require some secret, such as an API key or username and password. An attacker who can get access to this secret will also have access to the service. This problem becomes more acute in a microservice architecture in which containers are constantly stopping and starting, as compared to an architecture with small numbers of long-lived VMs. Solutions for sharing secrets were previously discussed in "Sharing Secrets".

Containers and Namespacing

In a much-cited article, Dan Walsh of Red Hat wrote that "containers do not contain" (*https://opensource.com/business/14/7/docker-security-selinux*). By this, he primarily meant that not all resources that a container has access to are *namespaced*. Resources that *are* namespaced are mapped to a separate value on the host (e.g., PID 1 inside a container is not PID 1 on the host or in any other container). In contrast, resources that are not namespaced are the same on the host and in containers.

Resources that are not namespaced include:

User IDs (UIDs)

Users inside a container have the same UID in the container and on the host. This means that if a container is running as the root user, and a container breakout occurs, the attacker will be root on the host. There is work in progress to map the root user in a container to a high-numbered user on the host, but this hasn't landed yet.

The kernel keyring

If your application or a dependent application uses the kernel keyring for handling cryptographic keys or something similar, it's *very* important to be aware of this. Keys are separated by UID; therefore, containers running with the same UID will have access to the same keys, as well as the equivalent user on the host.

The kernel itself and any kernel modules

If a container loads a kernel module (which requires extra privileges), the module will be available across all containers and the host. This includes the Linux Security Modules discussed later.

Devices
> Including disk drives, sound-cards, and graphics processing units (GPUs).

The system time
> Changing the time inside a container changes the system time for the host and all other containers. This is only possible in containers that have been given the `SYS_TIME` capability, which is not granted by default.

The simple fact is that both Docker and the underlying Linux kernel features it relies on are still young and nowhere near as battle hardened as the equivalent VM technology. For the time being at least, containers do not offer the same level of security guarantees as VMs.[2]

Defense-in-Depth

So what can you do? Assume vulnerability and build defense-in-depth. Consider the analogy of a castle, which has multiple layers of defense, tailored to thwart various kinds of attack. Typically, a castle has a moat, or exploits local geography, to control access routes to the castle. The walls are thick stone, designed to repel fire and cannon blasts. There are battlements for defenders and multiple levels of keeps inside the castle walls. Should an attacker get past one of set of defenses, there will be another to face.

The defenses for your system should also consist of multiple layers. For example, your containers will most likely run in VMs so that if a container-breakout occurs, another level of defense can prevent the attacker from getting to the host or containers belonging to other users. Monitoring systems should be in place to alert admins in the case of unusual behavior. Firewalls should restrict network access to containers, limiting the external attack surface.

Least Privilege

Another important principle to adhere to is *least privilege*; each process and container should run with the minimum set of access rights and resources it needs to perform

---

2 There is an interesting argument about whether containers will ever be as secure as VMs. VM proponents argue that the lack of a hypervisor and the need to share kernel resources mean that containers will always be less secure. Container proponents argue that VMs are more vulnerable because of their greater attack surface, pointing to the large amounts of complicated and privileged code in VMs required for emulating esoteric hardware (as an example, see the recent VENOM vulnerability (*http://venom.crowdstrike.com/*) that exploited code in floppy-drive emulation).

its function.[3] The main benefit of this approach is that if one container is compromised, the attacker should still be severely limited in being able to access further data or resources.

In regards to least privilege, you can take many steps to reduce the capabilities of containers, such as:

- Ensure that processes in containers do not run as root so that exploiting a vulnerability present in a process does not give the attacker root access.
- Run filesystems as read-only so that attackers cannot overwrite data or save malicious scripts to file.
- Cut down on the kernel calls a container can make to reduce the potential attack surface.
- Limit the resources a container can use to avoid DoS attacks where a compromised container or application consumes enough resources (such as memory or CPU) to bring the host to a halt.

Docker Privileges == Root Privileges

This chapter focuses on the security of running containers, but it is important to point out that you also have to be careful about who you give access to the Docker daemon. Any user who can start and run Docker containers effectively has root access to the host. For example, consider that you can run the following:

```
$ docker run -v /:/homeroot -it debian bash
...
```

And you can now access any file or binary on the host machine.

If you run remote API access to your Docker daemon, be careful about how you secure it and who you give access to. If possible, restrict access to the local network.

Securing Identidock

In order to provide some context to this chapter, let's take a look at how we could secure the identidock application for production. Identidock doesn't store any sensitive information, so the main concern is an attacker getting in and repurposing the

---

3 The concept of least privilege was first articulated as, "Every program and every privileged user of the system should operate using the least amount of privilege necessary to complete the job," by Jerome Saltzer in "Protection and the Control of Information Sharing in Multics" (*Communications of the ACM*, vol. 17). Recently, Diogo Mónica and Nathan McCauley from Docker have been championing the idea of "least-privilege microservices" based on Saltzer's principle.

server for spam or similar. I am assuming that identidock is of some value and has a user base that would be at least mildly disappointed if identidock stopped working.[4]

The major things I would make sure are in place include:

- The identidock containers run in a VM or on a dedicated host to avoid exposing other users or services to attack (see "Segregate Containers by Host").
- The loadbalancer/reverse proxy is the only container that exposes a port to the outside world, cutting out a large amount of attack surface. Any monitoring or logging services should only be exposed via private interfaces or VPN (see "Limit Container Networking").
- All identidock images define a user and do not run as root (see "Set a User").
- All identidock images are downloaded by hash or otherwise obtained in a secure and verified manner (see "Image Provenance").
- Monitoring and alerting is in place for detecting unusual traffic or behavior (see Chapter 10).
- All containers are running with up-to-date software and in production mode with debug information turned off (see "Applying Updates").
- AppArmor or SELinux is enabled if available on the host (see "AppArmor" and "SELinux").
- Add some form of access control or password protection to Redis.

Given enough time, I would:

- Remove any unneeded setuid binaries from the identidock images. This reduces the risk of attackers who gain access to a container being able to increase their privileges (see "Remove Setuid/Setgid Binaries").
- Run filesystems as read-only where possible. The dnmonster, identidock, and redis containers can run with a read-only container filesystem, but the redis volume must be writable (see "Limit Filesystems").
- Drop unneeded kernel privileges. Both the dnmonster and identidock containers will run with all capabilities dropped (see "Limit Capabilities").

If I was feeling more paranoid, or running a more security sensitive service, I would:

- Limit memory on each container with the -m flag. This would prevent some DoS attacks and memory leaks. Requires profiling of the containers to determine the maximum memory usage, or very loose limits.

---

4 Again, it's easiest if you play along…

- Run SELinux with specialized types for the containers. This can be a very effective security measure but represents a significant amount of work and is only possible if running with the devicemapper storage driver (see "SELinux").

- Apply a `ulimit` on the number of processes. This limit is applied to the user of the container, so it is more tricky to use than it may sound. It will cut out the threat of fork bombs being used as a DoS attack (see "Apply Resource Limits (ulimits)").

- Encrypt internal communications to make it harder for attackers to tamper with data.

In addition, there should be periodic audits of the system to make sure everything is up to date and no containers are hogging resources. Even in a toy application like identidock, there are a lot of security measures that should be put in place and a lot more that can be considered.

The rest of this chapter will go into detail about how to implement these defenses and more. The key point to remember is that the more checks and boundaries you have in place, the greater the chances of stopping an attack before it can do real harm. Used incorrectly, Docker will reduce the security of the system by opening up new attack vectors. Used correctly, it will improve security by adding further levels of isolation and limiting the scope of applications to damage the system.

Segregate Containers by Host

If you have a multitenancy setup where you are running containers for multiple users (whether these are internal users in your organization or external customers), ensure each user is placed on a separate Docker host, as shown in Figure 13-1. This is less efficient than sharing hosts between users and will result in a higher number of VMs and/or machines than reusing hosts but is important for security. The main reason is to prevent container breakouts resulting in a user gaining access to another user's containers or data. If a container breakout occurs, the attacker will still be on a separate VM or machine and unable to easily access containers belonging to other users.

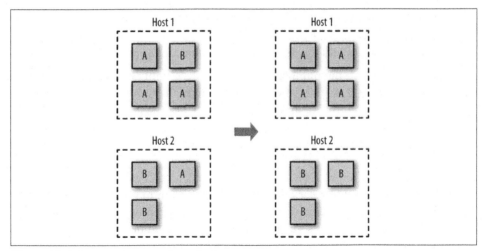

Figure 13-1. Segregating containers by host

Similarly, if you have containers that process or store sensitive information, keep them on a host separate from containers handling less sensitive information, and in particular, away from containers running applications directly exposed to end users. For example, containers processing credit card details should be kept separate from containers running the Node.js frontend.

Segregation and use of VMs can also provide added protection against DoS attacks; users won't be able to monopolize the memory on the host and starve out other users if they are contained within their own VM.

In the short to medium term, the vast majority of container deployments will involve VMs. Although this isn't an ideal situation, it does mean we can combine the efficiency of containers with the security of VMs.

Applying Updates

The ability to quickly apply updates to a running system is critical to maintaining security, especially when vulnerabilities are disclosed in common utilities and frameworks.

The process of updating a containerized system roughly involves the following steps:

1. Identify images that require updating. This includes both base images and any dependent images. See "Getting a List of Running Images" for how to do this with the CLI.

2. Get or create an updated version of each base image. Push this version to your registry or download site.

3. For each dependent image, run `docker build` with the `--no-cache` argument. Again, push these images.

4. On each Docker host, run `docker pull` to ensure that it has up-to-date images.

5. Restart the containers on each Docker host.

6. Once you've determined that everything is functioning correctly, remove the old images from the hosts. If you can, also remove them from your registry.

Some of these steps sound easier than they are. Identifying images that need updating may require some grunt work and shell fu. Restarting the containers assumes you have in place some sort of support for rolling updates or are willing to tolerate down-time. At the time of writing, functionality to completely remove images from a registry and reclaim the disk space is still being worked on.[5]

If you use the Docker Hub to build your images, note that you can set up *repository links* that will kick off a build of your image when any linked image changes. By setting a link to the base image, your image will automatically get rebuilt if the base image changes.

Getting a List of Running Images

The following gets the image IDs for all running images:

```
$ docker inspect -f "{{.Image}}" $(docker ps -q)
42a3cf88f3f0cce2b4bfb2ed714eec5ee937525b4c7e0a0f70daff18c3f2ee92
41b730702607edf9b07c6098f0b704ff59c5d4361245e468c0d551f50eae6f84
```

We can use a little more shell fu to get some more information:

```
$ docker images --no-trunc | \
    grep $(docker inspect -f "-e {{.Image}}" $(docker ps -q))
nginx    latest    42a3cf88f...    2 weeks ago    132.8 MB
debian   latest    41b730702...    2 weeks ago    125.1 MB
```

To get a list of all images and their base or intermediate images (use `--no-trunc` for full IDs):

```
$ docker inspect -f "{{.Image}}" $(docker ps -q) | \
    xargs -L 1 docker history -q
41b730702607
3cb35ae859e7
42a3cf88f3f0
e59ba510498b
50c46b6286b9
ee8776c93fde
439e7909f795
```

---

5 A workaround is to pull all the images you want to keep, then push them in to a new, clean registry.

```
0b5e8be9b692
e7e840eed70b
7ed37354d38d
55516e2f2530
97d05af69c46
41b730702607
3cb35ae859e7
```

And you can extend this again to get information on the images:

```
$ docker images | \
    grep $(docker inspect -f "{{.Image}}" $(docker ps -q) | \
        xargs -L 1 docker history -q | sed "s/^/\-e /")
nginx   latest   42a3cf88f3f0   2 weeks ago   132.8 MB
debian  latest   41b730702607   2 weeks ago   125.1 MB
```

If you want to get details on the intermediate images as well as named images, add the
-a argument to the docker images command. Note that this command has a significant gotcha—if your host doesn't have a tagged version of a base image, it won't show
up in the list. For example, the official Redis image is based on debian:wheezy, but
the base image will appear as <None> in docker images -a unless the host has separately and explicitly pulled the debian:wheezy image (and it is exactly the same version of that image).

When you need to patch a vulnerability found in a third-party image, including the
official images, you are dependent on that party providing a timely update. In the
past, providers have been criticized for being slow to respond. In such a situation, you
can either wait or prepare your own image. Assuming you have access to the Dockerfile and source for the image, rolling your image may be a simple and effective temporary solution.

This approach should be contrasted with the typical VM approach of using configuration management (CM) software such as Puppet, Chef, or Ansible. In the CM
approach, VMs aren't re-created but are updated and patched as needed, either
through SSH commands or an agent installed in the VM. This approach works, but it
means that separate VMs are often in different states, and involves significant complexity in tracking and updating the VMs. This is necessary to avoid the overhead of
re-creating VMs and maintaining a master or golden image for the service. The CM
approach can be taken with containers as well but adds significant complexity for no
benefit—the simpler golden image approach works well with containers because of
the speed at which containers can be started and the ease of building and maintaining
images.[6]

---

6 This is very similar to modern ideas of *immutable infrastructure*, where infrastructure—including bare metal,
  VMs, and containers—is never modified and is instead replaced when a change is required.

Label Your Images

Identifying images and what they contain can be made a lot easier by liberal use of labels when building images. This feature appeared in 1.6 and allows the image creator to associate arbitrary key-value pairs with an image. This can be done in the Dockerfile:

```
FROM debian
LABEL version 1.0
LABEL description "A test image for describing labels"
```

You can take things further and add data such as the Git hash that the code in the image was compiled from, but this requires using some form of templating tool to automatically update the value.

Labels can also be added to a container at runtime:

```
$ docker run -d --name label-test \
                    -l group=a debian sleep 100
1d8d8b622ec86068dfa5cf251cbaca7540b7eaa67664a13c620006...
$ docker inspect -f '{{json .Config.Labels}}' label-test
{"group":"a"}
```

This can be useful when you want to handle certain events at runtime, such as dynamically allocating containers to load-balancer groups.

At times, you will need to update the Docker daemon to gain access to new features, security patches, or bug fixes. This will force you to either migrate all containers to a new host or temporarily halt them while the update is applied. It is recommended that you subscribe to either the docker-user (*http://bit.ly/1XLSu8X*) or docker-dev (*http://bit.ly/1XLSx4y*) Google groups to receive notifications of important updates.

Avoid Unsupported Drivers

Despite its youth, Docker has already gone through several stages of development, and various features have been deprecated or unmaintained. Relying on such features is a security risk, as they will not be receiving the same attention and updates as other parts of Docker. The same goes for drivers and extensions depended on by Docker.

In particular, do not use the legacy LXC execution driver. By default, this is turned off, but you should check that your daemon isn't running with the -e lxc argument.

Storage drivers are another major area of development and change. At the time of writing, Docker is moving from AUFS to Overlay as the preferred storage driver. The AUFS driver is being taken out of the kernel and is no longer under development. Users of AUFS are encouraged to move to Overlay in the near future.

Image Provenance

To safely use images, we need to have guarantees about their *provenance* (i.e., where they came from and who created them). We need to be sure that we are getting exactly the same image the original developer tested and that no one has tampered with it, either during storage or transit. If we can't verify this, the image may have become corrupted or—much worse—replaced with something malicious. Given the previously discussed security issues with Docker, this a major concern; you should assume that a malicious image has full access to the host.

Provenance is far from a new problem in computing. The primary tool in establishing the provenance of software or data is the *secure hash*. A secure hash is something like a fingerprint for data—it is a (comparatively) small string that is unique to the given data. Any changes to the data will result in the hash changing. Several algorithms are available for calculating secure hashes, with varying degrees of complexity and guarantees of the uniqueness of the hash. The most common algorithms are SHA (which has several variants) and MD5 (which has fundamental problems and should be avoided). If we have a secure hash for some data and the data itself, we can recalculate the hash for the data and compare it. If the hashes match, we can be certain the data has not been corrupted or tampered with. However, one issue remains—why should we trust the hash? What's to stop an attacker from modifying both the data and the hash? The best answer to this is *cryptographic signing* and public/private key pairs.

Through cryptographic signing, we can verify the identify of the publisher of an artifact. If a publisher signs an artifact with their *private key*,[7] any recipient of that artifact can verify it came from the publisher by checking the signature using the publisher's *public key*. Assuming the client has already obtained a copy of the publisher's key, and that publisher's key has not been compromised, we can be sure the content came from the publisher and has not been tampered with.

Docker Digests

Secure hashes are known as *digests* in Docker parlance. A digest is a SHA256 hash of a filesystem layer or manifest, where a manifest is a metadata file describing the constituent parts of a Docker image. As the manifest contains a list of all the image's layers identified by digest,[8] if you can verify that the manifest hasn't been tampered with, you can safely download and trust all the layers, even over untrustworthy channels (e.g., HTTP).

---

7 A full discussion of public-key cryptography is fascinating but out of scope here. For more information, see *Applied Cryptography* by Bruce Schneier (Wiley).

8 A similar construct is used in protocols such as BitTorrent and Bitcoin and is known as a *hash list*.

Docker Content Trust

Docker introduced content trust in 1.8. This is Docker's mechanism for allowing publishers[9] to sign their content, completing the trusted distribution mechanism. When a user pulls an image from a repository, she receives a certificate that includes the publisher's public key, allowing her to verify that the image came from the publisher.

When content trust is enabled, the Docker engine will only operate on images that have been signed and will refuse to run any images whose signatures or digests do not match.

Let's see content trust in action. We'll start by trying to pull signed and unsigned images:

```
$ export DOCKER_CONTENT_TRUST=1 ❶
$ docker pull debian:wheezy
Pull (1 of 1): debian:wheezy@sha256:c584131da2ac1948aa3e66468a4424b6aea2f33a...
sha256:c584131da2ac1948aa3e66468a4424b6aea2f33acba7cec0b631bdb56254c4fe: Pul...
4c8cbfd2973e: Pull complete
60c52dbe9d91: Pull complete
Digest: sha256:c584131da2ac1948aa3e66468a4424b6aea2f33acba7cec0b631bdb56254c4fe
Status: Downloaded newer image for debian@sha256:c584131da2ac1948aa3e66468a4...
Tagging debian@sha256:c584131da2ac1948aa3e66468a4424b6aea2f33acba7cec0b631bd...
$ docker pull amouat/identidock:unsigned
No trust data for unsigned
```

❶ In Docker 1.8, content trust must be enabled by setting the environment variable DOCKER_CONTENT_TRUST=1. In later versions of Docker, this will become the default.

Here we can see that the official, signed, Debian image has pulled successfully. In contrast, Docker has refused to pull the unsigned image amouat/identidock:unsigned.

So what about pushing signed images? It's surprisingly easy:

```
$ docker push amouat/identidock:newest
The push refers to a repository [docker.io/amouat/identidock] (len: 1)
...
843e2bded498: Image already exists
newest: digest: sha256:1a0c4d72c5d52094fd246ec03d6b6ac43836440796da1043b6ed8...
Signing and pushing trust metadata
You are about to create a new root signing key passphrase. This passphrase
will be used to protect the most sensitive key in your signing system. Please
choose a long, complex passphrase and be careful to keep the password and the
key file itself secure and backed up. It is highly recommended that you use a
password manager to generate the passphrase and keep it safe. There will be no
```

---

9 In the context of this chapter, anyone who pushes an image is a publisher; it is not restricted to large companies or organizations.

```
way to recover this key. You can find the key in your config directory.
Enter passphrase for new offline key with id 70878f1:
Repeat passphrase for new offline key with id 70878f1:
Enter passphrase for new tagging key with id docker.io/amouat/identidock ...
Repeat passphrase for new tagging key with id docker.io/amouat/identidock ...
Finished initializing "docker.io/amouat/identidock"
```

Because this is the first time I've pushed to this repository with content trust enabled, Docker has created a new *root signing key* and a *tagging key*. We'll come back to the tagging key in a minute, but note the importance of keeping the root key safe and secure. Life becomes very difficult if you lose this; all users of your repositories will be unable to pull new images or update existing images without manually removing the old certificate.

Now we can download our image using content trust:

```
$ docker rmi amouat/identidock:newest
Untagged: amouat/identidock:newest
$ docker pull amouat/identidock:newest
Pull (1 of 1): amouat/identidock:newest@sha256:1a0c4d72c5d52094fd246ec03d6b6...
sha256:1a0c4d72c5d52094fd246ec03d6b6ac43836440796da1043b6ed81ea4167eb71: Pul...
...
7e7d073d42e9: Already exists
Digest: sha256:1a0c4d72c5d52094fd246ec03d6b6ac43836440796da1043b6ed81ea4167eb71
Status: Downloaded newer image for amouat/identidock@sha256:1a0c4d72c5d52094...
Tagging amouat/identidock@sha256:1a0c4d72c5d52094fd246ec03d6b6ac43836440796d...
```

If you haven't downloaded an image from a given repository before, Docker will first retrieve the certificate for the publisher of that repository. This is done over HTTPS and is low risk, but can be likened to connecting to a host via SSH for the first time; you have to trust that you are being given the correct credentials. Future pulls from that repository can be verified using the existing certificate.

Back Up Your Signing Keys!

Docker will encrypt all keys at rest and takes care to ensure private material is never written to disk. Due to the importance of the keys, it is recommended that they are backed up on two encrypted USB sticks kept in a secure location. To create a TAR file with the keys, run:

```
$ umask 077
$ tar -zcvf private_keys_backup.tar.gz \
             ~/.docker/trust/private
$ umask 022
```

The umask commands ensure file permissions are set to read-only.

Note that as the root key is only needed when creating or revoking keys, it can—and should—be stored offline when not in use.

Back to the tagging key. A tagging key is generated for each repository owned by a publisher. The tagging key is signed by the root key, which allows it to be verified by any user with the publisher's certificate. The tagging key can be shared within an organization and used to sign any images for that repository. After generating the tagging key, the root key can and should be taken offline and stored securely.

Should a tagging key become compromised, it is still possible to recover. By rotating the tagging key, the compromised key can be removed from the system. This process happens invisibly to the user and can be done proactively to protect against undetected key compromises.

Content trust also provides freshness guarantees to guard against *replay attacks*. A replay attack occurs when an artifact is replaced with a previously valid artifact. For example, an attacker may replace a binary with an older, known vulnerable version that was previously signed by the publisher. As the binary is correctly signed, the user can be tricked into running the vulnerable version of the binary. To avoid this, content trust makes use of *timestamp keys* associated with each repository. These keys are used to sign metadata associated with the repository. The metadata has a short expiration date that requires it to be frequently resigned by the timestamp key. By verifying that the metadata has not expired before downloading the image, the Docker client can be sure it is receiving an up-to-date (or fresh) image. The timestamp keys are managed by the Docker Hub and do not require any interaction from the publisher.

A repository can contain both signed and unsigned images. If you have content trust enabled and want to download an unsigned image, use the `--disable-content-trust` flag:

```
$ docker pull amouat/identidock:unsigned
No trust data for unsigned
$ docker pull --disable-content-trust amouat/identidock:unsigned
unsigned: Pulling from amouat/identidock
...
7e7d073d42e9: Already exists
Digest: sha256:ea9143ea9952ca27bfd618ce718501d97180dbf1b5857ff33467dfdae08f57be
Status: Downloaded newer image for amouat/identidock:unsigned
```

If you want to learn more about content trust (*https://docs.docker.com/security/trust/content_trust/*), see the official Docker documentation, as well as The Update Framework (*http://theupdateframework.com/*), which is the underlying specification used by content trust.

While this is a reasonably complex infrastructure with multiple sets of keys, Docker has worked hard to ensure it is still simple for end users. With content trust, Docker has developed a user-friendly, modern security framework providing provenance, freshness, and integrity guarantees.

Content trust is currently enabled and working on the Docker Hub. To set up content trust for a local registry, you will also need to configure and deploy a Notary server (*https://github.com/docker/notary*).

Notary

The Docker Notary project (*https://github.com/docker/notary*) is a generic server-client framework for publishing and accessing content in a trustworthy and secure manner. Notary is based on The Update Framework specification, which provides a secure design for distributing and updating content.

Docker's content trust framework is essentially an integration of Notary with the Docker API. By running both a registry and a Notary server, organizations can provide trusted images to users. However, Notary is designed to be standalone and usable in a wide range of scenarios.

A major use case for Notary is to improve the security and trustworthiness of the common `curl | sh` approach, which is typified by the current Docker installation instructions:

```
$ curl -sSL https://get.docker.com/ | sh
```

If such a download is compromised either on the server or in transit, the attacker will be able to run arbitrary commands on the victim's computer. The use of HTTPS will stop the attacker from being able to modify data in transit, but they may still be able to prematurely end the download, thereby truncating the code in a potentially dangerous way. The equivalent example of using Notary looks something like this:

```
$ curl http://get.docker.com/ | notary verify docker.com/scripts v1 | sh
```

The call to `notary` compares a checksum for the script with the checksum in Notary's trusted collection for *docker.com*. If it passes, we have verified that the script does indeed come from *docker.com* and has not been tampered with. If it fails, Notary will bail out, and no data will be passed to `sh`. What's also notable is that the script itself can be transferred over insecure channels—in this case, HTTP—without worry; if the script is altered in transit, the checksum will change and Notary will throw an error.

If you are using unsigned images, it is still possible to verify images by pulling by digest, instead of by name and tag. For example:

```
$ docker pull debian@sha256:f43366bc755696485050ce14e1429c481b6f0ca04505c4a3093d\
fdb4fafb899e
```

This will pull the `debian:jessie` image as of the time of writing. Unlike the `debian:jessie` tag, it is guaranteed to always pull exactly the same image (or none at all). If the digest can be securely transferred and authenticated in some manner (e.g., sent via a PGP signed email from a trusted party), you can guarantee the authenticity of the image. Even with content trust enabled, it is still possible to pull by digest.

If you don't trust either a private registry or the Docker Hub to distribute your images, you can always use the docker load and docker save commands to export and import images. The images can be distributed by an internal download site or simply by copying files. Of course, if you go down this route, you are likely to find yourself re-creating many of the features of the Docker registry and content-trust components.

Reproducible and Trustworthy Dockerfiles

Ideally, Dockerfiles should produce exactly the same image each time. In practice, this is hard to achieve. The same Dockerfile is likely to produce different images over time. This is clearly a problematic situation, as again, it becomes hard to be sure what is in your images. It is possible to at least come close to entirely reproducible builds by adhering to the following rules when writing Dockerfiles:

- Always specify a tag in FROM instructions. FROM redis is bad, because it pulls the latest tag, which is expected to change over time, including major version changes. FROM redis:3.0 is better but can still be expected to change with minor updates and bug fixes (which may be exactly what you want). If you want to be sure you are pulling exactly the same image each time, the only choice is to use a digest, as described previously. Using a digest will also protect against accidental corruption or tampering. For example:

```
FROM redis@sha256:3479bbcab384fa343b52743b933661335448f8166203688006...
```

- Provide version numbers when installing software from package managers. apt-get install cowsay is OK, as cowsay is unlikely to change; but apt-get install cowsay=3.03+dfsg1-6 is better. The same goes for other package installers such as pip—provide a version number if you can. The build will fail if an old package is removed, but at least this gives you a warning. Also note that a problem still remains: packages are likely to pull in dependencies, and these dependencies are often specified in >= terms and can hence change over time. To completely lock down the version of things, have a look at tools like aptly (*http://www.aptly.info/*), which allows you to take snapshots of repositories.

- Verify any software or data downloaded from the Internet. This means using checksums or cryptographic signatures. Of all the guidelines listed here, this is the most important. If you don't verify downloads, you are vulnerable to accidental corruption as well as attackers tampering with downloads. This is particularly important when software is transferred with HTTP, which offers no guarantees against man-in-the-middle attacks. The following section offers specific advice on how to do this.

Most Dockerfiles for the official images provide good examples of using tagged versions and verifying downloads. They also typically use a specific tag of a base image but do not use version numbers when installing software from package managers.

Securely downloading software in Dockerfiles

In the majority of cases, vendors will make signed checksums available for verifying downloads. For example, the Dockerfile for the official Node.js image includes the following:

```
RUN gpg --keyserver pool.sks-keyservers.net \
        --recv-keys 7937DFD2AB06298B2293C3187D33FF9D0246406D \
                    114F43EE0176B71C7BC219DD50A3051F888C628D ❶

ENV NODE_VERSION 0.10.38
ENV NPM_VERSION 2.10.0
RUN curl -SLO "http://nodejs.org/dist/v$NODE_VERSION/\
node-v$NODE_VERSION-linux-x64.tar.gz" \ ❷
   && curl -SLO "http://nodejs.org/dist/v$NODE_VERSION/SHASUMS256.txt.asc" \ ❸
   && gpg --verify SHASUMS256.txt.asc \ ❹
   && grep " node-v$NODE_VERSION-linux-x64.tar.gz\$" SHASUMS256.txt.asc \
   | sha256sum -c - ❺
```

❶ Gets the GPG keys used to sign the Node.js download. Here we do have to trust that these are the correct keys.

❷ Downloads the Node.js tarball.

❸ Downloads the checksum for the tarball.

❹ Uses GPG to verify that the checksum was signed by whoever owns the keys we obtained.

❺ Checks that the checksum matches the tarball by using the sha256sum tool.

If either the GPG test or the checksum test fails, the build will abort.

In some cases, packages are available in third-party repositories, which means they can be installed securely by adding the given repository and its signing key. For example, the Dockerfile for the official Nginx image includes the following:

```
RUN apt-key adv --keyserver hkp://pgp.mit.edu:80 \
                --recv-keys 573BFD6B3D8FBC641079A6ABABF5BD827BD9BF62
RUN echo "deb http://nginx.org/packages/mainline/debian/ jessie nginx" \
        >> /etc/apt/sources.list
```

The first command obtains the signing key for Nginx (which is added to the keystore), and the second command adds the Nginx package repository to the list of repositories to check for software. After this, Nginx can be simply and securely installed with `apt-get install -y nginx` (preferably with a version number).

Assuming no signed package or checksum is available, creating your own is straightforward. For example, to create a checksum for a Redis release:

```
$ curl -s -o redis.tar.gz http://download.redis.io/releases/redis-3.0.1.tar.gz
$ sha1sum -b redis.tar.gz ❶
fe1d06599042bfe6a0e738542f302ce9533dde88 *redis.tar.gz
```

❶ Here we're creating a 160-bit SHA1 checksum. The `-b` flag tells the `sha1sum` utility that we are dealing with binary data, not text.

Once you've tested and verified the software, you can add something like the following to your Dockerfile:

```
RUN curl -sSL -o redis.tar.gz \
        http://download.redis.io/releases/redis-3.0.1.tar.gz \
    && echo "fe1d06599042bfe6a0e738542f302ce9533dde88 *redis.tar.gz" \
    | sha1sum -c -
```

This downloads the file as *redis.tar.gz* and asks `sha1sum` to verify the checksum. If the check fails, the command will fail, and the build will abort.

Changing all these details for each release is a lot of work if you release often, so automating the process is worthwhile. In many of the official image repositories, such as this one (*http://bit.ly/1QMyDVf*), you can find *update.sh* scripts for this purpose.

Security Tips

This section contains actionable tips on securing container deployments. Not all the advice is applicable to all deployments, but you should become familiar with the basic tools you can use.

Many of the tips describe various ways in which containers can be limited so that they are unable to adversely affect other containers or the host. The main issue to bear in mind is that the host kernel's resources—CPU, memory, network, UIDs, and so forth—are shared among containers. If a container monopolizes any of these, it will starve out other containers. Worse, if a container can exploit a bug in kernel code, it may be able to bring down the host or gain access to the host and other containers. This could be caused either accidentally, through some buggy programming, or maliciously, by an attacker seeking to disrupt or compromise the host.

Set a User

Never run production applications as root inside the container. That's worth saying again: *never run production applications as root inside the container*. If you don't follow this advice, an attacker who breaks the application will have full access to the container, including its data and programs. Worse, an attacker who manages to break out of the container will have root access on the host. You wouldn't run an application as root in a VM or on bare metal, so don't do it in a container.

To avoid running as root, your Dockerfiles should always create a nonprivileged user and switch to it with a USER statement or from an entrypoint script. For example:

```
RUN groupadd -r user_grp && useradd -r -g user_grp user
USER user
```

This creates a group called `user_grp` and a new user called `user` who belongs to that group. The USER statement will take effect for all of the following instructions and when a container is started from the image. You may need to delay the USER instruction until later in the Dockerfile if you need to first perform actions that need root privileges such as installing software.

Many of the official images create an unprivileged user in the same way but do not contain a USER instruction. Instead, they switch users in an entrypoint script, using the *gosu* utility. For example, the entrypoint script for the official Redis image looks like this:

```
#!/bin/bash
set -e
if [ "$1" = 'redis-server' ]; then
        chown -R redis .
        exec gosu redis "$@"
fi

exec "$@"
```

This script includes the line `chown -R redis .`, which sets the ownership of all files under the images data directory to the redis user. If the Dockerfile had declared a USER, this line wouldn't work. The next line `exec gosu redis "$@"` executes the given redis command as the redis user. The use of exec means the current shell is replaced with redis, which becomes PID 1 and has any signals forwarded appropriately.

Use gosu, not sudo

The traditional tool for executing commands as another user is sudo. While sudo is a powerful and venerable tool, it has some side effects that make it less than ideal for use in entrypoint scripts. For example, we can see what happens if we run sudo ps aux inside an Ubuntu[10] container:

```
$ docker run --rm ubuntu:trusty sudo ps aux
USER        PID %CPU ... COMMAND
root          1  0.0       sudo ps aux
root          5  0.0       ps aux
```

We have two processes, one for sudo and one for the command we ran.

In contrast, if we install gosu into an Ubuntu image:

```
$ docker run --rm amouat/ubuntu-with-gosu \
                      gosu root ps aux
USER        PID %CPU ... COMMAND
root          1  0.0       ps aux
```

we have only one process running—gosu has executed the command and gotten out of the way completely. Importantly, the command is running as PID 1, so it will correctly receive any signals sent to the container, unlike the sudo example.

If you have an application that insists on running as root (and you can't fix it), consider using tools such as sudo, SELinux (see "SELinux"), and fakeroot to constrain the process.

Limit Container Networking

A container should open only the ports it needs to use in production, and these ports should be accessible only to the other containers that need them. This is a little trickier than it sounds, as by default, containers can talk to each other whether or not ports have been explicitly published or exposed. We can see this by having a quick play with the Netcat tool:[11]

```
$ docker run --name nc-test -d amouat/network-utils nc -l 5001 ❶
f57269e2805cf3305e41303eafefaba9bf8d996d87353b10d0ca577acc731186
$ docker run \
    -e IP=$(docker inspect -f {{.NetworkSettings.IPAddress}} nc-test) \
    amouat/network-utils sh -c 'echo -n "hello" | nc -v $IP 5001' ❷
Connection to 172.17.0.3 5001 port [tcp/*] succeeded!
```

---

10 I'm using Ubuntu instead of Debian here as the Ubuntu image includes sudo by default.

11 We're using the OpenBSD version here.

```
$ docker logs nc-test
hello
```

❶ Tells the Netcat utility to listen to port 5001 and echo any input.

❷ Sends "hello" to the first container using Netcat.

The second container is able to connect to nc-test despite there being no ports published or exposed. We can change this by running the Docker daemon with the **--icc=false** flag. This turns off inter-container communication, which can prevent compromised containers from being able to attack other containers. Any explicitly linked containers will still be able to communicate.

Docker controls inter-container communication by setting IPtables rules (which requires that the --iptables flag is set on the daemon, as it should be by default).

The following example demonstrates the effect of setting **--icc=false** on the daemon:

```
$ cat /etc/default/docker | grep DOCKER_OPTS=
DOCKER_OPTS="--iptables=true --icc=false" ❶
$ docker run --name nc-test -d --expose 5001 amouat/network-utils nc -l 5001
d7c267672c158e77563da31c1ee5948f138985b1f451cd2222cf248006491139
$ docker run \
    -e IP=$(docker inspect -f {{.NetworkSettings.IPAddress}} nc-test)
    amouat/network-utils sh -c 'echo -n "hello" | nc -w 2 -v $IP 5001' ❷
nc: connect to 172.17.0.10 port 5001 (tcp) timed out: Operation now in progress
$ docker run \
    --link nc-test:nc-test \
    amouat/network-utils sh -c 'echo -n "hello" | nc -w 2 -v nc-test 5001'
Connection to nc-test 5001 port [tcp/*] succeeded!
$ docker logs nc-test
hello
```

❶ On Ubuntu, the Docker daemon is configured by setting DOCKER_OPTS in */etc/default/docker*.

❷ The -w 2 flag tells Netcat to time out after two seconds.

The first connection fails, as intercontainer communication is off and no link is present. The second command succeeds, as we have added the link. If you want to understand how this works under the hood, try running sudo iptables -L -n on the host with and without linked containers.

When publishing ports to the host, Docker publishes to all interfaces (0.0.0.0) by default. You can instead specify the interface you want to bind to explicitly:

```
$ docker run -p 87.245.78.43:8080:8080 -d myimage
```

This reduces the attack surface by only allowing traffic from the given interface.

Remove Setuid/Setgid Binaries

Chances are that your application doesn't need any setuid or setgid binaries.[12] If we can disable or remove such binaries, we stop any chance of them being used for privilege escalation attacks.

The `find` command can be used to generate a list of such binaries. For example:

```
$ docker run debian find / -perm +6000 -type f -exec ls -ld {} \; 2> /dev/null
-rwsr-xr-x 1 root root   10248 Apr 15 00:02 /usr/lib/pt_chown
-rwxr-sr-x 1 root shadow 62272 Nov 20  2014 /usr/bin/chage
-rwsr-xr-x 1 root root   75376 Nov 20  2014 /usr/bin/gpasswd
-rwsr-xr-x 1 root root   53616 Nov 20  2014 /usr/bin/chfn
-rwsr-xr-x 1 root root   54192 Nov 20  2014 /usr/bin/passwd
-rwsr-xr-x 1 root root   44464 Nov 20  2014 /usr/bin/chsh
-rwsr-xr-x 1 root root   39912 Nov 20  2014 /usr/bin/newgrp
-rwxr-sr-x 1 root tty    27232 Mar 29 22:34 /usr/bin/wall
-rwxr-sr-x 1 root shadow 22744 Nov 20  2014 /usr/bin/expiry
-rwxr-sr-x 1 root shadow 35408 Aug  9  2014 /sbin/unix_chkpwd
-rwsr-xr-x 1 root root   40000 Mar 29 22:34 /bin/mount
-rwsr-xr-x 1 root root   40168 Nov 20  2014 /bin/su
-rwsr-xr-x 1 root root   70576 Oct 28  2014 /bin/ping
-rwsr-xr-x 1 root root   27416 Mar 29 22:34 /bin/umount
-rwsr-xr-x 1 root root   61392 Oct 28  2014 /bin/ping6
```

You can then "defang" the binaries with `chmod a-s` to remove the suid bit. For example, we can create a defanged Debian image with the following Dockerfile:

```
FROM debian:wheezy

RUN find / -perm +6000 -type f -exec chmod a-s {} \; || true ❶
```

❶ The `|| true` allows us to ignore any errors from the find command.

Build and run it:

```
$ docker build -t defanged-debian .
...
Successfully built 526744cf1bc1
$ docker run --rm defanged-debian \
  find / -perm +6000 -type f -exec ls -ld {} \; 2> /dev/null | wc -l
0
$
```

It's more likely that your Dockerfile will rely on a setuid/setgid binary than your application. Therefore, you can always perform this step near the end, after any such

---

12 Setuid and setgid binaries run with the privileges of the owner rather than the user. These are normally used to allow users to temporarily run with the escalated privileges required to execute a given task, such as setting a password.

calls and before changing the user (removing setuid binaries is pointless if the application runs with root privileges).

Limit Memory

Limiting memory protects against DoS attacks and applications with memory leaks that slowly consume all the memory on the host (such applications can be restarted automatically to maintain a level of service).

The `-m` and `--memory-swap` flags to `docker run` limit the amount of memory and swap memory a container can use. Somewhat confusingly, the `--memory-swap` argument sets the *total* amount of memory—that is, memory *plus* swap memory rather than just swap memory. By default, no limits are applied. If the `-m` flag is used but not `--memory-swap`, then `--memory-swap` is set to double the argument to `-m`. This is best explained with an example. Here we'll use the `amouat/stress` image that includes the Unix stress utility (*http://people.seas.harvard.edu/~apw/stress/*) used to test what happens when resources are hogged by a process. In this case, we will tell it to grab a certain amount of memory:

```
$ docker run -m 128m --memory-swap 128m amouat/stress \
    stress --vm 1 --vm-bytes 127m -t 5s ❶
stress: info: [1] dispatching hogs: 0 cpu, 0 io, 1 vm, 0 hdd
stress: info: [1] successful run completed in 5s
$ docker run -m 128m --memory-swap 128m amouat/stress \
    stress --vm 1 --vm-bytes 130m -t 5s ❷
stress: FAIL: [1] (416) <-- worker 6 got signal 9
stress: WARN: [1] (418) now reaping child worker processes
stress: FAIL: [1] (422) kill error: No such process
stress: FAIL: [1] (452) failed run completed in 0s
stress: info: [1] dispatching hogs: 0 cpu, 0 io, 1 vm, 0 hdd
$ docker run -m 128m amouat/stress \
    stress --vm 1 --vm-bytes 255m -t 5s ❸
stress: info: [1] dispatching hogs: 0 cpu, 0 io, 1 vm, 0 hdd
stress: info: [1] successful run completed in 5s
```

❶ These arguments tell the stress utility to run one process that will grab 127 MB of memory and timeout after five seconds.

❷ This time we try to grab 130 MB, which fails because we are only allowed 128 MB.

❸ This time we try to grab 255 MB, and because `--swap-memory` has defaulted to 256 MB, the command succeeds.

Limit CPU

If an attacker can get one container, or one group of containers, to start using all the CPU on the host, that attacker will be able to starve out any other containers on the host, resulting in a DoS attack.

In Docker, CPU share is determined by a *relative* weighting with a default value of 1,024; therefore, by default, all containers will receive an equal share of CPU.

The way it works is best explained with an example. Here we start four containers with the amouat/stress image we saw earlier, except this time they will all attempt to grab as much CPU as they like, rather than memory.

```
$ docker run -d --name load1 -c 2048 amouat/stress
912a37982de1d8d3c4d38ed495b3c24a7910f9613a55a42667d6d28e1da71fe5
$ docker run -d --name load2 amouat/stress
df69312a0c959041948857fca27b56539566fb5c7cda33139326f16485948bc8
$ docker run -d --name load3 -c 512 amouat/stress
c2675318fefafa3e9bfc891fa303a16e72caf221ec23a4c222c2b889ea82d6e2
$ docker run -d --name load4 -c 512 amouat/stress
5c6e199423b59ae481d41268c867c705f25a5375d627ab7b59c5fbfbcfc1d0e0
$ docker stats $(docker inspect -f {{.Name}} $(docker ps -q))
CONTAINER        CPU %     ...
/load1           392.13%
/load2           200.56%
/load3           97.75%
/load4           99.36%
```

In this example, the container load1 has a weighting of 2,048, load2 has the default weighting of 1,024, and the other two containers have weightings of 512. On my machine with 8 cores and hence a total of 800% CPU to allocate, this results in load1 getting approximately half the CPU, load2 getting a quarter, and load3 and load4 getting an eighth each. If only one container is running, it will be able to grab as much resources as it wants.

The relative weighting means it shouldn't be possible for any container to starve out the others with the default settings. However, you may have "groups" of containers that dominate CPU over other containers, in which case you can assign containers in that group a lower default value to ensure fairness. If you do assign CPU shares, make sure you bear the default value in mind so that any containers that run without an explicit setting still receive a fair share without dominating other containers.

Alternatively, CPU can be shared by using the *Completely Fair Scheduler* (CFS) by using the --cpu-period and --cpu-quota flags. In this method, containers are given a set CPU quota (defined in microseconds) they can use in a given period. If a container exceeds its CPU quota for a given period, it must wait until the next period before it can continue execution. For example:

```
$ docker run -d --cpu-period=50000 --cpu-quota=25000 myimage
```

This container would be allowed to use half the CPU every 50 ms, assuming a 1 CPU system. For more information on CFS, see the Linux kernel documentation (*https:// www.kernel.org/doc/Documentation/scheduler/sched-bwc.txt*).

Limit Restarts

If a container is constantly dying and restarting, it will waste a large amount of system time and resources, possibly to the extent of causing a DoS. This can be easily prevented by using the on-failure restart policy instead of the always policy. For example:

```
$ docker run -d --restart=on-failure:10 my-flaky-image
...
```

This causes Docker to restart the container up to a maximum of 10 times. The current restart count can be found under .RestartCount in the metadata returned by docker inspect:

```
$ docker inspect -f "{{ .RestartCount }}" $(docker ps -lq)
0
```

Docker employs an exponential backoff when restarting containers (it will wait for 100 ms, then 200 ms, then 400 ms, and so forth, on subsequent restarts). By itself, this should be effective in preventing DoS attacks that try to exploit the restart functionality.

Limit Filesystems

Stopping attackers from being able to write to file prevents several attacks and generally makes life harder for hackers. They can't write a script to file and trick your application into running it or overwrite sensitive data or configuration files.

Starting with Docker 1.5, you can pass the --read-only flag to docker run, which makes the container's filesystem entirely read-only:

```
$ docker run --read-only debian touch x
touch: cannot touch 'x': Read-only file system
```

You can do something similar with volumes by adding :ro to the end of the volume argument:

```
$ docker run -v $PWD:/pwd:ro debian touch /pwd/x
touch: cannot touch '/pwd/x': Read-only file system
```

The majority of applications need to write out files and won't operate in a completely read-only environment. In such cases, you can find the folders and files the application needs write access to and use volumes to mount only those files.

Adopting such an approach has huge benefits for auditing; if I can be sure my container's filesystem is exactly the same as the image it was created from, I can perform a single offline audit on the image rather than auditing each separate container.

Limit Capabilities

The Linux kernel defines sets of privileges—called *capabilities*—that can be assigned to processes to provide them with greater access to the system. The capabilities cover a wide range of functions, from changing the system time to opening network sockets. Previously, a process either had full root privileges or was just a user, with no in-between. This was particularly troubling with applications such as ping, which required root privileges only for opening a raw network socket. This meant that a small bug in the ping utility could allow attackers to gain full root privileges on the system. With the advent of capabilities, it is possible to create a version of ping that only has the privileges it needs for creating a raw network socket rather than full root privileges, which means would-be attackers gain much less from exploiting any bugs.

By default, Docker containers run with a subset of capabilities.[13] So, for example, a container will not normally be able to use devices such as the GPU and soundcard or insert kernel modules. To give extended privileges to a container, start it with the `--privileged` argument to `docker run`.

In terms of security, what we really want to do is limit the capabilities of containers as much as we can. We can control the capabilities available to a container by using the `--cap-add` and `--cap-drop` arguments. For example, if we want to change the system time (don't try this unless you want to break things!):

```
$ docker run debian date -s "10 FEB 1981 10:00:00"
Tue Feb 10 10:00:00 UTC 1981
date: cannot set date: Operation not permitted
$ docker run --cap-add SYS_TIME debian date -s "10 FEB 1981 10:00:00"
Tue Feb 10 10:00:00 UTC 1981
$ date
Tue Feb 10 10:00:03 GMT 1981
```

In this example, we can't modify the date until we add the SYS_TIME privilege to the container. As the system time is a non-namespaced kernel feature, setting the time inside a container sets it for the host and all other containers as well.[14]

A more restrictive approach is to drop all privileges and just add back the ones we need:

---

13 These are CHOWN, DAC_OVERRIDE, FSETID, FOWNER, MKNOD, NET_RAW, SETGID, SETUID, SETFCAP, SETPCAP, NET_BIND_SERVICE, SYS_CHROOT, KILL, and AUDIT_WRITE. Dropped capabilities notably include (but are not limited to) SYS_TIME, NET_ADMIN, SYS_MODULE, SYS_NICE, and SYS_ADMIN. For full information on capabilities, see man capabilities.

14 If you run this example, you'll have a broken system until you set the time correctly. Try running sudo ntpdate or sudo ntpdate-debian to change back to the correct time.

```
$ docker run --cap-drop all debian chown 100 /tmp
chown: changing ownership of '/tmp': Operation not permitted
$ docker run --cap-drop all --cap-add CHOWN debian chown 100 /tmp
```

This represents a major increase in security; an attacker who breaks into a container will still be hugely restricted in which kernel calls she is able to make. However, some problems exist:

- How do you know which privileges you can safely drop? Trial and error seems to be the simplest approach, but what if you accidentally drop a privilege your application only needs rarely? Identifying required privileges is easier if you have a full test suite you can run against the container and are following a microservices approach that has less code and moving parts in each container to consider.

- The capabilities are not as neatly grouped and fine-grained as you may wish. In particular, the SYS_ADMIN capability has a lot of functionality; kernel developers seemed to have used it as a default when they couldn't find (or perhaps couldn't be bothered to look for) a better alternative. In effect, it threatens to re-create the simple binary split of admin user versus normal user that capabilities were designed to take us away from.

Apply Resource Limits (ulimits)

The Linux kernel defines resource limits that can be applied to processes, such as limiting the number of child processes that can be forked and the number of open file descriptors allowed. These can also be applied to Docker containers, either by passing the --ulimit flag to docker run or setting container-wide defaults by passing --default-ulimit when starting the Docker daemon. The argument takes two values, a soft limit and a hard limit separated by a colon, the effects of which are dependent on the given limit. If only one value is provided, it is used for both the soft and hard limit.

The full set of possible values and meanings are described in full in man setrlimit (but note that the as limit can't be used with containers). Of particular interest are the following values:

cpu

  Limits the amount of CPU time to the given number of seconds. Takes a soft limit (after which the container is sent a SIGXCPU signal) followed by a SIGKILL when the hard limit is reached. For example, again using the stress utility from "Limit Memory" and "Limit CPU" to maximize CPU usage:

```
$ time docker run --ulimit cpu=12:14 amouat/stress stress --cpu 1
stress: FAIL: [1] (416) <-- worker 5 got signal 24
stress: WARN: [1] (418) now reaping child worker processes
stress: FAIL: [1] (422) kill error: No such process
```

```
stress: FAIL: [1] (452) failed run completed in 12s
stress: info: [1] dispatching hogs: 1 cpu, 0 io, 0 vm, 0 hdd

real  0m12.765s
user  0m0.247s
sys 0m0.014s
```

The ulimit argument killed the container after it used 12 seconds of CPU.

This is potentially useful for limiting the amount of CPU that can be used by containers kicked off by another process (e.g., running computations on behalf of users). Limiting CPU in such a way may be an effective mitigation against DoS attacks in such circumstances.

nofile

The maximum number of file descriptors[15] that can be concurrently open in the container. Again, this can be used to defend against DoS attacks and ensure an attacker isn't able to read or write to the container or volumes. (Note that you need to set nofile to *one more* than the maximum number you want.) For example:

```
$ docker run --ulimit nofile=5 debian cat /etc/hostname
b874469fe42b
$ docker run --ulimit nofile=4 debian cat /etc/hostname
Timestamp: 2015-05-29 17:02:46.956279781 +0000 UTC
Code: System error

Message: Failed to open /dev/null - open /mnt/sda1/var/lib/docker/aufs...
```

Here, the OS requires several file descriptors to be open, although cat only requires a single file descriptor. It's hard to be sure of how many file descriptors your application will need, but setting it to a number with plenty of room for growth offers some protection against DoS attacks, compared to the default of 1,048,576.

nproc

The maximum number of processes that can be created by the user of the container. On the face of it, this sounds useful, because it can prevent fork bombs and other types of attack. Unfortunately, the nproc limits are not set per container but rather for the user of the container across all processes. For example:

```
$ docker run --user 500 --ulimit nproc=2 -d debian sleep 100
92b162b1bb91af8413104792607b47507071c52a2e3128f0c6c7659bfbb84511
```

---

15 A *file descriptor* is a pointer into a table recording information on the open files on the system. An entry is created whenever a file is accessed, recording the mode (read, write, etc.) the file is accessed with and pointers to the underlying files.

```
$ docker run --user 500 --ulimit nproc=2 -d debian sleep 100
158f98af66c8eb53702e985c8c6e95bf9925401c3901c082a11889182bc843cb
$ docker run --user 500 --ulimit nproc=2 -d debian sleep 100
6444e3b5f97803c02b62eae601fbb1dd5f1349031e0251613b9ff80871555664
FATA[0000] Error response from daemon: Cannot start container 6444e3b...
[8] System error: resource temporarily unavailable
$ docker run --user 500 -d debian sleep 100
f740ab7e0516f931f09b634c64e95b97d64dae5c883b0a349358c5995806e503
```

The third container couldn't be started because two processes already belong to
UID 500. However, by simply dropping the --ulimit argument, we can continue
to create processes as the user. While this is a major drawback, nproc limits may
still be helpful in situations where you use the same user across a limited number
of containers.

Also note that you can't set nproc limits for the root user.

Run a Hardened Kernel

Beyond simply keeping your host operating system up to date and patched, you may
want to consider running a hardened kernel, using patches such as those provided by
grsecurity (*https://grsecurity.net/*) and PaX (*https://pax.grsecurity.net/*). PaX provides
extra protection against attackers manipulating program execution by modifying
memory (such as buffer overflow attacks). It does this by marking program code in
memory as nonwritable and data as nonexecutable. In addition, memory is randomly
arranged to mitigate against attacks that attempt to reroute code to existing procedures (such as system calls in common libraries). grsecurity is designed to work
alongside PaX and adds patches related to role-based access control (RBAC), auditing, and various other miscellaneous features.

To enable PaX and/or grsecurity, you will probably need to patch and compile the
kernel yourself. This isn't as daunting as it sounds, and plenty of resources are available, including WikiBooks (*http://bit.ly/1QMzhC1*) and InsanityBit (*http://bit.ly/
1QMzntt*).

These security enhancements may cause some applications to break. PaX will conflict
with any programs that generate code at runtime. Also, a small overhead is incurred
by the extra security checks and measures. Finally, if you use a precompiled kernel,
you will need to ensure that it is recent enough to support the version of Docker you
want to run.

Linux Security Modules

The Linux kernel defines the Linux Security Module (LSM) interface, which is implemented by various modules that want to enforce a particular security policy. At the

time of writing, several implementations exist, including AppArmor, SELinux, Smack, and TOMOYO Linux. These security modules can be used to provide another level of security checks on the access rights of processes and users, beyond that provided by the standard file-level access control.

The modules normally used with Docker are SELinux (typically with Red Hat–based distributions) and AppArmor (typically with Ubuntu and Debian distributions). We'll take a look at both of these modules now.

SELinux

The SELinux, or *Security Enhanced Linux*, module was developed by the National Security Agency (NSA) in the United States as an implementation of what it calls Mandatory Access Control (MAC), in contrast to the standard Unix model of Discretionary Access Control (DAC). In somewhat plainer language, there are two major differences between the access control enforced by SELinux and the standard Linux access controls:

- SELinux controls are enforced based on *types*, which are essentially labels applied to processes and objects (files, sockets, etc.). If the SELinux policy forbids a process of type A to access an object of type B, that access will be disallowed regardless of the file permissions on the object or the access privileges of the user. SELinux tests occur after the normal file-permission checks.
- It is possible to apply multiple levels of security, similar to the governmental model of confidential, secret, and top-secret access. Processes belonging to a lower level cannot read files written by processes of a higher level, regardless of the file permissions or which directory the files resides in. So a top-secret process could write a file to /tmp with chmod 777 privileges, but a confidential process would still be unable to access the file. This is known as *Multi-Level Security* (MLS) in SELinux, which also has the closely related concept of *Multi-Category Security* (MCS). MCS allows categories to be applied to processes and objects and denies access to a resource if it does not belong to the correct category. Unlike MLS, categories do not overlap and are not hierarchical. MCS can be used to restrict access to resources to subsets of a type (e.g., by using a unique category, a resource can be restricted to use by only a single process).

SELinux comes installed by default on Red Hat distributions and should be simple to install on most other distributions. You can check whether SELinux is running by executing sestatus. If that command exists, it will tell you whether SELinux is enabled or disabled and whether it is in permissive or enforcing mode. When in permissive mode, SELinux will log access-control infringements but will not enforce them.

The default SELinux policy for Docker is designed to protect the host from containers, as well as containers from other containers. Containers are assigned the default process type `svirt_lxc_net_t`, and files accessible to a container are assigned `svirt_sandbox_file_t`. The policy enforces rules that mean containers are only able to read and execute files from *usr* on the host and cannot write to any file on the host. It also assigns a unique MCS category number to each container, intended to prevent containers from being able to access files or resources written by other containers in the event of a breakout.

Enabling SELinux

If you're running a Red Hat–based distribution, SELinux should be installed already. You can check whether it's enabled and enforcing rules by running `sestatus` on the command line. To enable SELinux and set it to enforcing mode, edit */etc/selinux/config*, so that it contains the line `SELINUX=enforcing`.

You will also need to ensure that SELinux support is enabled on the Docker daemon. The daemon should be running with the flag `--selinux-enabled`. If not, it should be added to the file */etc/sysconfig/docker*.

You must be using the devicemapper storage driver to use SELinux. At the time of writing, getting SELinux to work with Overlay and BTRFS is an ongoing effort, but they are not currently compatible.

For installation on other distributions, refer to the relevant documentation. Note that SELinux needs to label all files in your filesystem, which takes some time. Do not install SELinux on a whim!

Enabling SELinux has an immediate and drastic effect on using containers with volumes. If you have SELinux installed, you will no longer be able to read or write to volumes by default:

```
$ sestatus | grep mode
Current mode:                   enforcing
$ mkdir data
$ echo "hello" > data/file
$ docker run -v $PWD/data:/data debian cat /data/file
cat: /data/file: Permission denied
```

We can see the reason by inspecting the folder's security context:

```
$ ls --scontext data
unconfined_u:object_r:user_home_t:s0 file
```

The label for the data doesn't match the label for containers. The fix is to apply the container label to the data by using the `chcon` tool, effectively notifying the system that we expect these files to be consumed by containers:

```
$ chcon -Rt svirt_sandbox_file_t data
$ docker run -v $PWD/data:/data debian cat /data/file
hello
$ docker run -v $PWD/data:/data debian sh -c 'echo "bye" >> /data/file'
$ cat data/file
hello
bye
$ ls --scontext data
unconfined_u:object_r:svirt_sandbox_file_t:s0 file
```

Note that if you only run chcon on the file and not the parent folder, you will be able to read the file but not write to it.

From version 1.7 and on, Docker automatically relabels volumes for use with containers if the :Z or :z suffix is provided when mounting the volume. The :z labels the volume as usable by *all* containers (this is required for data containers that share volumes with multiple containers), and the :Z labels the volume as only usable by that container. For example:

```
$ mkdir new_data
$ echo "hello" > new_data/file
$ docker run -v $PWD/new_data:/new_data debian cat /new_data/file
cat: /new_data/file: Permission denied
$ docker run -v $PWD/new_data:/new_data:Z debian cat /new_data/file
hello
```

You can also use the --security-opt flag to change the label for a container or to disable the labeling for a container:

```
$ touch newfile
$ docker run -v $PWD/newfile:/file --security-opt label:disable \
        debian sh -c 'echo "hello" > /file'
$ cat newfile
hello
```

An interesting use of SELinux labels is to apply a specific label to a container in order to enforce a particular security policy. For example, you could create a policy for an Nginx container that only allows it to communicate on ports 80 and 443.

Be aware that you will be unable to run SELinux commands from inside containers. Inside the container, SELinux will appear to be turned off, which prevents applications and users from trying to run commands such as setting SELinux policies that will get blocked by SELinux on the host.

A lot of tools and articles are available for helping to develop SELinux policies. In particular, be aware of audit2allow, which can turn log messages from running in permissive mode into policies that allow you to run in enforcing mode without breaking applications.

The future for SELinux looks promising; as more flags and default implementations are added to Docker, running SELinux-secured deployments should become simpler.

The MCS functionality should allow for the creation of secret or top-secret containers for processing sensitive data with a simple flag. Unfortunately, the current user experience with SELinux is not great; newcomers to SELinux tend to watch everything break with "Permission Denied" and have no idea of what's wrong and no idea how to fix it. Developers refuse to run with SELinux enabled, leading back to the problem of having different environments between development and production—the very problem Docker was meant to solve. If you want or need the extra protection that SELinux provides, you will have to grin and bear the current situation until things improve.

AppArmor

The advantage and disadvantage of AppArmor is that it is much simpler than SELinux. It should just work and stay out of your way but cannot provide the same granularity of protection as SELinux. AppArmor works by applying profiles to processes, restricting which privileges they have at the level of Linux capabilities and file access.

If you're using an Ubuntu host, chances are it is running right now. You can check this by running `sudo apparmor_status`. Docker will automatically apply an AppArmor profile to each launched container. The default profile provides a level of protection against rogue containers attempting to access various system resources, and can normally be found at */etc/apparmor.d/docker*. At the time of writing, the default profile cannot be changed, as the Docker daemon will overwrite it when it reboots.

If AppArmor interferes with the running of a container, it can be turned off for that container by passing `--security-opt="apparmor:unconfined"` to `docker run`. You can pass a different profile for a container by passing `--security-opt="apparmor:PROFILE"` to `docker run`, where `PROFILE` is the name of a security profile previously loaded by AppArmor.

Auditing

Running regular audits or reviews on your containers and images is a good way to ensure that your system is kept clean and up to date and to double-check that no security breaches have occurred. An audit in a container-based system should check that all running containers are using up-to-date images and that those images are using up-to-date and secure software. Any divergence in a container from the image it was created from should be identified and checked. In addition, audits should cover other areas nonspecific to container-based systems, such as checking access logs, file permissions, and data integrity. If audits can be largely automated, they can run regularly to detect any issues as quickly as possible.

Rather than having to log in to each container and examine each individually, we can instead audit the image used to build the container and use `docker diff` to check for any drift from the image. This works even better if you use a read-only filesystem (see "Limit Filesystems") and can be sure that nothing has changed in the container.

At a minimum, you should check that the versions of software used are up to date with the latest security patches. This should be checked on each image and any files identified as having changed by `docker diff`. If you are using volumes, you will also need to audit each of those directories.

The amount of work involved in auditing can be seriously reduced by running minimal images that only contain the files and libraries essential to the application.

The host system also needs to be audited just as you would a regular host machine or VM. Making sure the kernel is correctly patched becomes even more critical in a container-based system that shares the kernel among containers.

Several tools are already available for auditing container-based systems, and we can expect to see more in the coming months. Notably, Docker released the Docker Bench for Security tool (*https://dockerbench.com*), which checks for compliance with many of the suggestions from the Docker Benchmark document from the Center for Internet Security (CIS) (*https://benchmarks.cisecurity.org/*). Also, the open source Lynis (*https://cisofy.com/lynis/*) auditing tool contains several checks related to running Docker.

Incident Response

Should something bad occur, you can take advantage of several Docker features to quickly respond to the situation and investigate the cause of the problem. In particular, `docker commit` can be used to quickly take a snapshot of the compromised system, and `docker diff` and `docker logs` can reveal changes made by the attacker.

A major question that needs to be answered when dealing with a compromised container is, "Could a container breakout have occurred?" (i.e., could the attacker have gained access to the host machine?). If you believe that this is possible or likely, the host machine will need to be wiped and all containers re-created from images (without some form of attack mitigation in place). If you are sure the attack was isolated to the container, you can simply stop that container and replace it. (*Never* put the compromised container back into service even if it holds data or changes not in the base image; you simply can't trust the container anymore.)

An effective way to prevent attack may be to limit the container in some way, such as dropping capabilities or running with a read-only filesystem.

Once the immediate situation has been dealt with and some form of attack mitigation put in place, the compromised image you committed can be analyzed to determine the exact causes and extent of the attack.

For information on how to develop an effective security policy covering incident response, read CERT's "Steps for Recovering from a UNIX or NT System Compromise" (*https://www.cert.org/historical/tech_tips/win-UNIX-system_compromise.cfm*) and the advice given on the ServerFault website (*https://serverfault.com/questions/218005/how-do-i-deal-with-a-compromised-server*).

Future Features

Several Docker features related to security are in the works (these features have been prioritized by Docker, so they might be available by the time you read this):

Seccomp
> The Linux seccomp (or *secure computing mode*) facility can be used to restrict the system calls that can be made by a process. Seccomp is most notably used by web browsers, including both Chrome and Firefox, to sandbox plugins. By integrating seccomp with Docker, containers can be locked down to a specified set of system calls. The proposed Docker seccomp integration would by default deny calls to 32-bit system calls, old networks, and various system functions that containers don't typically need access to. In addition, other calls could be explicitly denied or allowed at runtime. For example, the following code would allow the container to make the `clock_adjtime` syscall needed for syncing the system time by using the Network Time Protocol daemon:

> ```
> $ docker run -d --security-opt seccomp:allow:clock_adjtime ntpd
> ```

User namespacing
> As mentioned previously, a few proposals exist for how to improve the issue of user namespacing, in particular with regard to the root user. We can expect to see support for mapping the root user to a nonprivileged user on the host soon.

In addition, I would expect to see some consolidation of the various security tools available to Docker, possibly in the form of a security profile for containers. At the moment, a lot of overlap exists between the various security tools and options (e.g., file access can be restricted by using SELinux, dropping capabilities, or using the `--read-only` flag).

Conclusion

As we've seen in this chapter, there are many aspects to consider when securing a system. The primary advice is to follow the principles of defense-in-depth and least privilege. This ensures that even if an attacker manages to compromise a component of the system, that attacker won't gain full access to the system and will have to penetrate further defenses before being able to cause significant harm or access sensitive data.

Groups of containers belonging to different users or operating on sensitive data should run in VMs separate from containers belonging to other users or running publicly accessible interfaces. The ports exposed by containers should be locked down, particularly when exposed to the outside world, but also internally to limit the access of any compromised containers. The resources and functionality available to containers should be limited to only that required by their purpose, by setting limits on their memory usage, filesystem access, and kernel capabilities. Further security can be provided at the kernel level by running hardened kernels and using security modules such as AppArmor or SELinux.

In addition, attacks can be detected early through the use of monitoring and auditing. Auditing in particular is interesting in a container-based system because containers can be easily compared to the images they were created from to detect suspicious changes. In turn, images can be vetted offline to make sure they are running up-to-date and secure versions of software. Compromised containers with no state can be quickly replaced with new versions.

Containers are a positive force in terms of security because of the extra level of isolation and control they provide. A system using containers properly will only be more secure than the equivalent system without containers.

Index

Symbols

.dockerignore file, 41
–a (docker run option), 57
–d (docker run option), 57
–e (docker run option), 57
–h (docker run option), 58
–i (docker run option), 57
–p (docker run option), 49, 58
–P (docker run option), 49, 59
–t (docker run option), 57
–u (docker run option), 59
–v (docker run option), 58
–w (docker run option), 59
––attach (docker run option), 57
––detach (docker run option), 57
––entrypoint (docker run option), 59
––env (docker run option), 57
––expose (docker run option), 58
––hostname (docker run option), 58
––interactive (docker run option), 57
––link (docker run option), 58
––name (docker run option), 58
––publish (docker run option), 58
––publish–all (docker run option), 59
––restart (docker run option), 57, 148
––rm (docker run option), 57
––tty (docker run option), 57
––user (docker run option), 59
––volume (docker run option), 58
––volumes–from (docker run option), 58
––workdir (docker run option), 59

A

A/B (multivariate) testing, 135

access controls, SELinux vs. standard Linux, 317
ADD instruction, 47
affinity filter, 258
aggregating logs, 176
alerting (see monitoring and alerting)
Amazon EC2 Container Service (ECS), 137, 162-165
Amazon Elastic Load Balancer, 164
ambassador containers (ambassadors), 206-210
    advantages and disadvantages, 206
    and amouat/ambassador image, 208
amouat/ambassador image, 208
amouat/network–utils image, 242
Ansible, 154-156
Apache Mesos (see Mesos)
AppArmor, 320
application groups, Marathon, 284
architecture, Docker, 35-39
auditing, 320
AUFS storage driver, 157
authentication of registry users, 110
Automated Builds, 102-104
awsElasticBlockStore (Kubernetes volume), 273
aws–vpc Flannel backend, 238

B

backup
    data, 32
    Jenkins, 132
base images, 44-46
bind mounts, 75
blue/green deployment, 135
boolean flags, 56

bridge networking mode, 226
BTRFS storage driver, 158
build (docker–compose command), 83
build context, 40-41
build slaves, 132
builds, triggering with Jenkins, 128

C

caching
    for identidock web app, 93-97
    of layers, 43
cAdvisor, 196
Calico, 243-247, 248
CAP theorem, 219
capabilities, limiting, 313
CFS (Completely Fair Scheduler), 311
cgroups, 36
CI (see Continuous Integration)
clustering and orchestration
    third–party solutions, 38
    tools for, 252-285
    with fleet, 260-266
    with Kubernetes, 266-274
    with Marathon, 275-284
    with Mesos, 274-285
    with Swarm, 252-260
clustering, defined, 252
clusters
    monitoring solutions, 197-200
    optimal size for etcd/Consul, 211
CMD instruction, 47
commands
    Compose, 83
    container information, 62
    container management, 59-61
    Docker, 20-24, 55-67
    Docker installation/usage information sub-
        commands, 62
    for image creation and manipulation, 63-66
    for registries, 66
    run, 56-59
Completely Fair Scheduler (CFS), 311
component tests, 133
Compose, 37
    automating development with, 81-84
    commands, 83
    extends keyword, 143
configuration files
    and Dockerfile, 80

with dockerize and docker–gen, 147
Configuration Management (CM) tool
    and security, 296
    for container deployment, 153-156
consensus, 210
constraint filter, 257
Consul, 219-223
    and CAP theorem, 219
    optimal cluster size, 211
consumer contract tests, 134
container breakouts, 288
container networking (see networking)
container networking mode, 228
Content Trust, 9, 114, 299-303, 302
Continuous Delivery, 171
Continuous Deployment, 171
Continuous Integration (CI), 115-136
    adding unit tests to identidock, 116-121
    creating Jenkins container for, 121-129
    hosted solutions for, 133
    pushing images, 129-132
    testing and microservices, 133-135
    testing in production, 135
COPY instruction, 47
CPU share, limiting, 311
cross–host networking, 230-247
    with Flannel, 237-242
    with Overlay, 231-233
    with Weave, 233-237
Crypt, 170
cryptographic signing, 298

D

DAC (Discretionary Access Control), 317
daemon (see Docker daemon)
data
    backing up, 32
    managing with volumes/data containers,
        51-55
    sensitive, 167-170
    sharing, 53
data containers, 54
defense–in–depth, 290
denial–of–service (DoS) attacks, 288
    limiting CPU to prevent, 311
    limiting memory to prevent, 310
    limiting restarts to prevent, 312
dependency filter, 258
deployment, container, 137-172

L

labels
  in Kubernetes, 266
  using when building images, 297
latest tag, 100
layers, 25
  caching, 43
  image, 41-43
least privilege principle, 290
libcontainer, 37
lifecycle, container, 57
link container (term), 50
links
  and guaranteed logging, 193
  breaking on restart of containers, 150
  for containers, 49-51
  forthcoming Docker changes, 32
Linux
  64-bit platform, 10
  installing Docker on, 13
  logrotate utility, 185
  seccomp, 322
Linux Containers (LXC) project, 6
Linux Security Modules (LSMs), 316-320
logging, 174-194
  aggregating logs, 176
  commercial solutions, 201
  default Docker, 174
  Docker events API, 188-189
  forwarding logs with rsyslog, 191-193
  guaranteed, 193
  log storage/rotation, 185
  with ELK stack, 177-186
  with raw logs on filesystem, 193
  with syslog, 187-193
logrotate utility, 185
logs (docker-compose command), 83
Logspout, 177
Logstash, 177, 196
LSMs (Linux Security Modules), 316-320
LXC (Linux Containers) project, 6
LXC execution driver, 297

M

MAC (Mandatory Access Control), 317
Mac OS, Docker installation on, 15
Machine (see Docker Machine)
MAINTAINER instruction, 48
management (container management)

defined, 252
Mandatory Access Control (MAC), 317
Marathon, 275-284
master container (term), 50
MCS (Multi-Category Security), 317
MD5 algorithm, 298
memory, limiting, 310
Mesos, 274-285, 285
  and Marathon, 275-284
  running Swarm or Kubernetes on, 285
Mesos Agent Nodes, 274
Mesos Frameworks, 274
Mesos Master, 274
microservices
  and identidock web app, 96
  and unit tests, 115
  monoliths vs., 11, 96
  testing of, 133-135
MLS (Multi-Level Security), 317
mock, 119
monitoring and alerting, 194-201
  cluster solutions, 197-200
  commercial solutions, 201
  getting stats on all running containers, 195
  with cAdvisor, 196
  with Docker tools, 194-196
  with Logstash, 196
  with Prometheus, 197-200
monoliths, microservices vs., 11, 96
multivariate (A/B) testing, 135
Multi-Category Security (MCS), 317
Multi-Level Security (MLS), 317

N

names, image, 99
namespaces/namespacing, 29, 37, 289
  future security features, 322
networking, 226-249
  ambassadors as alternative to, 206-210
  and container deployment, 170
  basic modes, 226-228
  bridge mode, 226
  container mode, 228
  cross-host solutions, 230-247
  defined in container context, 205
  forthcoming Docker changes, 32, 50
  forthcoming Docker features, 228-230
  host mode, 227
  in Kubernetes, 266

root privileges, 15
root signing key, 300
rsyslog, 191-193
run (docker–compose command), 83
run command (see docker run command)
RUN instruction, 48
runc driver, 36

S

SANs (Subject Alternative Names), 107
scaling, monoliths vs. microservices, 11
scheduled runs, 134
seccomp (secure computing mode), 322
secret (Kubernetes volume), 273
secrets (see sensitive data)
secure hash, 298
security, 287-323
    and Docker Content Trust, 299-303
    and Docker digests, 298
    and unsupported drivers, 297
    and USER statement in Dockerfiles, 78
    AppArmor, 320
    applying resource limits, 314-316
    applying updates, 294-297
    auditing, 320
    containers and namespacing, 289
    defense–in–depth, 290
    forthcoming Docker features, 322
    getting lists of running images, 295
    image provenance, 298-305
    important issues, 288-290
    incident response, 321
    least privilege principle, 290
    limiting capabilities, 313
    limiting CPU, 311
    limiting filesystems, 312
    limiting memory, 310
    limiting restarts, 312
    LSMs, 316-320
    Notary project, 302
    of identidock, 291-293
    removing setuid/setgid binaries, 309
    reproducible/trustworthy Dockerfiles, 303-305
    running a hardened kernel, 316
    segregating containers by host, 293
    SELinux, 317-320
    setting a user, 306-307
    tips, 305-316

SELinux security module, 317-320
    AppArmor vs., 320
    enabling, 318
    Linux access controls vs., 317
    running in permissive mode, 14
sensitive data
    compromising, 289
    key–value store for, 169
    passing via environment variables, 168
    passing via volumes, 169
    saving in the image, 167
    sharing, 167-170
service discovery, 210-226, 247
    ambassadors as alternative to, 206-210
    and CAP theorem, 219
    defined, 205
    DNS–based pros and cons, 224
    registration, 223
    third–party solutions, 38
    with Consul, 219-223
    with docker–discover, 225
    with etcd, 210-214
    with Eureka, 225
    with SkyDNS, 214-219
    with SmartStack, 225
    with WeaveDNS, 225
    with ZooKeeper, 225
services, in Kubernetes, 267
setuid/setgid binaries, removing, 309
SHA algorithm, 298
shadowing, 135
sharing data, 53
shell format, exec format vs., 46
signing keys, 300
SkyDNS, 214-219
    and fleet, 262
slim images, 73
SmartStack, 225
socket activation, 261
staging images, 131
state variables, 155
stop (docker–compose command), 83
stopped containers, 23, 26
storage drivers
    and host configuration, 157
    and UFS, 37
    security issues, 297
    switching, 159
stub, 119

About the Author

Adrian Mouat is the chief scientist for Container Solutions, a pan-European services company that specializes in Docker and Mesos. Previously, he was an applications consultant at EPCC, part of the University of Edinburgh.

Colophon

The animal on the cover of *Using Docker* is a bowhead whale (*Balaena mysticetus*). It is a dark-colored, stocky whale, notable for its lack of dorsal fin. Bowhead whales live their lives in Arctic and sub-Arctic waters, unlike other whales that migrate to low-latitude waters to feed or reproduce.

Bowhead whales are large and robust, growing up to 53 feet (males) and 59 feet (females). They have massive, triangular skulls that they use to break through Arctic ice in order to breathe. Bowhead whales have strongly bowed, white lower jaws and narrow upper jaws, which house the longest baleen of any whale (at 9.8 feet) and is used to strain tiny prey from the water. Paired blowholes are found at the highest point of the whale's head; they can spout water 20 feet high. It boasts the thickest blubber of any animal, ranging from 17–20 inches thick.

Bowhead whales travel alone or in small pods of six. They can remain underwater for up to an hour, but tend to limit their single dives to 4–15 minutes. These whales typically travel about 2–5 kilometers per hour—slow for a whale—but when in danger, they can reach speeds of 10 km/hr. Despite not being very social, bowhead whales are the most vocal of large whales. They communicate using underwater sounds while traveling, socializing, and feeding. During mating season, bowheads make long, complex songs as mating calls.

These whales are known as the longest-living mammals, with an average lifespan of over 200 years. In 2007, a 49-foot bowhead whale was caught off the coast of Alaska with an explosive harpoon head found embedded in its neck blubber. The weapon was traced back to a major whaling center in New Bedford, Massachusetts, and determined to have been manufactured in 1890. Other bowhead whales have been aged between 135 and 172 years old. Once in danger of extinction, bowhead whales have increased since commercial whaling ceased. Small numbers (25–40) are still hunted during subsistence hunts by Alaska natives, but this level of hunt is not expected to affect the population's recovery.

Many of the animals on O'Reilly covers are endangered; all of them are important to the world. To learn more about how you can help, go to *animals.oreilly.com*.

The cover image is from *Braukhaus Lexicon*. The cover fonts are URW Typewriter and Guardian Sans. The text font is Adobe Minion Pro; the heading font is Adobe Myriad Condensed; and the code font is Dalton Maag's Ubuntu Mono.

Have it your way.

O'Reilly eBooks

- Lifetime access to the book when you buy through oreilly.com

- Provided in up to four, DRM-free file formats, for use on the devices of your choice: PDF, .epub, Kindle-compatible .mobi, and Android .apk

- Fully searchable, with copy-and-paste, and print functionality

- We also alert you when we've updated the files with corrections and additions.

oreilly.com/ebooks/

Safari Books Online

- Access the contents and quickly search over 7000 books on technology, business, and certification guides

- Learn from expert video tutorials, and explore thousands of hours of video on technology and design topics

- Download whole books or chapters in PDF format, at no extra cost, to print or read on the go

- Early access to books as they're being written

- Interact directly with authors of upcoming books

- Save up to 35% on O'Reilly print books

See the complete Safari Library at safaribooksonline.com

©2014 O'Reilly Media, Inc. O'Reilly logo is a registered trademark of O'Reilly Media, Inc. 14373

Get even more for your money.

Join the O'Reilly Community, and register the O'Reilly books you own. It's free, and you'll get:

- $4.99 ebook upgrade offer
- 40% upgrade offer on O'Reilly print books
- Membership discounts on books and events
- Free lifetime updates to ebooks and videos
- Multiple ebook formats, DRM FREE
- Participation in the O'Reilly community
- Newsletters
- Account management
- 100% Satisfaction Guarantee

Signing up is easy:

1. Go to: oreilly.com/go/register
2. Create an O'Reilly login.
3. Provide your address.
4. Register your books.

Note: English-language books only

To order books online:
oreilly.com/store

For questions about products or an order:
orders@oreilly.com

To sign up to get topic-specific email announcements and/or news about upcoming books, conferences, special offers, and new technologies:
elists@oreilly.com

For technical questions about book content:
booktech@oreilly.com

To submit new book proposals to our editors:
proposals@oreilly.com

O'Reilly books are available in multiple DRM-free ebook formats. For more information:
oreilly.com/ebooks

O'REILLY®

©2014 O'Reilly Media, Inc. O'Reilly logo is a registered trademark of O'Reilly Media, Inc. 14373

CPSIA information can be obtained
at www.ICGtesting.com
Printed in the USA
BVOW09s1029251017
498626BV00014B/564/P